The Complete Book

of

Hot Rodding

The Complete Book
of
Hot Rodding

by

Robert E. Petersen

and

The Editors of Hot Rod Magazine

Prentice-Hall, Inc.

Englewood Cliffs, N. J.

LIBRARY OF CONGRESS CATALOG CARD NUMBER 59-6699

First printing . . . . April, 1959
Second printing . . . . July, 1960
Third printing . . . . December, 1960
Fourth printing . . . . October, 1961

PRINTED IN THE UNITED STATES OF AMERICA
15742-T

Contents

Acknowledgments

Any book involving such a broad subject as hot rodding obviously could not have been compiled without expert technical knowledge and assistance. The author is deeply indebted to Don Francisco, who acted as technical editor for the entire project; to the staff of HOT ROD magazine, for their valuable assistance and cooperation, particularly in regard to many of the illustrations to be found throughout the book; and to James E. Potter, who acted as editorial production coordinator on the project.

ROBERT E. PETERSEN

CHAPTER ONE

The Hot Rod Story

Its beginning, development,

and its organized activities.

What is drag racing all about?

HOT ROD, HOT RODDER, HOT RODDING — three terms you won't find in many dictionaries. What do they mean? They mean different things to different people. To those who understand them they are the terms that describe a healthy, interesting, and rapidly growing sport; a sport not necessarily limited to the boundaries of any certain country. To those who don't understand them they often stand for an activity that should, one way or another, be suppressed.

Hot rodding is the term that identifies the sport, or art, of modifying production automobile engines to enable them to create more torque and horsepower than they did in their stock form. The idea of hot rodding is, of course, to make the cars in which the modified engines are installed accelerate more rapidly and go faster. A hot rodder is a person who is engaged in the sport of hot rodding, and a hot rod is the car a hot rodder uses for his sport.

When did hot rodding begin? It began when the first automobile was built. To some this may seem to be a bold statement because, although it is easy for a modern hot rodder to remember when he first became involved in the sport, it may be difficult for him to realize that hot rodding was firmly established long before he became acquainted with it.

Hot rodding was firmly entrenched as an automotive sport when Model T Fords were popular. Proof of this is in the many makes and types of special equipment that were made for T engines: Frontenac, Rajo, and Winfield cylinder heads; Ruckstell transmissions; Rocky Mountain brakes; centrifugal water pumps, etc. Most Model T's were probably hopped-up for track use but I've listened to many men tell stories of fantastic highway races in their hopped-up "T-bones." To say what was popular before the Model T would, for us, be only conjecture but no doubt there were many four-cylinder bombs roaming the countryside years before Henry ever dreamed of the Model T.

After the Model T, the engine that caught the hot rodder's fancy was another Ford product. This was the Model A with a four-cylinder engine very much akin to the T but sturdier. All sorts of special equipment became available for Model A's: overhead valve cylinder heads, special flat heads, reground camshafts, ignition distributors and magnetos, intake manifolds for multiple carburetors, etc. They were converted to full-pressure lubrication for longer bearing and crankshaft life and their cylinders were bored to increase their displacement.

During the latter part of the Model T reign,

before the A's came into the picture, four-cylinder Chevrolets found favor with many hot rodders but their popularity never equalled that enjoyed by Ford engines. Chevy four-bangers had overhead valves but all but the '28 model, which was the last of them, had only one exhaust port in their cylinder heads. A vast improvement in the performance of a single-port engine could be had by replacing its stock cylinder head with an Oldsmobile "three-port" head. Olds heads had three exhaust ports and they bolted to Chevrolet cylinder blocks without alterations. The vintage of the Olds heads is still a mystery to us. As with Model T's and A's, many other modifications were made to Chevy four-bangers to make them potent performers for their day.

In 1932 the all-time champion of hot rod engines began rolling off the production lines of the Ford Motor Company. This was the new flathead V8 that was eventually to force all four-bangers out of the competition picture. Ford built this engine, without changing its basic design but with minor improvements and displacement increases that eventually doubled its advertised horsepower. During this period every hot rodder in the country had at least one of the engines and any number of the special parts made for them.

Although Ford brought out an improved four-cylinder engine with the V8 (the Model B), the reign of the four-barrels expired when the V8's came out. But because of their simplicity and the fact that they were the first to be used for all-out hot rod modifications, there was, and is, much automotive "romance" connected with four-cylinder engines.

If credit can be given to any engine for starting the thriving business of manufacturing hot rod parts as we know it today, it must be given to the flathead Ford V8. This was when such well-known names as Edelbrock, Weiand, Navarro, Kong, Weber, Harman & Collins, etc., were added to the vocabularies of every performance-minded youth in the nation. These are the men who built the special cylinder heads, intake manifolds, ignition distributors, and pistons, and who reground camshafts, stroked crankshafts, and made or remade all the other parts these engines needed to develop their maxmium possible horsepower.

The life of the flathead was long and colorful, and, for that matter, it isn't over yet. Flatheads are getting pushed around a lot by the more modern ohv V8's that are now so numerous. In many sections of the country, however, they are still

Most popular engine in the early days of hot rodding was Ford Motor Company's flathead V8.

strong contenders at competition meets of all sorts.

Overhead valve V8's first became a menace to the flatheads in 1949 when Oldsmobile brought out their first engine of this design. The threat to the flatheads has grown stronger each year as the overheads have become better and better and as their displacement has grown. But as far as out-and-out vehicle performance is concerned, ohv V8's may still have a long way to go to equal the flatheads on a cubic-inch-per-cubic-inch basis. The wildest and hairiest flathead was approximately equal in displacement to the smallest of the early ohv engines. Now, with stock ohv's of 430 cubic inches, and bored and stroked versions of many of them well above this and not too far from 500 cubic inches, a flathead's displacement is insignificant.

Problems for the hot rodder changed somewhat when he turned his interest from flathead engines to ohv models. Although the engines are basically the same in that they both operate on the four-stroke cycle principle, use liquid fuel, have spark ignition, and so forth, the ohv models presented problems and different procedures the average hot rodder hadn't encountered before. For instance, to raise the compression ratio of

his flathead engine he installed special cylinder heads, or had his stock heads milled, domed, and flycut; now he has to work with his stock heads because there aren't any special heads available. He found that he can raise the compression ratio of his ohv engine by milling its cylinder heads and then fighting the intake manifold misalignment and other factors affected by head milling, or he can install pistons that have special domed heads in its cylinders, or he can bore and stroke the engine to increase its displacement, thereby raising the ratio.

Porting and relieving were standard procedures in flatheads to enable them to breathe at high engine speeds but there isn't anything to relieve in the overheads. In some overheads it is wise to enlarge the combustion chambers around the valve seats but this is considerably different than the relieving operation hot rodders were accustomed to doing in flathead blocks. Intake and exhaust ports in some of the earlier ohv jobs could and should have been enlarged but now about all that is necessary is a light grinding to smooth the surfaces of the ports and passages. There were other things the hot rodder had to learn but in most instances he is a sturdy, highly adaptable organism that takes things of this na-

Overhead valve V8's first became a menace to the flatheads when Oldsmobile produced an engine of that design in 1949.

In the early days of hot rodding, someone discovered the flat-surfaced dry lakes in Southern California to be ideal for acceleration and all-out speed trials. Here a "belly tank" type vehicle is seen going through the "traps" at Muroc Dry Lake.

ture in stride. Things that were problems not long ago are simple matters now.

Organized Activities

Hot rodders of the Model T days weren't as fortunate as those of today. The only places they had to test and prove their handiwork and make experimental runs so they could determine what to do to improve their engines further were on race tracks at some fair grounds or on public highways. Highways in those days weren't what we're accustomed to now. They were dirt roads; they were narrow; they had ruts; and for any speed greater than that provided by a two-horse team, they were down-right dangerous. One thing in their favor, however, was that there wasn't much traffic on them. Testing a car on a track required considerably more skill than straightaway running if the driver were to keep his car right side up and out of the fence. If he were really bold he could enter a race on Sunday and maybe win himself a dollar or two.

During the 1920's Southern California's hot rodders got the break of their lives when someone discovered that Muroc dry lake, located in

the Mojave desert close to Los Angeles, was an ideal spot for finding out just how fast a car could go. The lake was long enough and wide enough so that a fellow could get on the throttle and let everything hang out until either he became bored or the engine came apart. It was some 20 miles from the nearest paved highway to the lake, but several times a year during the dry season hot rodders from Southern and Central California would gather on the lake on Sundays and have it out. This was paradise for hot rodders because they could make as much noise as they cared to and drive as fast as their cars would go; there wasn't anyone to bother them. Sometimes it was a little dangerous because the lake was so large that fellows going in different directions on test runs wouldn't know there was anyone else around until they came together.

In the late thirties, after a few bad accidents on the lake, a group of fellows banded together and formed an organization for the protection of everyone who used the lake and to contribute some kind of order and an organized spirit of competition to the sport. This association, which

Top speed record course in the nation and possibly the world is the Bonneville salt flats in Utah. Each year since 1949 a S.C.T.A. sponsored week-long affair is held. All types are tested, but the best known are the "streamliners," shown here.

is still active, was named the "Southern California Timing Association." The S.C.T.A. brought together under a common governing body the many clubs to which most of the hot rodders who were using Muroc as a test ground belonged. It then set up rules and regulations for the use of the lake. The association further whetted competition between the clubs by making it possible for them to vie for points that would determine the champion club and car at the end of each competition season. Success of the S.C.T.A. is proven by its uninterrupted existence from the date of its formation.

The S.C.T.A. and other associations, such as Russetta Timing Association and one or two others that formed at later dates, faced a major problem when Muroc was taken over by the military arm of the federal government to be used as an aircraft test center. During the years Muroc has been off-limits to hot rodders it has become what is perhaps the world's greatest testing ground for military aircraft. There was no place better suited for this purpose; however, if it hadn't been for El Mirage, Rosamond, and

another dry lake or two in the area, the loss of Muroc would have put a huge damper on the hot rod movement.

El Mirage, the next scene of competition, was much smaller than Muroc and not nearly as ideal but it had to do. It was in the same general area as Muroc and just as easy to get to. Then, in 1949, the first annual Bonneville Speed Trials were held on the Bonneville salt flats in Utah. This was a week-long affair sponsored by the S.C.T.A. It was a terrific success and since the first meet it has been held annually.

Bonneville is an ideal course for high-speed events. The world's land speed record was established there, as have been all major hot rod records. But Bonneville Speed Trials are held only once a year. In the early fifties this left hot rodders with no other choice but to run on El Mirage, or on other lakes that were even less suitable, if they were to enjoy their sport. The poor surfaces of these lakes increased the sport's danger to the point where a substitute activity of some sort was sought. This substitute, organized drag racing, soon proved to be the most popular.

Organized drag racing was another Southern California first. The strip at Santa Ana, California, was the first in the nation and it opened with the blessings of the local police. The strip is an extra landing strip at the Orange County Airport just outside Santa Ana. Because of the nature of the sport and the convenient location of the strip, it was possible to run every Sunday, unless it was raining, and the popularity of drag racing sky-rocketed. Now, there are nearly 200 drag strips in the United States and new ones are being opened from time to time.

Drag racing differs from dry lake and Bonneville competition in that the course is only a quarter of a mile long. At Bonneville it's possible to run as far as three miles before entering the timing trap and at El Mirage the approach to the trap is usually a mile. These flying-start runs for all-out top speed differ greatly from the standing-start quarter-mile of drag racing.

Stock and near-stock cars are the backbone of drag racing but the sport has fostered a very highly specialized type of car designed to propel its driver over a quarter-mile course in the shortest time and to attain the highest possible speed at the end of the course. These cars are called "dragsters." Dragsters are built as light as possible because acceleration is dependent on a car's weight-to-horsepower ratio and their weight is distributed so that most of it is carried by their rear wheels. Placing most of the weight on the rear wheels enables the wheels to get maximum traction on the strip. Some fantastic creations have been pushed to the starting lines of the nation's strips and a few of them have established equally fantastic elapsed times for the quarter-mile and top speeds considered impossible not too long ago.

A true dragster is out of place anywhere but on a drag strip but some competition cars are suitable for either drag racing, dry lake, or Bonneville use. Among these are stock-bodied roadsters, coupes, sedans, and versions of these cars with modified bodies. Classes have been established for cars of these types so they can compete fairly in both straightaway and drag

Today, organized drag racing has become one of the nation's most popular weekend sports. Nearly 200 drag strips are in the U.S. and new ones are being opened. "Dragsters" are built light as possible with much of the weight on the rear wheels.

events. Some of the cars with modified bodies are just as fantastic as the dragsters and many of them perform remarkably well.

The usual procedure at a drag strip is to run the cars individually in the morning so that each of them can be classified as to its speed potential. Then, in the afternoon, the cars are run off in pairs in elimination matches according to their competition class and previous speed. Eventually, only the fastest car in each class — fastest in that it can get from the starting line to the finish line quicker than the others — remains undefeated. At most strips the winner in each class is presented a trophy of some kind for his victory. Also, there is usually a trophy for the "top eliminator," which is the fastest car of the day regardless of class. This, of course, usually goes to a dragster if there are any running on that particular day.

Organized drag racing has become an important tool used by law enforcement officials to help bring illegal drag racing under control. Before drag strips became popular it was common for groups of rodders to meet at a specified place on a certain night of the week and then run drag races on a little-used street or highway. This, under the best of conditions, was dangerous and few of the fellows who participated in such unlawful competition realized the seriousness of what they were doing.

Despite the many drag strips where a fellow can run safely, and with the blessing of the law, a small amount of street dragging still persists in some areas. It is sheer stupidity to engage in such a practice. At the speeds modern automobiles are capable of traveling at the end of a quarter or half-mile acceleration run a car is actually out of control if something unexpected should happen, and on a highway unexpected things are the order of the day. In addition to the possibility of an accident of some sort that might kill the driver of one or both of the cars or, worse yet, kill an innocent bystander, is the chance that illegal drags can give a fellow a chance to sit out a few days in the local pokey. As there isn't a jail in the country that was designed with the comfort of its customers in mind, there are many other places where it is much more enjoyable to spend a vacation.

Not long after organized drag racing showed an indication of catching on and becoming a major hot rod sport, an association with the pri-

This drag coupe is typical of the type of reengineered machinery to be found on the local drag strips of the country. In their quest for performance, chopped tops, smaller frontal areas, and the like are ideas commonly employed.

mary purpose of organizing hot rodders in general and drag racers in particular was founded. This was the National Hot Rod Association. During the time since its organization the NHRA has received much praise and an equal amount of criticism but the fact remains that it has been highly beneficial to drag racing. By sending well-informed men to different areas of the country for the sole purpose of selling city officials and law enforcement men on the value of drag racing to their communities, it has made possible the establishment of many drag strips that would never have made the grade without its assistance.

As with any other good thing, there are imitators of the NHRA. The advertised purpose of the associations formed after the NHRA was to promote hot rodding but the activities of some of them would seem to indicate that this aim is secondary to advertising a company or product, or to just plain making money.

Each year the NHRA holds a gigantic drag meet. The meet is held somewhere near the geographical center of the nation to make it easier for rodders from all over the nation to attend and compete. Attendance is terrific and many records for speed and elapsed time are established during the meets. The 1958 event, which was the fourth, was held over the Labor Day weekend at Oklahoma City, Oklahoma. None of the 500 cars entered were passenger cars and 95 of them were dragsters.

CHAPTER TWO

Hot Rodders Tackle the World's Engines

The why for more

power and methods used

to get it.

A HOT RODDER HAS TWO PURPOSES in mind when he installs special equipment on the engine in his car and reworks its inner parts: to make the car accelerate faster and to give it a higher top speed. Immediate acceleration adds greatly to the safety factor of a car used for everyday driving and for drag racing it is everything. In recent years the top-speed factor has become less important for engines in passenger cars because most stock automobiles will run fast enough in high gear for anything but competition purposes.

Before a fellow can understand the things that must be done to an engine to enable it to develop greater torque and horsepower outputs, he must know the purpose of its various parts and how they function. When these things are understood, the air of mysticism that stands between many beginners and the purpose of normal hot rod procedures is blown away.

Engines used in American automobiles since the turn of the century have utilized the "Otto" cycle. The Otto cycle is nothing more than the four-stroke cycle that is so familiar to all of us.

It gained its name from Dr. N. A. Otto, a German engineer who patented the principle in 1876.

A four-stroke cycle engine can have any number of cylinders, from one up. Automobile engines built in the United States since the introduction of the Model T have had either four, six, or eight cylinders. There are no four-cylinder engines in current full-size automobiles and sixes are in a definite minority. The trend is toward eight cylinders arranged in a V formation.

Four-stroke cycle refers to the number of strokes each piston in an engine must make to create one "power" stroke. A piston makes a stroke when it travels from the top the the bottom of its cylinder or vice-versa. Therefore, in a four-stroke engine a piston travels from the top to the bottom of its cylinder twice and from the bottom to the top of the cylinder twice for every power stroke it creates.

Each of the strokes has a name. The first one in the normal sequence leading up to a power stroke is the "intake" stroke. On this stroke the piston moves from the top to the bottom of the

FOUR STROKES OF FOUR-CYCLE ENGINE

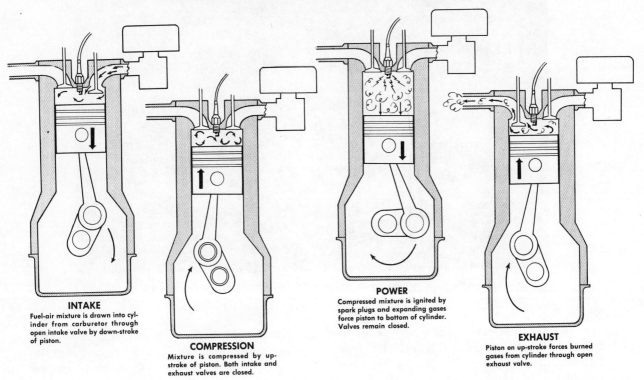

INTAKE
Fuel-air mixture is drawn into cylinder from carburetor through open intake valve by down-stroke of piston.

COMPRESSION
Mixture is compressed by up-stroke of piston. Both intake and exhaust valves are closed.

POWER
Compressed mixture is ignited by spark plugs and expanding gases force piston to bottom of cylinder. Valves remain closed.

EXHAUST
Piston on up-stroke forces burned gases from cylinder through open exhaust valve.

cylinder. When the piston starts back up the cylinder, it is on its "compression" stroke. The next stroke, again from the top to the bottom of the cylinder, is the power stroke, on which work is done, and then the piston moves back to the top of the cylinder on its "exhaust stroke," completing the cycle.

Any engine, regardless of the number of cylinders it has, is merely a group of single cylinders connected together on a common crankshaft; therefore, if one understands the functions of the parts in a single cylinder he should have no trouble visualizing the functions of the parts in an engine that has any number of cylinders.

An engine is built around its cylinders, where the energy in a liquid fuel is converted to mechanical energy. Cylinders are made of cast iron and in most modern engines they have an inner bore approximately four inches in diameter. The actual bore diameter depends on the make and model of the engine. Cylinder bores are made as round as possible and with a fairly smooth surface. The lower end of each cylinder is open but the upper end is sealed with a "cylinder head."

Fitted to the inside of each cylinder is a "piston." Pistons for passenger car engines are now made of aluminum alloys. A piston is cylindrical in shape and its end nearest the top of the cylinder, or its "head," is closed and its other end is open. The outer diameter of the piston is a few thousandths of an inch smaller than the cylinder bore so the piston can move through its strokes without excess friction.

A piston's purpose is to form the third and last wall of a sealed chamber. One wall of this chamber is the inner surface of the cylinder head, another is the wall of the cylinder, and the third is the head of the piston. As the piston moves up the cylinder, the chamber becomes smaller, and as the piston moves down the cylinder, the chamber becomes larger. When the piston is as high as it can go in the cylinder it is at "top dead center" (TDC) and when it is as low as it can go it is at "bottom dead center" (BDC). When the piston is at TDC, the volume of the chamber remaining is the "combustion chamber." In most engines the total volume of the combustion chamber remaining is the "combustion cham-

These are four of the eight cylinders in a late-model Chevrolet engine, as viewed from the left side.

ber." In most engines the total volume of the combustion chamber is in the cylinder head; however, in some of the newer engines the upper end of the cylinder is used as the combustion chamber. The ratio of the volume of the chamber when the piston is at BDC to the volume of the combustion chamber is the engine's "compression ratio."

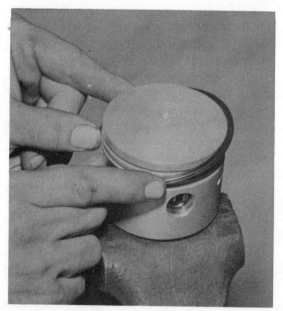

An automobile piston is fitted with rings that form gas-and-oil tight seals in the cylinders of the power plant.

Fitted in grooves around the upper end of the piston are "piston rings" made of cast iron or steel. The rings bear against the cylinder wall to form gastight and oiltight seals between the combustion chamber and the area below the piston.

A "crankshaft" controls the length of movement of the piston in its cylinder. Bearings in the "crankcase," which is the portion of the engine's structure that supports the cylinder, support the crankshaft in such a manner that the shaft can rotate.

Crankshafts are made of steel or special types of cast iron so they will have adequate strength for their job. A shaft for a single-cylinder engine has a "main bearing journal" at each of its ends. These journals rest in the bearings in the crankcase. Between the journals is a "crankpin" supported by two arms that extend out from the main bearing journals. A crankpin and its two arms is a "throw." The distance from the center of the journals to the center of the crankpin would be equal to one-half the piston stroke.

A "connecting rod," which has a bearing at its lower end that can be clamped around the crankpin and a bore in its upper end for a "piston pin," is the mechanical link between the crankshaft and the piston. Connecting rods in modern V8 engines vary in length but the distance between the crankpin bearing bore in their lower end and the center of the piston pin bore in their upper end is usually between six and seven inches.

Piston pins in modern engines are tubular and approximately one inch in diameter. They are made as light as feasible but with adequate strength to transmit pressures from the pistons to the connecting rods. Their outer surface is highly polished as it acts as a bearing surface.

Pins are installed by inserting them through bores in the skirt of the piston and the bore in the upper end of the connecting rod. They are held in place by lock rings in the piston bores or by friction between their outer surface and the bore in the rod. Pins held in place by friction are a press fit in the rods.

With the connecting rod linking the piston to

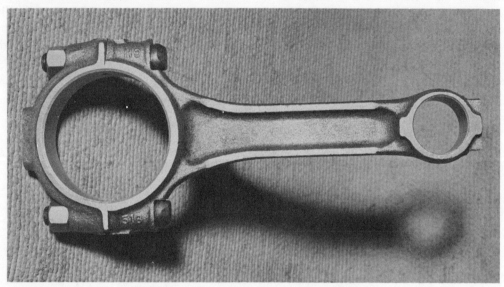

Connecting rods couple the pistons to the crankshaft.

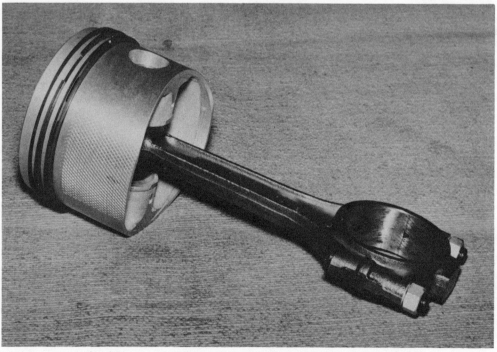

This shows an assembly of piston, rings, connecting rod and piston pin.

the crankpin, it can be seen that as the crankshaft is rotated, the piston will move up and down in the cylinder. Conversely, if one of the pistons should be forced to move down its cylinder, it will force the crankshaft to rotate. This is the mechanical principle around which the engine is built. Up and down, or "reciprocating," motion of the piston is converted to rotating, or "rotary," motion of the crankshaft.

Force to move the piston down its cylinder so it will rotate the crankshaft is created in the sealed portion of the cylinder above the piston. But before this pressure can be created it is necessary to fit the cylinder with "valves" and their related parts. Valves in modern engines are

called "poppet" valves. A poppet valve consists of a stem, approximately ⅜-inch in diameter, fitted with a disc-shaped head on one of its ends. Diameters of the heads vary for different makes of engines and depending on whether the valves are to be used as "intake" or "exhaust" valves. Heads of intake valves for some modern engines are two inches in diameter. Exhaust valves are usually a quarter-inch or so smaller than intakes.

Valves are installed in the cylinder heads of "overhead valve" engines and in the cylinder blocks of "L-head" engines so that their heads are in the combustion chambers. In overhead valve engines the stems of the valves extend up through "valve guides" in the heads. In most

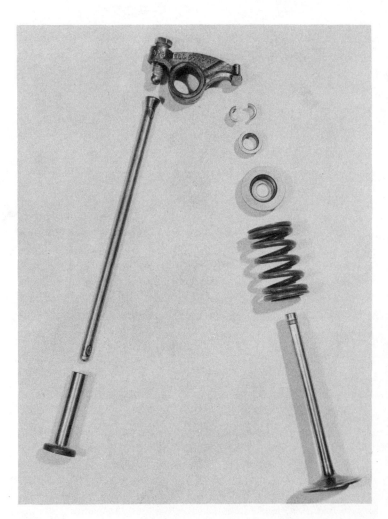

Valve (lower right) and actuating parts is from an overhead valve engine.

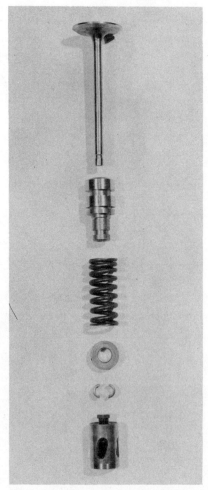

Valve, actuating parts from L-head engine.

The camshaft functions to open the valves in the engine in the proper sequence.

engines the valve guides are so positioned that they are in a line parallel to the centerline of the crankshaft.

The purpose of valves is to open and close passages in the cylinder heads of overhead valve engines and in the cylinder blocks of L-head engines. The passage sealed by the intake valve is the "intake" passage and the passage sealed by the exhaust valve is the "exhaust" passage. To make the chamber above the piston airtight when the valves are closed, a beveled seat is ground on the combustion chamber ends of the intake and exhaust passages (these ends of the passage are "valve ports") and faces to match the seats are ground on the underside of the valve heads. When a valve is closed, the face on its head rests on the seat on the end of the valve port. The angle of the seats for intake valves is either 45 or 30 degrees, as measured from the surface of the valve head, and usually 45 degrees for exhause valves.

When the crankshaft is rotated to force the piston to move down the cylinder, a low pressure is created in the chamber above the piston. This is because the volume of the chamber becomes greater but the chamber still contains the same quantity of air it contained before the piston was moved. By opening the intake valve while the piston is moving down the cylinder, atmospheric pressure outside the engine forces air through the intake passage and into the cylinder to equalize the pressure in the cylinder with that of the air surrounding the engine.

As the piston is moved from the bottom to the top of the cylinder after the intake valve closes, the volume of the chamber above it is reduced and air in the chamber is compressed to a higher pressure than that of the air surrounding the engine. If the exhaust valve is opened while the piston is moving from the bottom to the top of the cylinder, air will be forced out of the cylinder through the exhaust passage in the head. By opening and closing the valves at the correct times in relation to movement of the pistons it is possible to cause air to flow from outside the engine and into the cylinders, to compress the air, and to force it out of the cylinders.

In an overhead valve engine the mechanism that controls the opening and closing of the valves is more complicated than it is in an L-head, or "flathead," engine. In engines of either type, rotary motion is converted to reciprocating motion to move the valves. This is accomplished by the "camshaft," which is supported by bearings in the crankcase in such a position that it is parallel to the crankshaft. The crankshaft drives the camshaft by means of sprockets and a chain or by gears. The ratio of the sprockets or gear is such that the camshaft rotates at one-half crankshaft speed.

There is a "cam" on the camshaft for each of the valves in the engine. Cams are elliptical in cross-sectional area and they have a "heel" and a "lobe." The heel is concentric with the center of the shaft and the high point of the lobe is a greater distance than the heel from the shaft's center. This difference in distance depends on the type of engine the camshaft is in and several other factors. Directly above the cams are bores that hold "cam followers," or as they are some-

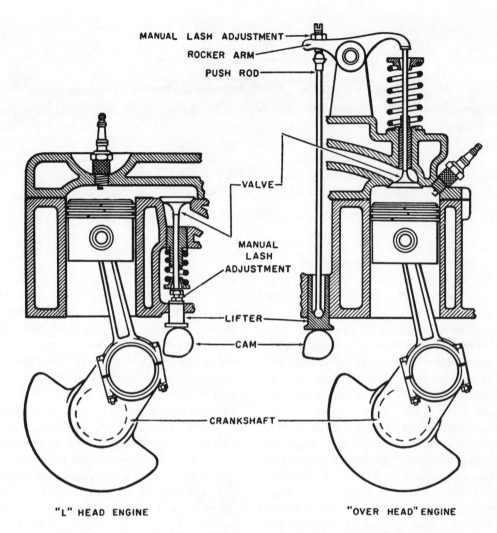

MANUAL LASH ADJUSTMENT
ROCKER ARM
PUSH ROD
VALVE
MANUAL LASH ADJUSTMENT
LIFTER
CAM
CRANKSHAFT

"L" HEAD ENGINE   "OVER HEAD" ENGINE

This diagram shows the difference between an L-head and an overhead-valve engine.

times called, "valve lifters," or "tappets." Cam followers vary in shape but the lower end of all of them has a diameter large enough to let it ride on the cam. As the camshaft is rotated by the crankshaft the cam followers move up and down in their bores as the cam lobes lift them and then allow them to drop down again.

In an L-head engine the valves are directly above the valve lifters. The upper ends of the lifters contact the ends of the valve stems directly. In an overhead valve engine of the type now popular it is necessary to have some sort of mechanism between the lifters and the ends of the valve stems to transmit lifter movement to the ends of the valves. This mechanism consists

of "pushrods" and "rocker arms." The lower ends of the pushrods seat in the lifters and their upper ends seat in one end of the rocker arms.

Rocker arm mounting methods vary but the principle is the same for all. In most engines the arms have a bore through their center through which is slipped a tubular steel shaft. The arms pivot on this shaft as they are moved by their pushrods. The end of the arm opposite that contacted by the pushrod rests on the upper end of the valve stem. As the valve lifter is lifted by the cam the pushrod moves with it and causes the rocker arm to rotate on its shaft. The rocker arm then forces the valve down and the valve's head leaves its seat in the cylinder head.

Rocker arms can open valves but they can't close them. Closing is accomplished by coil springs of the compression type that fit around the upper ends of the valve stems and are locked to the stems with special washers and split locks. After a valve has been opened by its rocker arm and the camshaft begins to let the valve lifter drop, the spring holds the end of the valve stem against the rocker arm and the valve closes.

This completes the mechanical part of the engine in which work is done to create power; however, an engine must have many more components before it can run. Among these are a carburetor and an ignition system.

Automobile engines are designed to use gasoline as their source of energy. Gasoline, in its natural form, is a liquid and as long as it remains a liquid it is of little use to the engine. But by vaporizing the liquid and mixing it with the correct weight of air, a rapid-burning mixture is formed. When this mixture is burned in an engine's combustion chamber the pressure resulting from the combustion is exerted on all surfaces of the chamber. As the piston head is the only surface of the chamber that can move, the pressure forces the piston to move down the cylinder and the piston's rod causes the crankshaft to rotate.

A carburetor is used to vaporize the gasoline and mix it with air. The carburetor is connected to the engine with an "intake manifold" so the air that flows through it can enter the cylinder by means of the cylinder's intake passage. In L-head engines the intake manifold is bolted to the cylinder block and in overhead valve engines it is bolted to the cylinder head. As the piston is moved down the cylinder on its intake stroke the intake valve opens and atmospheric pressure around the engine forces air through the carburetor. As the air passes through the carburetor gasoline flows from discharge nozzles and mixes with it. This mixture then enters the cylinder. As the crankshaft continues to rotate, the piston finishes its intake stroke and starts back up the cylinder on its compression stroke. The intake valve closes, and as the exhaust valve was already closed, the fuel and air mixture is compressed. Compression is an important part of the four-stroke cycle because the pressure exerted by the furning fuel and air is dependent on the pressure of the mixture prior to its ignition.

The compressed mixture is ignited at the correct time by a high voltage electrical spark between the contacts of a "spark plug" screwed into the cylinder head. Voltage for this spark originates in an "induction coil" and is delivered to the cylinder at the correct time by an "ignition distributor." The distributor is usually driven by the engine's camshaft.

As the mixture burns and expands it forces the piston back down the cylinder on its power stroke. This is the only time during the four strokes of the cycle that the piston contributes positive pressure to the crankshaft. At the end of the power stroke the piston starts back up the cylinder and the exhaust valve opens so the gases remaining after the combustion of the fuel and air mixture can be forced out of the cylinder. When the piston reaches the top of the cylinder on its exhaust stroke the four strokes of the cycle have been completed.

Multi-cylinder engines are formed by joining together the desired number of single cylinders. This is done by casting the cylinders in a common cylinder block. The crankshaft is lengthened and additional throws and crankpins are added to it to accommodate the cylinders in the block. At one time it was common practice to have all an engine's cylinders in line. An engine of this type is an "in-line" engine. Now the practice is to place the cylinders in two banks joined together on a common crankshaft. An engine with a block of this type is a "V" engine. Advantages of the V layout are a shorter engine and a shorter, stiffer crankshaft. Engine length is important to the passenger car designer, and crankshaft length and strength are important to the engine designer.

Other parts of the engine lubricate its moving parts, carry away combustion heat absorbed by its structure, revolve its crankshaft so it can be started, and convert rotating to electrical energy to maintain the car's battery in a charged condition. As these parts have no direct influence on the engine's ability to create torque and power, they won't be discussed.

It should be apparent by now that an automobile engine is a complex machine and that its ability to create torque and horsepower is dependent on the perfect synchronization of the

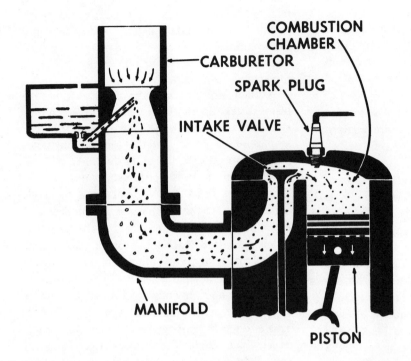

The carburetor mixes fuel and air before it enters the cylinders.

functions of its parts. Also, as the amount of force exerted on the crankshaft by a piston is dependent on the quantity of fuel and air mixture in the cylinder and the pressure of the mixture at the time of ignition, it should be clear that the torque and horsepower an engine can create are dependent on the amount of highly compressed fuel and air mixture it can burn efficiently in a given length of time. For this reason most of the modifications made to engines by hot rodders are aimed at enabling the cylinders to induct the greatest possible quantity of fresh mixture on each of their intake strokes. The mixture is then compressed as tightly as possible, within the limitations of the fuel to resist detonation, so that the pressure in the cylinders after combustion will be as high as conditions will permit.

Another factor on which the quantity of mixture an engine can consume is dependent is the speed of rotation of its crankshaft. This determines the number of intake and power strokes a piston can make during a given period of time. There is, however, a maximum crankshaft speed at which any engine will run efficiently. This is

determined by the ability of the engine's cylinders to induct fresh mixture and to exhaust the gases in the cylinders after combustion. This is an engine's "breathing" ability. At speeds below the practical maximum, breathing ability is better than it is at speeds above the maximum.

Because of the similarity of automobile engines of different makes, a broad basic formula that can be applied to any of them to increase their performance has worked itself out through the years. Methods of applying the formula vary because no two makes of engines are exactly alike but the basic principle of improvement is the same for all.

The formula can be divided into two parts. Steps in one of the parts have to do with increasing the quantity of fuel and air mixture the engine can consume and those in the other have to do with getting the greatest possible percentage of the energy created in the engine's cylinders to its flywheel. The second part of the formula is just as important as the first because energy created in the cylinders is of no value as far as moving a car is concerned if it must be used to over-

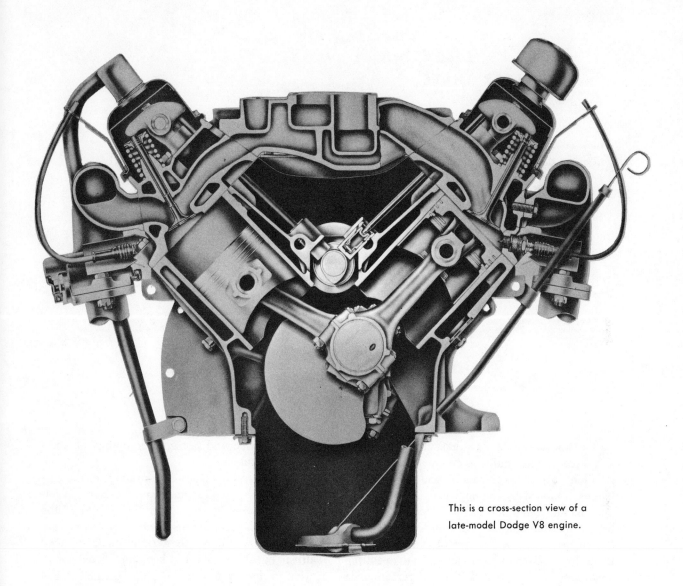

This is a cross-section view of a
late-model Dodge V8 engine.

come friction in the engine's many moving parts. Any reduction made in the amount of torque required to overcome an engine's internal friction is automatically added to the torque delivered by its flywheel. This is almost like getting something for nothing.

Normal steps in the first part of the formula are boring and stroking; enlarging and polishing intake and exhaust ports and passages; installing oversize valves; increasing the air flow and fuel flow capacities of the carburetion system; regrinding the cams on the camshaft so they will open the valves sooner and faster, hold them open longer, and allow them to close later and faster; raising the compression ratio; improving the exhaust system to provide an unrestricted path between the cylinders and the atmosphere; and improving the ignition system so it will be able to fire the highly compressed mixture in the cylinders at the high crankshaft speeds the engine will be capable of running after it has been reworked.

Steps in the second part of the formula have to do with the correct alignment of the engine's moving parts with each other and the cylinder block, increasing main and connecting rod bearing clearances, and establishing correct piston to cylinder wall clearances.

CHAPTER THREE

The True Facts About Horsepower

Horsepower and torque: What it is,
how it's determined, how it's
applied to your car.

AVAILABLE FOR EVERY INTERNAL COMBUS-TION ENGINE built for commercial purposes is a long list of specifications and performance figures compiled by the engineers who designed and manufactured the engine. Included in this list is everything one would want to know about the engine, from the number of cylinders it has to its fuel consumption under certain operating conditions. These specifications and performance figures are the yardstick an engineer who is buy-ing an engine for a specific installation uses to· determine which one is the most suitable for his purpose.

The average man who buys an automobile dif-fers from the purchaser of a commercial engine in that he isn't an engineer. Automobile manu-facturers have taken this into consideration and as a result they haven't confused the purchasers of their products with detailed engine specifica-tions. If it weren't for advertising purposes the purchaser probably wouldn't be told anything but the price of the car; however, with the adver-tising business and automotive competition what they are, great emphasis has recently been placed on the torque and horsepower ratings of auto-mobile engines.

Torque and horsepower are ratings of the per-formance ability of engines and, therefore, of rel-ative acceleration and speed capabilities of the cars in which they are installed. These ratings are items of importance to a performance-minded driver but their value has been minimized some-what in the last few years by exaggerated claims made by over-zealous advertising men striving to top the competition.

To the average hot rodder, torque and horse-power are almost sacred terms. He uses them every day in his conversations and he quotes them faithfully. But whether he is just quoting figures or talking about things he understands is something else again.

Torque and horsepower are listed in specifica-tions as individual items. Each has its own rating, torque being in pounds-feet and horsepower in horsepower, and each rating is at a different en-gine speed. When they are listed this way it is apparent that an engine develops its maximum torque at a crankshaft speed lower than that at

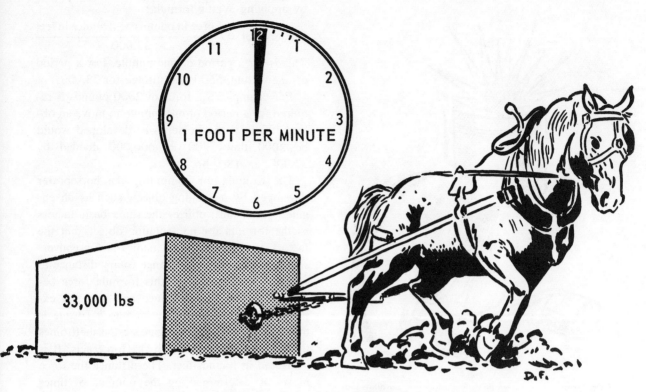

1 FOOT PER MINUTE

33,000 lbs

After extensive experiments with dray horses, 33,000 ft. lbs. of work per minute was established by James Watt, in 1873, as the equivalent of one horsepower.

which it develops its maximum horsepower. Listing torque and horsepower in this manner and showing that they reach their maximum values at different engine speeds might lead one to believe that they have nothing to do with each other. This would be a false assumption because in any engine torque and horsepower are as related as feet and inches on a yardstick; one cannot exist without the other. An engine cannot develop horsepower without creating torque, nor can it create torque without developing horsepower.

Both horsepower and torque are measures of performance but horsepower differs from torque in that the element of time must be considered when it is computed. To thoroughly understand these terms and their relationship to each other it is necessary to understand other related terms such as force, work, and pounds-feet. One must also know that horsepower developed by rotating objects is computed with a different formula than that used for non-rotating objects.

The term horsepower was supposedly originated by James Watt, who in 1873 adopted the value of 33,000 foot-pounds of work per minute as the equivalent of one horsepower. Watt had determined during extensive experiments that a strong dray horse could move the equivalent of 33,000 pounds a distance of one foot in one minute. With this information he established the three basic factors necessary for horsepower computations: force, distance, and time.

Force, the first of the power factors, refers to the effort exerted on an object in an effort to change the object's position. For example, a horse applies force to move a wagon by pushing against its harness. Force can be created by men, animals, or machines. For horsepower computations force is measured in pounds.

The distance factor refers to the distance the object on which the force is exerted is moved by the force. Distance is measured in feet. By themselves the factors of force and distance are of no consequence but combined they serve as a measure of "work." Work is done when a force moves an object. If the object is not moved, no work is done, regardless of the amount of force exerted.

The unit of measure for work is "pounds-feet,"

Force created in an engine's cylinders by burning fuel and air mixture is converted to torque at crankshaft.

by applying Watt's formula:

$$\text{Horsepower} = \frac{\text{Force in pounds} \times \text{distance in feet}}{33,000}$$

This is for a period of one minute. For a period of one second, 550 is substituted for 33,000.

For example, if a force of 2000 pounds is required for a period of one minute to move an object 300 feet, the horsepower developed would be 2000 times 300 = 600,000 divided by 33,000 = 18.1 hp.

The formula for computing the horsepower developed by a rotating object, such as an engine's crankshaft, utilizes the same basic factors as the formula for non-rotating objects but the factors are given different names and a conversion factor is added to change rotary distance to straight-line distance. In this formula force becomes "torque" and distance and time are expressed as "revolutions per minute." Torque is the force exerted by an engine's crankshaft times the leverage through which the force acts. It is measured in pounds-feet. The distance the force moves is determined by the number of times the crankshaft rotates in one minute. This is measured in revolutions per minute by a "tachometer."

Converting the factors of torque and revolutions per minute to pounds-feet of work per minute is accomplished by adding the conversion factor "2 pi" to the horsepower formula. Pi is the ratio of the circumference of a circle to its diameter. Its numerical value is accepted as 3.1416. A circle's circumference is found by multiplying its diameter by pi, or by multiplying its radius, which is one half its diameter, by 2 pi, or 6.2832.

Multiplying the product of torque and revolutions per minute by 2 pi converts the total rotary distance through which the torque force acts for a period of one minute to straight-line force. This is because the straight-line distance through which the torque force acts is equal to the distance around the circle the force would follow if it were free to rotate with the crankshaft, multiplied by the number of times it would travel around the circle. As torque is measured in pounds-feet, the radius of the circle followed by the force could be considered as one foot. Therefore, it is possible to compute the pounds-

or as it is sometimes used, "foot-pounds." This unit is the equivalent of a force of one pound moving an object a distance of one foot. Pounds-feet of work done in any particular instance is computed by multiplying the force exerted, in pounds, by the distance, in feet, the object on which the force was exerted moved. If, for instance, a force of 20 pounds moved an object 15 feet, 300 pounds-feet of work were done.

Time, the remaining factor, is easily understood as it is merely the period during which the work is being done. Time, combined with work, gives horsepower. Horsepower computations are usually made on a time basis of one minute, although one second can also be used if desired. For a period of one minute, 33,000 pounds-feet of work must be done to develop one horsepower; for one second, 1/60th of 33,000, or 550, pounds-feet of work must be done.

Horsepower developed by a non-rotating object for any specific job can be easily computed feet of work done during one crankshaft revolution by multiplying the pounds-feet value of the torque by 2 pi. Then, by multiplying this product by the number of revolutions per minute turned by the crankshaft, the total pounds-feet of work done in one minute is found. Dividing this figure by 33,000 gives the horsepower developed by the engine. This makes the formula for computing the horsepower developed by a rotating object:

$$\text{Horsepower} = \frac{2\text{Pi} \times \text{Torque} \times \text{RPM}}{33,000}$$

The formula can be simplified by reducing its numerical factors. This reduces it to:

$$\text{Horsepower} = \frac{\text{Torque} \times \text{RPM}}{5252}$$

Measuring the torque created by an engine's crankshaft is by no means a simple problem because the shaft's rotary force must be converted to a stationary force before it can be measured accurately. This problem was first approached by Baron Gaspar deProny, a French engineer who lived from 1755 to 1839. The Baron constructed a device, subsequently called "Prony brake," consisting of a wooden clamp designed to fit the outer circumference of an engine's flywheel. A torque arm attached to the clamp prevented the clamp from rotating with the flywheel and movement of the torque arm was restricted by stops on a stationary object.

When the engine was running, force was transmitted from the flywheel to the clamp by the friction created between their contacting surfaces. Measurements of the force transmitted to the clamp were made by attaching suitable weights to the outer end of the torque arm. Multiplying the value of the weight in pounds, necessary to hold the arm in a stationary position by the arm's effective length, in feet, gave the pounds-feet of torque delivered by the flywheel. The effective length of a torque arm is the distance from a vertical line drawn through the center, or axis of rotation, of the power absorption unit to which it is attached to another vertical line drawn through the point of application of the weight on the arm.

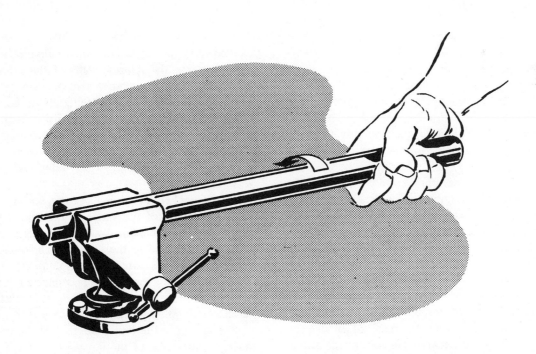

Torque is created when a force is exerted on an object in such a manner as to cause the object to rotate on its axis.

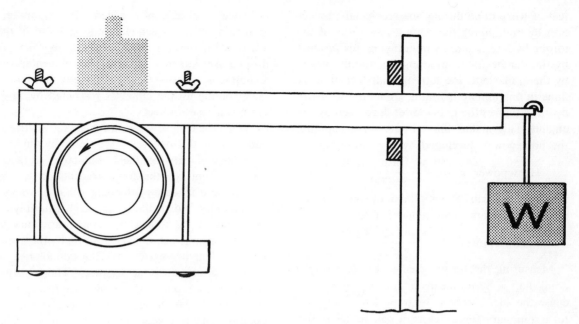

The Prony brake was used to measure torque by adding sufficient weight to the end of its torque arm to hold the arm steady.

Although inadequate means of dissipating heat generated by the friction between the flywheel and the brake made the Prony brake unsuitable for anything but quick torque readings, it was the first instrument of its kind and as such it served the purpose of pointing the way for further development work in the search for more practical torque measuring instruments.

Modern engine testing dynamometers utilize either electric or hydraulic absorption units capable of absorbing high torque loads for long periods of time. Electric absorption units consist of a large generator with a suitable coupling for connecting the generator's armature shaft to the crankshaft of an engine. The frame, or outer housing, of the generator is supported on ball bearings so it is free to rotate about the axis of the armature's shaft. Rotation of the frame is restricted by a torque arm. The outer end of the arm is connected to a weighing device that measures the force transmitted to the arm.

Transmission of torque from the revolving armature to the frame is the result of an electro-magnetic reaction between the coils in the armature and the field coils attached to the frame. Accompanying this reaction is the generation, in the armature coils, of an electric current. This

current is dissipated by converting it to heat, either by using it to light incandescent bulbs or by directing it through some other type of resistance unit.

An absorbtion unit for a hydraulic dynamometer consists of an impeller in a suitable housing. Cast into the interior walls of the housing are pockets that resist movement of water in the housing when the water is agitated by the impeller. The housing is mounted on ball bearings so it is free to rotate on the axis of the impeller shaft. Rotation of the housing is restricted by a torque arm connected at its outer end to a weighing device.

As the pockets in the wall of the housing restrict movement of the water in the unit, force imparted to the impeller by the engine's crankshaft is transferred to the housing. This enables the force to be measured by the weighing device to which the unit's torque arm is connected. Raising or lowering the water level in the housing varies the load imposed on the engine by the unit. The higher the level, the greater the resistance to movement of the impeller.

The weighing device on which the torque arm of any absorption unit acts can be a spring scale, a beam scale, a platform scale, or any other device calibrated to indicate a force in pounds or to indicate directly the pounds-feet of torque being transferred from the engine to the dynamometer. A direct-reading scale, rather than one that requires the juggling of sliding or loose weights, is generally used to speed the process of determining the torque load. If the weighing device indicates the force in pounds, a computation involving the length of the torque arm must be made for each of the force readings taken. At the same time a torque reading is being taken, the speed of rotation of the crankshaft, as indicated by a tachometer driven by the engine or the driven shaft of the absorption unit, is recorded.

The accuracy of horsepower measurements depends on the accuracy of the dynamometer's instrumentation but horsepower measurements made in different localities will vary with altitude and atmospheric conditions. To enable comparisons to be made between dynamometer tests conducted under different conditions of altitude, temperature, and humidity, it is necessary to ap-

ply correction factors to the conditions. A formula containing these factors has been standardized by the Society of Automotive Engineers. By applying this formula to the conditions under which a test was conducted, the result is converted to that which would have been obtained if the test had been run with dry air at sea level atmospheric pressure and with an air temperature of 60°F.

When the factors and formulas for computing horsepower are understood it becomes apparent that torque and horsepower cannot be separated, nor can one be increased at any given engine speed without increasing the other. This is because horsepower is directly proportional to the product of torque and crankshaft speed. It increases or decreases proportionately as either torque or crankshaft speed increases or decreases.

An engine's maximum torque and its maximum horsepower are developed at two widely varying speeds of crankshaft rotation. The 430 cubic-inch 1958 Mercury engine, for instance, develops its maximum torque of 480 pounds-feet

ENGINE PERFORMANCE

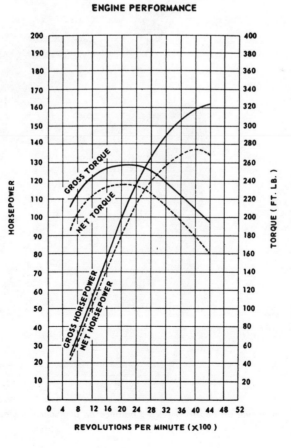

These are horsepower and torque curves of a standard Chevrolet V8 engine of 1955 vintage. "Gross" and "net" curves are explained in the text.

at 3000 revolutions per minute, compared to 360 horsepower at 4600 rpm. This variance is caused by the "volumetric efficiency" characteristics of internal combustion engines. An engine's volumetric efficiency is the ratio of the volume of fresh mixture in its cylinders at the end of intake strokes to the volume of the cylinders. The higher the volumetric efficiency, the greater will be the pressure exerted on the pistons on power strokes.

Due to the many factors that affect the flow of fresh mixture and exhaust gases in and out of an engine's cylinders, volumetric efficiency is comparatively low at low crankshaft speeds, becomes higher and reaches its maximum as the speed increases, and then drops off as the speed continues to increase above the point of maximum efficiency. It is at the point of maximum volumetric efficiency that the torque output of the engine reaches its highest value. Horsepower developed at this point, however, is low in comparison to the maximum rating because the crankshaft speed is low. The Mercury, for example, develops approximately 274 horsepower

A technician adjusts the scale balance on a modern engine test dynamometer.

at its speed of maximum torque output. As crankshaft speed increases, the horsepower increases, despite the fact that the torque is decreasing, until the point is reached where the proportional increase in crankshaft speed is matched by the proportional decrease in torque. In other words, when the result of multiplying the torque value by the crankshaft speed reaches its maximum, the horsepower output of the engine is at its maximum. As crankshaft speed increases beyond this point, the figure derived from multiplying the torque and speed together begins to become numerically smaller, meaning that the horsepower peak has been passed.

Horsepower measured with a dynamometer is the "actual" or "brake" horsepower developed by the engine. It is the power available at the engine's flywheel to do work. Brake horsepower should not be confused with mathematically computed horsepower ratings such as those used in many states for determining tax and license fees. These formulas are generally based on an engine's bore, stroke, and number of cylinders. Brake horsepower cannot be computed from engine dimensions because of the many variables involved in engine performance.

Horsepower ratings released by automobile manufacturers for each model of their engines sometimes specify whether or not the standard accessories used on the engine when it is installed in an automobile were on it when the horsepower was measured. An engine without its accessories is a "bare" engine and its horsepower in this condition is its "gross" power. A bare engine does not have a fan, water pump, or generator to turn, nor does it have a fuel pump or carburetor air cleaner or any of the other pumps or power-consuming devices that operate the many accessories so popular on modern automobiles. The exhaust system used for most dynamometer tests is usually a better system than the one the engine will have when it is in a chassis.

The horsepower an engine delivers when equipped with all accessories and installed in a chassis is called its "net" horsepower. This is the horsepower rating that determines performance but is seldom quoted in sales spiels.

Another horsepower rating that is seldom published but is nevertheless measured as a matter of course by engineers is the engine's "friction" horsepower. This is the power required to move the parts in the engine through their power-producing functions. It is a necessary evil that can not be eliminated, although usually it can be reduced somewhat.

The horsepower rating that is generally used by advertising and sales departments is the gross rating because it is as much as 20 percent higher than the net rating. It has been known for a company to add the friction rating to the gross rating. This is a strange form of mathematics but it makes for a high horsepower rating and easy-to-get sales appeal.

Something else that boosts factory horsepower ratings is that the engines used for test purposes at the factories are usually hand-built to the exact specifications set down by the engineering department. These engines aren't exposed to assembly line tolerances and assembly methods, which makes them considerably better products than units off the line. This adherence to specifications and the more careful assembly could be good for several horsepower at the flywheel.

During the past few years a new type of dynamometer designed for use in automotive service shops has become popular. This is the "chassis" dynamometer. Whereas engine dynamometers are used to measure the horsepower available at an engine's flywheel, the chassis dynamometer measures the horsepower available at an automobile's rear wheels.

A chassis dynamometer consists of a set of rollers so arranged that power transmitted to the rollers by the drive wheels of the car is indicated on a direct-reading horsepower meter. Rear wheel horsepower is the real measure of vehicle performance, for regardless of the horsepower available at an engine's flywheel, performance will not be good unless there is adequate horsepower at the car's driving wheels. The drastic difference found between flywheel and rear wheel horsepower outputs is the result of power losses in the transmission, driveline, and rear axle assembly.

CHAPTER FOUR

Getting More Horsepower from Your Engine

Facts about boring and stroking,
porting, oversize valves, reground camshafts,
valve springs, carburetion, exhaust systems.

STEPS IN THE FIRST PART of the formula for reworking an engine for greater torque and horsepower outputs are concerned entirely with improving its breathing ability. They are many and varied and they must be applied correctly and in the proper combinations if the desired results are to be obtained.

Boring and Stroking

Boring and stroking are methods used to enlarge the displacement of an engine's cylinders. Larger cylinder displacement improves breathing ability because it enables the cylinders to induct and consume greater quantities of air/fuel mixture. Boring and stroking are individual operations that can be applied singly or together. The maximum displacement increase will, of course, be realized if the engine is both bored and stroked; however, in some instances, such as when building an engine for a particular competition class for which displacement is limited, the permissible displacement increase may limit the modifications to either boring or stroking, or to small amounts of each.

Boring is the act of enlarging the diameter of an engine's cylinders by removing material from the walls of the cylinders. This is a simple matter if one has equipment; however, there are limitations to the amount of material that can be removed from the cylinder walls of any engine and if this limitation is exceeded it is possible that a portion or all of the walls will be bored away. Sometimes a cylinder may appear to be sound after it has been bored to a large oversize but after the engine is fired up its wall may crack or a section may be blown out of it. When this happens it is sometimes possible to save the block by installing a sleeve in the cylinder but usually the wisest thing to do is discard the block and start over with another one, trying a smaller bore diameter for safety's sake.

Cylinder blocks for most late model engines have adequate cylinder wall thickness for an overbore of 1/8-inch. Sometimes cylinders are bored more than this and are used without difficulty but a fellow who does this is taking a chance on ruining his block. To be on the safe side, if there is any doubt as to how much the cylinders in a particular block can be bored, it is a good idea before having the boring done to check with someone who has had experience with that type of block. Another good idea is to find out what sizes of special pistons are available for the engine. In many instances this will give an idea as to how much the cylinder can be bored; however, this isn't a positive rule because some piston manufacturers make and sell pistons for cylinder bores of extremely risky diameters. Stock replacement oversize pistons cannot be used as a gauge of how much a block can be bored because generally the maximum diameter of pistons made for this purpose is only .060-inch greater than that of stock cylinders. Most engine manufacturers recommend that a block with cylinders that must be bored larger than .060-inch be discarded and replaced with a new one.

Stroking is more complicated than boring in that it is a process than involves reworking the engine's crankshaft. This must be done in a shop equipped with welding and crank grinding equipment and by competent workmen. The principle

Cylinder boring machine is used to enlarge diameter of stock engine cylinders.

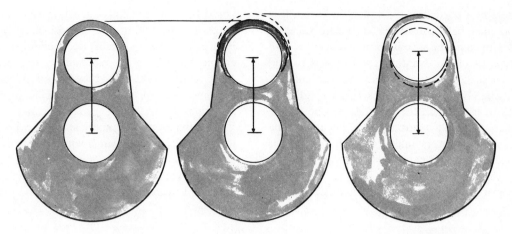

Sketch shows how crankshaft is built up and reground to increase crank "throw" and stroke length.

of stroking is to move the center of a crankshaft's crankpins farther from the center of its main bearing journals than they were originally. This increases the distance the pistons move in the cylinders as the shaft rotates.

When stroking first became popular, crankpins to be stroked were merely ground to a new diameter, with their center moved farther away from the axis of the crankshaft, and connecting rods made for the smaller crankpins were used on them. This method of stroking was made possible by the Ford Motor Company. Then, Ford was making crankshafts for their Ford V8 and Mercury engines that were interchangeable as far as their main bearing journal diameters were concerned but that had crankpins of different diameters. After the Merc pins had been ground to the standard Ford diameter, Ford bearings and connecting rods were used on them.

Mercury crankpins were .140-inch larger than Ford pins, making it possible to move their center one-half this distance, or .070-inch farther from the crankshaft's axis by grinding them to the Ford diameter. This made a stroke increase of twice .070-inch, or .140-inch possible but .125-inch became the standard increase. Stroking only .125-inch gave the fellow doing the grinding a little extra material he could use to allow for wear on the crankpins; also, it enabled him to allow for throws that didn't have exactly the correct stock stroke length and to correct the location of pins that weren't spaced exactly 90 degrees from each other. It wasn't uncommon to find such manufacturing errors on these shafts.

When engine manufacturers stopped making connecting rods designed for different diameter crankpins that could be used interchangeably in modern V8 engines, a way of restoring stroked crankpins to their original diameter so stock rods and bearings could be used on them had to be found. Many methods for doing this have been developed. The latest, and so far the best, is the welding method.

First of the many operations required to stroke a crank by the welding method is applying bead after bead of welding rod to the side of the crankpins farthest from the main bearing journals. In this way the pins are made oval in shape. Welding rod of a material that will bond well to the crankpins and provide a good wearing surface is used. After sufficient welding material has been applied to the pins, and while it is still hot, it is peened with an air hammer to relieve stresses in it and to increase its density. Heat absorbed by the shaft during the welding operation throws its main bearing journals out of alignment, making it necessary to straighten the shaft with a press before any grinding can be done to its crankpins.

After being straightened, the shaft is chucked in a crankshaft grinder adjusted to the new stroke length and the crankpins are rough-ground to a diameter slightly larger than the diameter to which they will be finished. Chucks in the grinding machine hold the shaft by its flywheel flange and front snout. The keyway in the snout for the sprocket or gear that drives the camshaft is used to index the shaft in the machine. After the first crankpin has been ground, the shaft is rotated exactly 90 degrees, as measured by some precision device, for each of the other crankpins.

During the rough grinding, considerable material is removed from the surface of the crankpins nearest the main bearing journals and the high spots are ground off the welded portion. As the grinding continues, the crankpins are changed from the oval shape they assumed when they were welded to round. If a cross section of one of these pins could be viewed after the grinding, the weld material would be seen in the form of a crescent adhering to the side of the pin farthest from the side of the main journals.

Further distortion in the shaft resulting from the rough grinding makes it necessary to straighten it again. Oil holes are then drilled through the weld material to intersect the original holes in the crankpins. This drilling is done from the outside of the crankpin rather than from the inside. The holes could be drilled from the inside by inserting a long drill through the oil passages from the main bearing journals but if they were drilled on the same angle as the passages they would penetrate the surface of the weld material at points too close to the center of the crankpin. Oil fed from holes in these positions would not lubricate the rod bearings as they should. By drilling the holes from outside the pins they can be placed in the center of the areas contacted by the bearings.

The crankpins are inspected and any pits or other imperfections found in the weld material are filled with welding beads to make them level with the rest of the surface. Surfaces of the crankshaft that weren't ground are cleaned with a portable grinder to remove any deposits of welding material that might be adhering to them. Next, the crankpins are again rough-ground, this time to within .010-inch of the diameter to which they will be finished. They are then inspected once more for pits or other imperfections. Any imperfections found are filled and the pins are ground to their finished diameter.

Factory specifications for crankpin and main bearing journal diameters generally allow a tolerance of .001 to .002-inch to cover variations due to mass production manufacturing methods. Crankpins on most stroked cranks are ground to the smaller diameter of the factory tolerance. The

reason for this is to provide the maximum clearance allowed by factory specifications between the pins and standard connecting rod bearings. Sometimes, for all-out engines to be used for competition where bearing life is of less importance than maximum horsepower output, the crankpins are ground even smaller than this to give the rod bearings still more clearance. This is something that shouldn't be done indiscriminately because it can increase the engine's rate of oil consumption as well as shorten bearing life.

Most stroked crankpins are lengthened a few thousandths of an inch over stock specifications. This is done by grinding the flanges at the ends of the pins. The reason for doing this is to provide slightly greater connecting rod end play on the pins and thereby enable greater quantities of oil to pass between the pins and the rod bearings. Oil cools as well as lubricates and the temperature of the bearings in a high-output engine must be kept within reasonable limits or the bearings will fail.

After the crankpins have been finished to size, the crankshaft is chucked in the crank grinder and its main bearing journals are ground to .010-inch undersize. The same amount of additional clearance ground into the crankpins is also ground into the main journals. After the main bearing journals have been ground, the rear surface of the flywheel flange is ground to guarantee its angularity with the shaft's axis. This is done to eliminate the possibility of flywheel runout in a fore and aft direction.

When a shaft's main bearing journals are ground, the center holes in the shaft's ends are

Welded material is applied to crank pins as the first step in altering crankshaft in pursuit for more horsepower.

First machining operation on altered crankshaft involves the rough grinding of the crank pins on the shaft.

used to center it in the grinder. However, quite often these holes aren't concentric with the shaft's snout and flywheel flange. To correct any misalignment at these points, a light cut is usually taken from the sides of the center holes while the shaft is supported in a lathe by its snout and flange. This guarantees that the center holes will be concentric with the snout and flange and that the main bearing journals will, therefore, also be concentric with the snout and flange and in their correct positions in relation to the crankpins.

To ensure maximum bearing life, each crankpin and main bearing journal is polished in a micro-finishing machine. This amounts to nothing more than dressing the pins and journals with a power-driven abrasive belt. Micro-finishing is a polishing operation that must remove only a fraction of a thousandth of an inch of material to be effective but it requires a certain amount of skill so the pins won't be made out-of-round or tapered by the removal of an uneven layer of material from their surfaces.

A crankshaft stroked as described by a competent workman and on a good grinder will be as good a shaft as one can possibly get as far as the alignment of its crankpins in relation to each other and to the main journals, and the diameters of the pins and journals are concerned. The crankpins will be exactly 90 degrees apart, the stroke length of each crank throw will be exactly as specified, and the crankpins and main bearing journals will be of the specified diameters and they will not be tapered.

In addition to making stroking possible in late model engines, enlarging stroked crankpins to their original diameter eliminated the restriction to the amount of stroke increase that was imposed by the diameters of the bearings in interchangeable connecting rods.

The only restriction, within reasonable limits, to the stroke increase possible with welded crankpins is the clearance in the crankcase. As the stroke is lengthened, the lower ends of the connecting rods describe a larger circle than they did originally. If the stroke is made too long parts of the rods will hit either the lower ends of the cylinder bores or some of the cam lobes on the camshaft. In some engines interference will occur at both these points. Some cylinder blocks will take a stroke increase of as much as ⅜-inch without difficulty but others will require modifications for this amount. The maximum stroke increase used in modern engines is approximately ½-inch.

Interference between connecting rods and the lower ends of the cylinders is usually easy to correct. As a rule the actual point of interference is between the nut on one of the rod's cap bolts and the lower end of the cylinder in the bank opposite the one in which the rod is installed. Points where interference might occur are found by temporarily installing the crankshaft and at least one connecting rod and piston assembly in each cylinder bank. The crankshaft is then rotated slowly and the points where the rods touch the block are marked. A notch is then ground in the bottom of all the cylinders in each bank in the same relative position indicated on the marked cylinders. The ground areas should be wide enough and deep enough to provide at least 1/16-inch clearance on all sides of the member that caused the interference. Grinding slots in these areas of the cylinder block seldom causes any difficulty because the material at the lower ends of the cylinders is usually quite thick.

Points of interference between the upper ends of the connecting rod bolts and the lobes on the camshaft's cams is checked with the crankshaft, all the rod and piston assemblies, and the camshaft and its drive sprockets and gears in the cylinder block. It is important that the camshaft be in time with the crankshaft, as it will be when the engine is assembled. The reason for this is that some of the rods may have sufficient clearance when the camshaft is in time with the crankshaft and not have clearance when the shafts aren't in time. It would be desirable for the rods to have clearance for all positions of the camshaft but it is absolutely necessary to have clearance only when the two shafts are in time.

Clearance between the rods and cams is checked by turning the crankshaft while watching the possible points of interference. Care must be taken to not bump the rods into any of the cam lobes. It would be possible to damage a lobe quite severely in this manner. Each of the rods should clear the camshaft by at least .030-inch. The blades of a thickness gauge can be used to check the clearance. If any rod does not have enough clearance, clearance must be provided by filing its area of interference. This must be done carefully so only enough material will be removed to provide clearance and not so much that the bolt head or the rod will be weakened.

In some Cadillac engines interference between upper ends of the rods and the cams is so bad that studs must be installed in place of one bolt in each rod. Studs must be custom-made for these installations. The bolt hole in the rod is threaded and after the stud has been screwed into the rod its upper end is welded to the rod so it can't unscrew. After studs have been installed it is necessary to have the rods reconditioned by a company that specializes in this type of work. This must be done so the bearing bores in the rods will be restored to their original round condition and diameter. Installing studs in rods is rather a costly procedure but in some engines it must be done if a stroked crankshaft is to be used.

Stroker Pistons

Special pistons must be used with stroked crankshafts. The reason for this is that the piston pin bores in the connecting rods attached to the crankpins of a stroked crankshaft rise to a higher position in the cylinders when the shaft rotates than they did originally. The distance the rods travel up the cylinders above their stock position is equal to one-half the amount the shaft was stroked. In other words, if a shaft had been stroked one-half inch, the rods would rise a

Final crank pin grinding is precision operation. Note dial micrometer used to gauge crankpin diameter during this operation.

Grinding surfaces of the flywheel flange to make it perpendicular to the axis of the crankshaft journals.

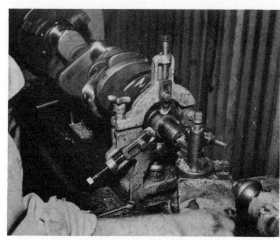

Machining center hole in crankshaft nose to guarantee concentricity of center with the main bearing journals.

quarter-inch higher in the cylinders than they did with a stock crankshaft. If stock pistons were installed on the rods their heads would be a quarter-inch higher in relation to the tops of the cylinders when they were in top center positions than they were with a stock crankshaft. In most engines this would cause interference between the pistons and the cylinder heads. This, of course, makes such an installation impossible.

The distance from the center of a piston's pin bore to the top of its head is the piston's "compression height." Compression height of "low crown" pistons made for use with stroked crankshafts is reduced one-half the amount the shaft was stroked. This reduced compression height places the top of a low crown piston when it is at top center in its cylinder at the same height as the head of a stock piston with a stock crankshaft. Low crown pistons are designated as ¼, 3/16, ⅛, or whatever the measurement may actually be, low crown. The figure used is the actual amount the compression height of the pistons is lower than that of a stock piston.

A piston used with a stroked crankshaft travels farther down a cylinder than it would with a stock crankshaft. This additional travel is also equal to one-half the stroke increase. To compensate for this, skirts on the pistons must be made shorter so they will not hit the counterweights on the crankshaft. It isn't wise to shorten a piston's skirt too much because if the skirt is too short in relation to the piston's diameter it won't

be able to stabilize the piston in the cylinder as it should. When a piston is not held square with the wall of its cylinder at all times the faces of its rings wear on a radius and then the rings are unable to hold compression and combustion pressures and oil as they should. Also, a piston with a short skirt has more of a tendency to knock as it travels through the strokes of its cycle. Up to now the necessary reduction in skirt length for crankshaft with maximum stroke increase hasn't created too much trouble; however, as cylinder bore diameters become greater, skirt length may become a problem.

Pistons for stroked crankshafts are usually made for a variety of cylinder bore diameters ranging up to the maximum oversize considered practical for the block for which they are made. Generally, the pistons are designed so that stock piston pins may be used in them. If pins aren't supplied with the pistons it would be a good idea to check with the piston manufacturer to determine which pins he recommends. In engines being converted for competition use it might be wise to try to find pins that are stronger than the stock type. Engine manufacturers are making pins larger and stronger as they raise the horsepower of their engines; this is an indication that pins should be given consideration when an engine is reworked. Pins seldom break but they will flex and crack their pistons if they aren't stiff enough for the loads they must carry. This can cause extensive engine damage.

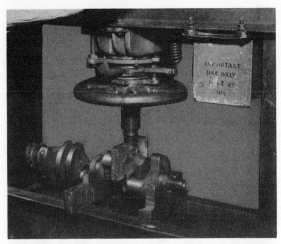

After grinding operations are complete, crankshaft is carefully straightened and aligned in a hydraulic press.

Eliminating points of interference with the new crankshaft may require hammered blisters in the engine's oil pan.

Stroker Kits

When crankshaft stroking first became popular the fellow who planned to stroke his engine was faced with the job of having its shaft stroked and then finding pistons and other related parts to go with it. Then, when he had assembled all these parts, he had to take them to someone who could balance them. Balancing is an extremely important operation in any V8 engine and its importance is multiplied when a shaft is stroked. Complete information is given on this part of the job in the chapter on balancing.

In recent years the popularity of stroking has made it possible for many shops that specialize in this sort of work to sell "stroker" kits. Contained in these kits are all the parts a fellow needs to stroke his engine. All he has to do is buy a kit, have the cylinders in his block bored, grind whatever clearance notches are necessary in the lower ends of the block's cylinders, and install the parts in the kit in the block.

Stroker kits contain a crankshaft with the desired stroke length, pistons for the desired cylinder bore diameter to match the stroke, piston pins, piston rings, connecting rods, connecting rod bearing inserts, and main bearing inserts. All the parts are balanced as an assembly. As a rule, crankshafts in kits are used; connecting rods are generally used but completely reconditioned, sometimes new; all other parts are new. The customer often has his choice of the makes of pistons available for such installations and of the brand of piston rings. There is usually a trade-in allowance for the customer's crankshaft and connecting rods if they can meet certain specifications. This makes it possible for a fellow who has these parts to save quite a bit of money on a kit and still take advantage of the convenience it offers. For the fellow who is starting from scratch and doesn't have any parts to trade in, a stroker kit is the answer because it saves him the trouble of canvassing the wrecking yards to find parts he can have reworked.

Porting

Porting is the operation of removing material from the walls of the intake and exhaust ports and passages to increase their cross-sectional area. This is done to make it easier for larger quantities of fresh fuel and air mixture to flow into the cylinders and for greater quantities of exhaust gases to be pumped out of the cylinders. An important part of the enlarging procedure is to eliminate any irregularities in the surfaces of the ports and passages and to give the surfaces a smooth finish. Irregularities are removed so there won't be restrictions in some of the ports that aren't in others and the surfaces are smoothed to minimize their resistance to the gases flowing through the passages.

At one time porting was one of the more important parts of an engine reworking job, especially if the engine had been bored and stroked.

Larger ports and passages were absolutely necessary in bored and stroked engines to handle the larger displacement of their cylinders. In the last two or three years porting has become less important for the simple reason that the ports and passages in engines built during this time are more than adequate in their stock form for reworked engines. However, in older engines porting is still a very necessary improvement.

The idea of porting is to remove as much material as possible from the walls of intake and exhaust passages so the flow capacity of the passages will be increased to the practical maximum. This material must be removed carefully. Only too frequently an over-zealous hot rodder will remove so much material from a passage wall that he will grind completely through it, or the wall will be made so thin that it will collapse when the engine is started. Ports and passages in the newer engines need only a light grinding job to remove irregularities and to give their surfaces a smooth finish.

If a fellow has a set of heads that require an old fashioned porting job and he doesn't have the equipment or experience to do the job, he would be wise to trust them to one of the porting experts that can be found in various parts of the country. A good porting job isn't too expensive and it might save the cost of a cylinder head or two.

Oversize Valves

Oversize valves, once considered necessary in any reworked engine, are seldom needed in the newer engines because the valves in most late model V8's are extremely large in their stock form. If an intake valve and its port are too large for their cylinder, they can be detrimental to the engine's performance. This is the result of the loss of velocity of the fresh fuel and air mixture through the port and past the valve head as it flows into the cylinder. When the velocity of the mixture drops to too low a value the cylinder will not receive as large a charge as it should. This particular factor of engine performance depends a great deal on the valve timing and lift provided by the engine's camshaft. For a happy combination of conditions in the intake side of the engine, velocity of the mixture past the valve head should be slightly greater than the velocity through the intake passage and valve port.

Mechanical limitations to the diameters of the valves that can be installed in any engine are the amounts the valve ports can be enlarged and the amount of clearance in the combustion chambers around the valve seats.

Installation of oversize valves has been simplified for many engines by the availability of special ready-to-install valves. Often, when special valves aren't available for an engine, it is possible to find valves for a different model of the same make of engine being worked on that can be used for oversize valve installations. It is important when substitutions of this type are being made that the new valves have stems exactly the same diameter as those on the valves they are to replace. Valve stem-to-guide clearance is important to the control of oil consumption and to smooth low speed operation. Also, grooves in the ends of the stems for valve spring washer locks must be in approximately the correct position in relation to the heads on the valves so that valve spring length can be adjusted correctly when the valves are in the cylinder heads. The stems must, of course, be the correct length so the rocker arms will contact them at the proper angle. Valve stems on special oversize valves made for a specific engine will be of the correct diameter and length and their spring retainer grooves will be in the correct position.

The amount of clearance in the combustion chambers around the valve seats is important to maximum engine performance because it has an influence on the quantity of fresh mixture and exhaust gases that can flow through the cylinder. When the valves are open there should be enough unrestricted area around their heads to pass the full flow capacity of the valve ports and the passages that serve them. Less area than this will restrict the engine's breathing. This is why it isn't wise to install oversize valves with extremely large heads in some engines. Although it might be mechanically possible to install such valves without any trouble, it is entirely possible that the engine would breathe better with smaller valves. Another thing about oversize valves that must be considered is that exhaust valves are opened against considerable pressure in the cylinders and as their head diameter becomes greater, the pressure on the valve actuating mechanism during this period also becomes greater. However, as valve spring pressures go up in new engines reason for concern for this condition becomes less important.

The amount to enlarge areas around valve seats can be something of a problem. They should be enlarged enough to provide adequate flow past the valve heads but it must be remembered that any material removed from the combustion chamber walls for this purpose also lowers the engine's compression ratio. This effect on compression ratio wouldn't matter in some engines because compensation could be made by other means to make the ratio as high as required. In other engines, especially those that are to be only

Stroker piston on left is shorter from the center of the pin to head than the stock piston shown on the right.

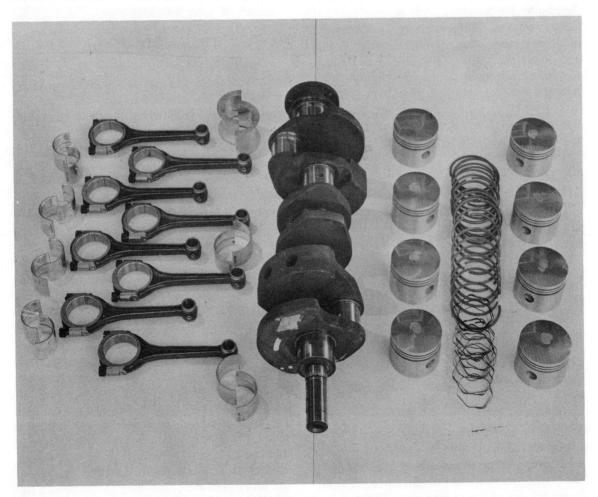

Complete stroker kit includes all parts necessary to stroke the engine.

Ports in the cylinder head are enlarged and polished with an electric hand grinder. This operation requires care.

ing and the grinding must be done accurately to ensure removal of the same amount of material from each of the combustion chambers. Most stock chambers have fairly uniform volumes and this uniformity must be preserved when the volumes of the chambers are changed in any way. If the volumes of the chambers are made unequal by removing unequal quantities of material from them, the compression ratios of the cylinders will vary and this will affect their detonation characteristics and power output.

Valves become heavier as their head diameter increases and valve weight has always been a problem in engines that must run at high crankshaft speeds. Oversize valves installed in some of the older engines and the large stock valves in many new engines must be lightened before they can be used in reworked engines that must run at high crankshaft speeds. Methods of removing weight from valves are described in the chapter on valve reconditioning.

Reground Camshafts

One of the oldest, and now the most common, method of increasing an engine's breathing ability is regrinding the cams on its camshaft. Camshaft regrinding has become big business for several companies.

Terms used to describe valve action are lift, opening and closing times, opening and closing rates, duration of opening, and overlap. Each of these factors has something to do with the way an engine runs. For maximum performance they must be combined in the correct proportions so that the engine can breathe as well as possible.

Lift is the amount a valve leaves its seat when it is opened by its cam. It is measured in thousandths of an inch. The quantity of fresh mixture or exhaust gases that can flow past a valve's head is dependent in part on the valve's lift. The higher the lift, up to a certain point, the greater the quantity. Lift is proportional to the difference in the distance from the center of the camshaft to the surface of the lobes of the cams and the distance from the center of the shaft to the surface of the heels of the cams. In an L-head engine lift is directly proportional to this difference and in an overhead valve engine that uses rocker arms it is proportional to the difference times the lift ratio of the arms. Most rocker arms have lift ratios ranging from 1.5 to 1 to 1.8 to 1.

mildly converted, the removal of material from the combustion chambers might become a critical factor; however, the highest useful compression ratio an engine can use is of little value if breathing around the heads of its valves is restricted.

Another limitation to the amount the areas around valve seats can be enlarged is the thickness of the combustion chamber walls. The walls must not be weakened by the removal of material to the point where they will crack or collapse under combustion pressures. Also, it wouldn't be wise to enlarge the chambers so much that they overlapped the cylinder bores. This condition is found in some stock engines, but it isn't good, especially under intake valves, because the overlapped area forms a lip that part of the incoming mixture strikes as it flows into the cylinder. This creates an unwanted turbulence in the mixture that may not be particularly beneficial to maximum breathing.

The best method of enlarging areas around valve seats is with large cutters that can be piloted in the valve guides. Cutters of this type can be rotated either by hand or with a power-driven machine. Areas machined in this manner can then be blended into the adjoining walls with small grinding stones. If cutters suitable for the job aren't available, the same results can be obtained by grinding away all the material that must be removed. Before this is done, the gasket surface of the head should be marked to indicate the boundaries of the ground areas. This mark-

Opening and closing times are determined by the position of the lobes on the camshaft and they are measured in degrees of crankshaft rotation before or after the pistons served by the valves reach top or bottom center in their cylinders. Top or bottom center piston position would depend on the stroke on which the valve function occurred. For instance, an intake valve that opens eight degrees before top center starts to leave its seat when the crankshaft reaches a point where eight more degrees of rotation will move the piston in the cylinder served by the valve to its top center position on its exhaust stroke. Intake valves close after the piston has passed its bottom center position on its intake stroke, exhaust valves open before the piston reaches bottom center on its power stroke, and exhaust valves close after the piston reaches top center on its exhaust stroke. Opening and closing times are determined by the shape of the cams.

Opening and closing rates are the speeds at which the valves leave their seats and move to their full open position, and vice-versa. These rates are measured in thousandths of an inch of valve movement per degree of crankshaft rotation. It is desirable to open and close valves as rapidly as possible so maximum advantage can be taken of their full-open position but there are certain limitations to the movement of valve actuating mechanisms that limit opening and closing rates. One of these is that valve lifters must be lifted comparatively slowly during their first few thousandths of an inch of movement so that the lash clearances required in the valve actuating mechanism when a valve is on its seat will be taken up slowly. If this clearance were taken up rapidly, the valve action would be noisy. Noise from this source can be tolerated in a competition engine but it would not be acceptable in a passenger car engine. After a valve has left its seat, its opening rate is speeded up. Closing action is similar to opening action except that it is reversed so the valve closes rapidly until it nears its seat and then is slowed so it will seat quietly.

Duration of opening is the number of degrees of crankshaft rotation during which a valve is off its seat. It is equal to the number of degrees of crankshaft rotation between a valve's opening and closing times.

Overlap is the number of degrees of crankshaft rotation at the end of exhaust strokes during which the intake and exhaust valves for the same cylinder are open at the same time. Overlap is made necessary by the comparatively slow rates of movement of the valves when they first start to open and when they are just closing and by the inertia of the fresh mixture that flows into the cylinder. Inertia has a tendency to prevent the mixture from starting to flow when the intake valve first opens and to try to keep it flowing when the piston has completed its intake stroke. If the intake valve were to start to open the instant the piston started its intake stroke, the piston would be well down the cylinder before the valve had opened an appreciable amount and atmospheric pressure outside the engine had gotten around to starting air flowing through the carburetor to overcome the low pressure in the cylinder. By starting to open the valve before the piston begins its stroke, the valve is far enough off its seat by the time the stroke does begin that mixture can start flowing past its head. This compensates for the valve's slow rate of movement when it is starting to open.

Overcoming inertia to start the mixture flowing into the cylinder also involves the exhaust valve's closing time. As exhaust gases flow out of a cylinder fitted with a free-flowing exhaust system, their movement through the valve port, exhaust passage in the head, and exhaust system creates an inertia in the gases that tends to keep them flowing. By holding the exhaust valve open after the piston has reached the end of its exhaust

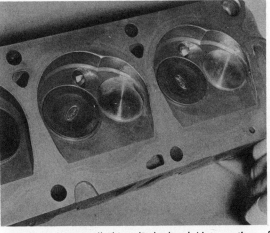

Oversize valves installed in cylinder head. Note portions of the head that have been machined for adequate clearance.

stroke, it's possible for this inertia to create a low pressure in the cylinder before the piston actually starts its intake stroke. If the intake valve is open at this time the cylinder's intake passages will also be subjected to this low pressure and mixture will start to flow into the cylinder. By the time the piston starts its intake stroke, inertia of the mixture has been overcome and its flows readily.

Valve overlap is beneficial to engine performance at high engine speeds only. At high speeds, the length of time a cylinder has to induct its fresh charge is so short that anything that can be done to start the mixture flowing into the cylinders sooner on intake strokes and to keep it flowing longer will have a beneficial effect on horsepower output. At low engine speeds overlap becomes detrimental to engine performance because the exhaust gases and fresh mixture don't have sufficient inertia to prevent dilution of the fresh mixture with exhaust gases. This causes the engine to run roughly at idle and low speeds and reduces its torque output until crankshaft speed reaches the point where the effect of overlap becomes beneficial. This point is very often quite high in the rpm range, making some cams undesirable for anything but high-speed running.

The closing time of the intake valve also has an effect on the quantity of mixture in the cylinder when the compression stroke starts. Inertia of the mixture as it flows into the cylinder tends to keep it moving after the piston has reached

the bottom of its intake stroke and started back up the cylinder on its compression stroke. By holding the valve open on the compression stroke until just before compression pressure in the cylinder becomes greater than the force of the mixture flowing into the cylinder, the greatest possible charge of mixture will be inducted.

The opening time of the exhaust valve has much to do with the amount of exhaust gas that will be expelled from the cylinder on the exhaust stroke. The idea is to open the valve near the end of the power stroke at the instant the combustion pressure in the cylinder drops to the point where it has lost its value as far as turning the crankshaft is concerned. Although the pressure in the cylinder at this time isn't high enough to do any useful work on the piston, it is considerably higher than atmospheric pressure so it starts the exhaust gas flowing out of the cylinder before the piston starts its exhaust stroke. By the time the exhaust stroke is started, the inertia of the gas in the cylinder's branch of the exhaust system has been overcome and the gas is flowing freely.

Of all the things that go on in an engine, the action of the valves has by far the most influence on how the engine will run at different speeds and on its torque and horsepower at those speeds. By hot rod standards valve timing in stock engines is very mild. It is made this way purposely to allow the engines to idle well and to run smoothly at low speeds. Mild valve action enables an en-

Cutting tool for valve clearance has pilot to center in valve guide. Many operations require special tools to do job.

The cutter is shown here removing metal from cylinder head for clearance for oversize valve installation.

gine to deliver its maximum torque at a crank-shaft speed where it will be of the most use for normal driving conditions. Maximum horsepower with mild valve action is developed at a modest crankshaft speed in comparison to the speed the engine is mechanically capable of turning. Mild action also has the advantage of being inherently quiet. This is important in a passenger car engine.

Despite the limitations that govern their design stock cams are surprisingly good, from the standpoint of performance. This has been proven in engine dynamometer tests made by men who regrind cams and others who do engine reworking. But when an engine is reworked to enable it to develop the maximum horsepower of which it is capable, its camshaft must be reground to enable full advantage to be taken of the many other modifications made to it.

The idea of regrinding cams is to make the various valve functions occur at the correct times in relation to piston movement so that at certain crankshaft speeds the engine will develop the maximum horsepower of which it is capable. It is necessary to change the contours of the cams to achieve this result. Effectiveness of new cam grinds is usually checked by running reground camshafts in an engine connected to a dynamometer. The actual results are then compared with the desired results and any changes in the cams indicated by the engine's performance are made in subsequent grinds.

If the people who build an engine can't design

The depth of the cut for valve clearance must be equal in each combustion chamber, requiring meticulous skill.

a camshaft for it that will allow it to idle smoothly and run well at low speeds and also deliver the maximum power of which it is capable at high speeds, it doesn't seem reasonable that anyone else could. Unfortunately, it's true that no one has been able to design such cams. This is why each company that regrinds camshafts has four or five or possibly more different grinds for each make of engine. Each grind is designed to allow the engine to run its best at a certain crankshaft speed. By having different grinds, these companies can supply a reground camshaft for the type of performance a specific customer may want. The customer may plan to run his engine on the road, on a drag strip, on a track, at the dry lakes or at Bonneville, or in a boat. A cam ground to provide maximum vehicle acceleration, such as for drag or track use, wouldn't be suitable in an engine to be used in a car designed for top speed straightaway runs or in a boat.

The variety of reground camshafts on the market makes it difficult for a fellow who is reworking an engine to choose the one best suited to his purpose. About all he can do is select a reliable grinder and discuss his needs with him. Most fellows who grind cams now are entirely reliable in this respect and they know from their own tests, or the experiences of their customers, what their grinds will do for an engine.

The mechanics of cam grinding are fairly simple. After a camshaft has been checked for straightness and, if necessary, been straightened, it is mounted in a special grinding machine equipped with a large-diameter grinding wheel. As the shaft is rotated by the machine it is automatically moved toward or away from the grinding wheel. This movement is controlled by a "master cam" on the machine and it determines the new contour of the cam being ground. Development of master cams is the difficult part of regrinding camshafts, and as the contours of the cams depend on the shape of the master cam, a new master must be made for each desired change in contour.

When the automotive industry first began to manufacture overhead valve engines on a mass production basis they encountered a cam lobe and valve lifter wear problem. The problem was most perplexing in that it didn't seem to follow any set pattern. Many theories were expounded

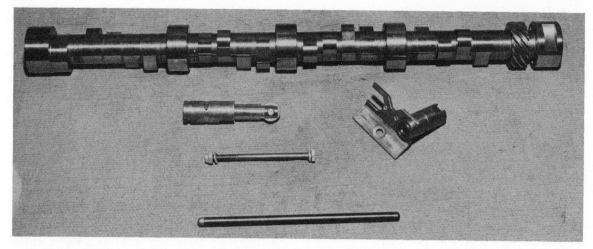

This shows camshaft and related parts for use with roller tappets. Note roller at lower end of the tappet.

but no one seemed to be able to actually pinpoint the reason that some cams and lifters would wear in a few hours of engine operation to the point where they would no longer open the valves while other cams and lifters of the same material and made with the same manufacturing process would run for many thousands of miles and show only normal wear.

In the past couple of years wear rates of stock cams and lifters seem to have abated somewhat but the men who regrind cams still find it a problem with some of their grinds. They have solved this problem with what they call a "hard-facing" process. Hard-facing is no more than the application by welding methods of a layer of a hard material of some kind to the cam lobes. Some grinders cover the full width of the lobe with hard material but others just fill a groove machined in the lobe. Lobes to be covered with a full-width layer must be rough-ground to a contour lower than that of their finished shape before the hard material is applied to them. The cams are then finish-ground so that the hard material blends into the cam material.

Hard-facing runs up the cost of a reground cam but it has been highly effective in combating wear. Many companies who supply hard-faced cams are so confident in their wearing ability that they sell them with a liberal guarantee. Usually this guarantee is good only if the valve lifters and springs recommended by the grinder are used with the cam. Most lifters sold for this purpose have chilled-iron faces. These have been found to have the best wearing qualities when used on most types of reground cams.

Some companies grind cams that are used with roller tappets. The shape of the cams necessary for roller tappets makes it necessary for them to be ground on "billet" shafts. Billet shafts are made in their entirety by the cam grinders. They are usually turned from lengths of round steel stock of alloys suitable for the application. Their cams and bearing surfaces are then ground. The tappets are also made in their entirety and their rollers are generally fitted with needle bearings to guarantee long life.

Roller-tappet camshafts have an advantage over flat-tappet types in that they can provide valve action of a radical nature without damage to their cams or lifters. In some engines this makes possible extremely high torque and horsepower outputs. However, flat-tappet cams have been known to perform as well as roller types.

Roller tappets have the additional advantage of rolling over the cam lobes instead of sliding over them as do flat tappets. This reduces wear on the lobes and tappets to the minimum. Disadvantages of roller-tappet camshafts are their price, which is quite high; the comparatively difficult installation of the tappets in the cylinder block; and the fact that most grinds are for competition engines only.

Valve Springs

Valve springs have much to do with cam lobe and lifter life and the way an engine runs. The pressure the springs exert on the stems of the valves must be great enough to make the valves and their actuating mechanism follow the cams at high engine speeds but it must not be so high that it creates excessive pressure on the valve lifters and cam lobes.

Most stock valve springs are not stiff enough for reworked engines. This is a matter of small consequence to the engine builder because springs capable of doing the job are available from companies who regrind camshafts. Most of these companies have at least two spring combinations, each of which is designed for certain of their cam grinds. It is imperative that the springs recommended for a specific grind be used if maximum cam and lifter life, and engine performance within the camshaft's limitation, are to be enjoyed.

Most cam regrinders recommend a single spring for their milder grinds. This spring is usually stiffer than the stock spring it will replace and it may have more or less difference between its valve-closed and valve-open pressures than the stock spring. Cams with more radical contours for competition engines usually require dual springs. Dual springs can exert considerably more pressure on a valve than is possible with a single spring because their total pressure is their combined pressure. Dual springs consist of an outer spring that is usually approximately the same diameter as a stock single spring and an inner spring small enough in diameter to fit inside the outer spring.

In addition to the high pressure they exert, dual valve springs provide a safety factor not possible with single springs. If one spring of a dual setup should break while the engine was running, the other spring would continue to close the valve. The valve wouldn't function as it should at high engine speeds but the engine would still run and the valve wouldn't be able to drop into the cylinder and punch a hole in the head of the piston, as it possibly could if a single spring should break.

Installation of dual valve springs on the heads of many late model engines creates something of a problem because of the "integral" valve guides that have been adopted by many engine manufacturers. Integral guides differ from the pressed-in guides used previously in all engines in that they are part of the head casting. The reason for the adoption of integral guides, as far as engine life is concerned, is that they are able to transmit more heat from the valve stems to the cooling water in the heads. This is said to increase valve life.

The as-cast outer circumference of the portion of integral guides that projects out of the heads makes it impossible to install inner valve springs on the valves until the guides are machined to a smaller diameter. This machining isn't too difficult if one has the correct tool for the job. Cutters for this purpose can be bought or borrowed from the companies that regrind camshafts. On some heads it is also necessary to enlarge the existing valve spring recess at the bottom of the guide so it will accomodate the new outer spring. Cutters for machining the guides will also enlarge the spring recess when this is needed.

Stock valve spring washers and split locks are generally used with single springs of any type. Special hardened-steel washers are usually recommended for dual-spring installations because of the pressure dual springs exert and also be-

Dual valve springs with related parts are available in kits.

Hollow end mill to machine integral guides for springs.

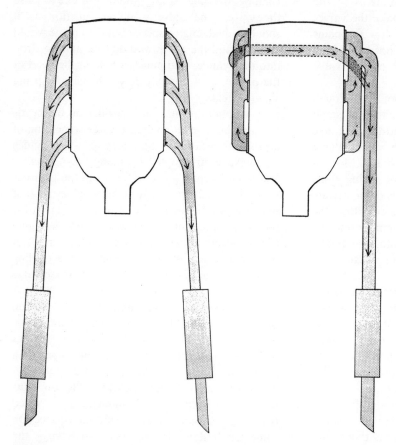

Comparison of single exhaust system for V8 engine to smooth-flowing dual system with special headers is shown in this diagramatic illustration.

cause they have a surface on which the upper end of the inner spring seats. Stock split locks are used with most special retainer washers.

Carburetion

Installation of additional carburetor capacity is the final improvement to the intake side of the engine's breathing system. All the modifications done to the inside of the engine to improve its breathing capacity would be wasted if the air flow and fuel flow capacities of its carburetion system and intake manifold were not enlarged accordingly.

Most late model V8 engines are equipped with a single four-throat carburetor. Of the remainder, most have a single two-throat. Dual four-throats and triple two-throats are available on some engines as optional equipment. Carburetion capacity of an engine equipped with a single four-throat or single two-throat is increased by installing multiple carburetors. This requires a special intake manifold. Manifolds for this pur-

pose are made to accomodate dual four-throat carburetors and three to eight two-throats. For some time now the trend in multiple-carburetor installations has favored two-throat carburetors.

For an engine to be used in a passenger car that is to be driven for normal use during the week and possibly on a drag strip on weekends, three two-throats are recommended. Three two-throats of the correct size will provide adequate carburetion for any engine to be used in a passenger car and they make possible the use of "progressive" throttle linkage. More than three two-throat carburetors are seldom installed on an engine to be used for normal driving but as many as eight are often installed on competition engines.

It might be wise to install a Hilborn fuel injector on an engine built for all-out competition use. These injectors are now available for either gasoline or alcohol fuel. They are not suitable for street driving. More information on multiple carburetor setups and fuel injectors will be found in their respective chapters.

Exhaust System

The duty of an engine's exhaust system is to provide a path from the exhaust passage of each cylinder to the atmosphere. The capacity of the system must be adequate for the volume of gases that must flow through it and its design must be such that the gases can move through it with the least possible difficulty.

When the flow capacity of an exhaust system is inadequate for an engine, "back pressure" is built up in the system when the engine is running at high speeds. Back pressure not only opposes the flow of exhaust gases through the system but it also opposes the flow of gases out of the engine's cylinders. The result is that an excessive quantity of exhaust gas remains in the cylinder after the completion of the exhaust stroke to dilute and heat the fresh charge of incoming mixture on the following intake stroke and to take up some of the space that should be available for the fresh mixture. Dilution and heating of the fresh mixture by exhaust gas and the reduction in the quantity of mixture that can be inducted into the cylinder lowers the pressure on the cylinder's piston on the following power stroke.

An ideal exhaust system would be one that was so designed that gases flowing through it would create a negative pressure, or vacuum, at the exhaust ports of the engine's cylinders. This would help the flow of gases out of the cylinders and when used with camshafts ground with considerable overlap it would also help the fresh mixture start to flow into the cylinders when the intake valves opened. An exhaust system of this type presents an extremely difficult engineering problem that requires many hours of experimentation with exhaust pipes of different diameters and lengths. Few hot rodders have the time or inclination to work on such a project.

Included in a stock passenger car exhaust system are the manifolds that bolt to the engine, the head pipes between the manifolds and the mufflers, and the "tail pipes" that run from the mufflers to the rear of the car. Some automobiles have only one muffler and tail pipe but many of them now have a muffler and tail pipe for each of the engine's cylinder banks. A system with two mufflers and tail pipes is usually adequate for a stock engine but it may not have the capacity for an engine that has been reworked.

Exhaust manifolds on modern engines are usually a compromise between what the engine really needs and what will fit in the chassis. Manifold design is also influenced by production cost, as is the design of many other engine components. However, regardless of the reasons for the shortcomings of stock manifolds, for a reworked engine to run as it should it is usually necessary to replace its stock manifolds with "headers."

Headers are special exhaust manifolds that are usually fabricated from steel tubing. They are designed to handle the flow of exhaust gases from an engine in an efficient manner. Good headers are available for some late model engines but not for all of them. Engines for which ready-made headers are not available pose a problem. There are companies that make custom-made headers for any engine but when a fellow buys headers of this type he must be careful to be sure he is getting a good product.

When headers first became popular thousands of sets for flathead Ford V8 and other engines were sold before anyone thought to check their efficiency. When someone finally tested a few representative models on a dynamometer it was found that most of the headers being made at that time weren't as efficient as stock manifolds. Now, however, a little more integrity has found its way into the header manufacturing business. Most of the companies offering ready-made

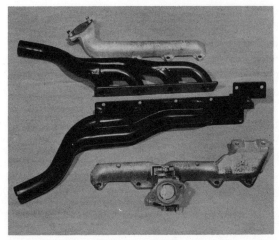

Special exhaust headers in center of photo are replacement for stock manifolds shown at top and bottom.

Straight individual exhaust stacks extend grotesquely at upward angle from extensively modified competition engine.

The owner of this competition hot rod prefers a collector-type exhaust system, with a single pipe running aft to rear.

headers for sale have conducted tests that have verified their products to be more efficient than the manifolds they replace. These findings are reflected by faster speeds and lower elapsed times on drag strips.

Head pipes and tail pipes on most late model cars are adequate for street use but some stock mufflers are too restrictive. Mufflers of this type should be replaced with special mufflers of the straight-through type. Straight-through mufflers are available in different lengths to give them different tone qualities. Contrary to common belief, an exhaust system doesn't have to be noisy to be efficient, and a fellow is showing good sense when he installs mufflers long enough to quiet the exhaust. A noisy exhaust system does nothing but attract attention and this is far from good when the attention attracted belongs to a law enforcement officer. This can lead to a traffic citation, wasted time in court, money out of pocket for the citation, and more money out of pocket to have the exhaust system quieted to acceptable standards.

An exhaust system in a passenger car to be used for any type of competition should be fitted with "lakes pipes." Lakes pipes are short stubs welded to stock head pipes that enable exhaust gases to leave the exhaust system without traveling through the mufflers and tail pipes. They are fitted with plugs or covers of some type that can be used to close them when the car is to be driven on the street. Lakes pipes can be installed so that they aren't noticeable from outside the car. This makes good sense because pipes that aren't noticeable don't attract attention to the car. This could be an asset in some localities where law enforcement officials frown on hot rod activities.

The design of an exhaust system for an engine in a competition machine depends on many things. Among these are the restrictions imposed by rules of the competition in which the engine is to be used and the amount of space available for the system. Ideas as to what constitutes the ideal exhaust system for a competition engine are as varied as the machines on which the systems are to be found. One group of builders favors an individual pipe for each of the engine's exhaust ports and another believes that a header that directs the exhaust gases from all the ports into a common collector pipe five or six feet long is the best. Cars with variations of both systems have performed well in all types of competition.

CHAPTER FIVE

Your Engine's Valves

How to disassemble, inspect
recondition, adjust. The complete
story on valves for better breathing.

NONE OF THE INTERNAL PARTS in a high-performance engine have an easy job but it's doubtful if any of them work harder or under more disagreeable conditions than the valves. Valves operate under conditions that approach the impossible. They are alternately exposed to the elevated temperatures of the burning fuel and the relatively cool charge of fresh mixture; they are expected to open and close as often as two thousand or more times per minute as a matter of course, often for hours at a time; and they must sometimes operate in combination with seats that become distorted when the engine's temperature reaches its normal level.

Valves have always had a difficult task and as compression ratios continue to rise the task becomes even more severe. This is because it is the valves' duty to seal compression and combustion pressures in the cylinders. As compression ratios go up, these pressures become greater. If valves did not prevent these pressures from escaping from the cylinders, the advantage of a high compression ratio would be lost.

Actually, compression ratio is merely a mathematical factor having to do with the relationship of the capacities of cylinders and combustion chambers to each other, whereas the pressure exerted on the pistons during power strokes is dependent on compression pressure. An engine cannot have a high compression pressure unless it has a high compression ratio but it can have a high compression ratio and at the same time have a low compression pressure because of leakage past its valves. Therefore, for an engine to utilize its compression ratio to the ratio's maximum advantage, its valves must effectively seal compression and combustion pressure in its cylinders during the thousands of compression and power strokes the pistons make each minute the engine runs.

The adverse conditions under which valves operate make it essential that they and their seats get as good a start in life as possible. This good start is in the hands of the engine's designer and the fellow who installs the valves when the engine is rebuilt or reworked for greater performance. It is the designer's problem to design an engine that will not distort out of proportion when it is operating under load, will have valves and seats of durable materials, have a camshaft that is not unduly severe on valves and their actuating mechanism, and have a valve actuating mechanism that will maintain valve lash clearances somewhere near their specified values under

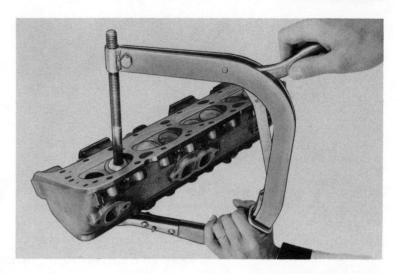

To remove valve springs from the head, a special compressor tool gives valuable assistance to the operation.

varying conditions of engine speed and load. These are not easy tasks; therefore it is seldom that all of them are achieved in any one engine. It is up to the man who assembles or reconditions the engine to do the necessary work on the valves, their seats, guides, and springs correctly and efficiently so they will be able to function as they should.

Engine design problems, as related to valves, are beyond the scope of a fellow who is reworking an engine to enable it to develop greater torque and horsepower. All he can do is be sure the engine receives the best possible valve job so the valves can perform to the best of their ability and have a reasonably long life. However, their duties and the conditions under which they operate make it impossible for valves to function indefinitely at peak performance; therefore, valves in a high-performance engine must be given frequent attention if the engine is to perform at its maximum capability.

There are two types of valve jobs. One of these is the installation or reconditioning of the valves and seats in an engine that has been reworked for better than stock performance, and the other is a job being done to a stock engine. Basic fundamentals of both jobs are similar because the components being worked on are similar but some of the steps required by the first type aren't necessary when working on a stock engine. However, many of the finer points of a valve job for a reworked engine can be applied with good results to stock engines. The steps and modifications described in this chapter will include those that would be done at the time an

engine was reworked. Those that wouldn't be necessary on a certain type of valve job will be easy to recognize.

Valve installation and reconditioning procedures vary somewhat between L-head and overhead valve engines due to the locations of the valves in the engines. In either engine access to the valves requires removal of its cylinder head, or heads, as the case may be. In an L-head engine the tappet chamber covers on the side of the cylinder block must also be removed. Overhead valve engines provide the advantage of enabling the head to be taken to a convenient work bench where the job can be done with maximum convenience: In an L-head engine the valves and their related parts can be difficult to reach and the job of cleaning up after the seats have been reconditioned is considerably more difficult. In other respects the jobs are somewhat similar and will be treated the same from here on.

A suitable valve spring compressor to simplify removal and installation of the valve springs is one tool that is almost indispensable when doing a valve job. Makeshift substitutions have been used for these jobs but such tools are usually clumsy and their use could result in damage to the springs or valves and possibly injury to their operator. Valve spring compressors aren't too expensive and the time they save makes them well worth their price.

As they are removed, valve spring retainer washers, the split locks for the washers, and the valve springs can be tossed into a common container. It doesn't matter if these parts become mixed. As the valves are removed from their guides they should be inserted in a valve stick, which is nothing more than an extra-heavy yardstick with holes along its length through which the valve stems can be inserted, so they will be kept together and will be less apt to be damaged. Gum and varnish deposits on their stems sometimes make it difficult to pull the valves through the guides. These deposits can often be removed with steel wool or some other mild abrasive.

When removing valves from flathead Ford and Mercury engines, it is necessary to remove each valve and its spring and guide as an assembly. The guide is locked in the block with a horseshoe-shaped clip that fits in a groove in its upper end. This lock seats in a shallow recess in the valve lifter chamber and positions the guide in the block in relation to the valve port. Special pullers are made to simplify the job of pulling the horseshoe locks and other tools are available for pushing or pulling the guides out of the block. Removing the guides sometimes becomes a problem because they can stick rather tightly in their bores. After the assemblies have been removed, another special tool, of which several types are available, is used to remove the spring washers from the valve stems. The assemblies can then be disassembled. Guides in some of these engines are split and their respective halves should be kept together.

A preliminary inspection should be made of the valves for readily noticeable signs of wear or other defects. Those with burned, cracked, or warped heads, bent or scored stems, or damaged lock grooves should be discarded. Intake valves should be inspected for unusually large accumulations of carbon under their heads because such accumulations are an indication of excessively worn valve guides. This carbon is caused by the mixture of lubricating oil and air drawn through the guides during intake strokes. Air drawn through guides in this manner can upset fuel and air mixtures in the cylinders, causing rough-running characteristics at low engine speeds. This condition cannot be corrected by adjusting the carburetor.

Valves that appear to be in usable condition can be cleaned with kerosene or solvent and, after drying, the carbon on their heads and upper ends of their stems can be removed with a wire brush rotated by an electric motor or bench grinder. Carbon removal can be often speeded by chipping away heavy incrustations with a suitable tool. A discarded valve makes an excellent tool for this purpose by using its stem as a handle to swing its head against the deposits. Safety glasses or goggles should be worn by the mechanic during chipping and wire brushing operations to prevent carbon particles or pieces of wire from the brush from flying into his eyes.

After all traces of carbon have been removed from the valves, they should be soaked in some kind of parts cleaning solution so gum and varnish deposits on their stems will be dissolved. After being rinsed and dried, the valves should be inspected again. Defects in their stems or heads that were not apparent before they were cleaned may now be visible. Valves that pass inspection are ready to be lightened or refaced.

Valve lightening is a job as old as hot rodding but it has never been more necessary than it is now because valves used in most modern big-displacement engines are monstrous and their weight has gone up with their size. Valve weight becomes more important as engine speeds go up. Valves that are too heavy aren't able to close fast enough at high engine speeds. This brings on the condition of valve float and all its attendant ills.

It's impossible to remove a lot of weight from any valve but this is one of those cases where every little bit helps. There isn't any place on a valve's stem where material can be removed to reduce weight, leaving only the surfaces of the head. Normal lightening processes require removal of material from both the top and bottom of the head. At the same time the weight is being reduced, it's possible to improve air flow past the heads when they are off their seats by slight improvements in their shape.

This is an excellent example of a badly burned valve.

Stock valves on left are compared to lightened valves on right.

Most valve heads are made of hard materials and the only means by which material can be removed from them is by grinding it away or by cutting it with a special cutting tool made for hard material. When the grinding method is used the valves are usually chucked in a lathe and the grinding is done with a suitable wheel on a tool post grinder. Grinding can be done in a valve refacing machine equipped with a special grinding wheel but this is the slow method. When a cutting tool is used it is necessary to chuck the valves in a lathe.

The important thing when lightening valves is to remove as much material as possible without causing the valves to be weakened. This requires a bit of common sense, and a little previous experience is a big help. Common practice on modern valves is to remove material from under their heads to eliminate bulky fillet areas between the stem and the heads and to blend the fillets gracefully into the head area. Lightened valves will be used on narrow seats so it is possible to extend the underhead trimming to the face and to remove some material from the face.

Material above the upper edge of the face is the valve's "margin." On most new valves the margin is thicker than it needs to be so the valves can be refaced for two or three reconditioning jobs without making them too thin. If the margin should become too thin for any reason the edge of the valve head might possibly overheat, or collapse from the pressure of the valve springs. A valve head that overheats can burn or warp and also be the cause of pre-ignition. The amount of material that can be removed from the top of a valve head to reduce the margin depends on the particular valve but usually half the head's thickness can be removed without causing difficulty.

After the margin has been thinned, additional material can usually be removed from an area on the top of the head extending from the head's center to within approximately a quarter of an inch from its outer edge. Sufficient material should be removed from this area to give the head a concave shape. The concave area can be an eighth-inch depth at its center, tapered in a gradual curve to the surface of the head.

This valve was destroyed as a result of improper lightening.

After all the valves have been machined, the sharp edges on their heads should be given a small radius and the machined areas should be polished with fine emery cloth or crocus cloth. The polishing can be done quite easily by holding the polishing cloth against the valves while they are being spun in a lathe or drill press. Sharp edges on a valve head have a tendency to overheat and possibly be the starting point for cracks, and rough surfaces may impede the flow of mixture and exhaust gases past the heads. The valves are now ready to be refaced.

Valve refacing is a precision machining operation that requires a special machine. Modern refacing machines are of the "wet" type, which means that a continuous flow of coolant is directed onto the valve face while it is being ground. Wet grinding is preferred over dry grinding because the valve and the grinding stone are kept cool by the flow of coolant. Keeping the valve head cool reduces its tendency to distort. Also, the coolant carries away small particles of steel and grit that might otherwise become imbedded in the grinding wheel, enabling the wheel to grind a smoother surface. The refacing machine must be in good condition and correctly adjusted to guarantee a seating surface that is of the correct angle, concentric with the valve stem, and free of chatter marks and roughness.

Warped or bent valves will be detected when they are rotated by the refacer. These valves must be discarded. Faces on valves that are straight are ground by feeding them back and forth across the grinding wheel until all grooves or pits in them are ground away and the entire surface of the face has been ground. Any valve that requires so much grinding to obtain a smooth face that its margin is reduced to a sharp edge should be discarded.

New valves to be used as replacements for worn or damaged valves must also be refaced before they are used. Quite often new valves have been subjected to rough handling after being refaced at the factory. Refaced valves should be placed in a valve stick so they will be protected from damage.

After the valve faces have been ground, the ends of their stems should be ground in an attachment on a refacing machine to make them smooth and parallel with the faces of the valves.

This is especially important in overhead valve engines where the stems are contacted by rocker arms because it isn't unusual for the arms to wear grooves in the ends of the stems. This makes valve lash adjustments difficult. After the tips have been ground, a narrow bevel should be ground at the sharp edge around their circumference. This will reduce the possibility of the tips scratching the bores in the valve guides when the stems are inserted in the guides.

Combustion chambers and valve seats and ports in the cylinder head or block must be cleaned thoroughly and inspected for cracks or other defects. Hard carbon deposits can be removed with suitable scrapers. A small rotary wire brush driven by a flexible shaft or electric drill can be used to remove the last traces of carbon. Care must be taken to prevent scratching or gouging the valve seat surfaces with the scrapers or wire brush. The surfaces should then be washed with kerosene or solvent to remove all traces of oil or carbon dust so any cracks or defects in the seats or ports will be visible. During these cleaning and subsequent grinding operations it is extremely important that carbon and other abrasive matter are not allowed to get into the cylinders or crankcase of an L-head engine. This can be prevented by covering the tops of the cylinders with a sheet of heavy wrapping paper taped to the block with masking tape and stuffing the oil drain holes in the bottom of the tappet chambers with clean rags.

Chances of finding cracks in the heads or block are comparatively slim unless the engine has been mistreated. Cracks around valve seats must be repaired before the seats can be reground. Cracks in parts that do not contain valve seats must be repaired before the parts can be reused. Crack repairing is a specialized job that should be done by men experienced in such matters. Although there are many types of satisfactory crack repairing methods, they all have the common fault of being expensive. When more than one crack must be repaired, the cost of the repair work should be balanced against the cost of replacement parts.

Before grinding the valve seats of cylinder heads or blocks equipped with valve guides, the bores of the guides must be checked for wear. In addition to being detrimental to engine performance because they allow excessive quantities of oil and air to flow into the cylinders on intake strokes, worn guides are unable to hold the valves in alignment with their seats. Guides can be checked by any one of several methods. The best of these is with a small-hole gauge and an outside micrometer. A small-hole gauge consists of a short handle with a spherical end. The spherical end can be expanded to increase its diameter by turning a knob on the end of the handle.

To check guides with a small-hole gauge, the spherical end of the gauge is inserted in a guide and then expanded so its sides lightly contact the sides of the guide's bore. The gauge is then withdrawn and its diameter measured with an outside micrometer. Guides should be checked in this manner at several points along their length so a true picture of their condition can be formed. Maximum wear in guides in overhead valve engines will usually be found in their upper ends in a line parallel to the rocker arm. This is the result of forces exerted on the valve stems by the arms. Guide diameters and tolerances vary between engines, making it necessary to consult a shop manual or the engine's manufacturer to determine whether the guides are within serviceable limits. Guides worn a measurable amount should not be used in an engine reworked for competition purposes.

Guides can also be checked with the solid pilots used with most valve seat grinders. These pilots are made in standard and oversize diameters. If a pilot with an oversize larger than the wear limit can be inserted in the guide, the guide should be replaced. Worn guides should be replaced in sets because it is more than likely that if some of them need replacing, the rest soon will.

Solid guides for flathead Ford and Mercury engines are checked in the same manner as other guides, but a different procedure must be used for split guides used in most of these engines. Split guides are checked by laying a valve with an unworn stem in a guide half and then measuring the combined thickness of the stem and the guide with an outside micrometer. If the measurement is less than that specified in the Ford manual, the guide must be replaced.

Methods of servicing valve guides differ now that many engines are using "integral" guides. Integral guides are part of the cylinder head casting and therefore they aren't removable. They are said to have the advantage over pressed-in guides of enabling valves to run cooler. This reduction in valve temperature is due to the uninterrupted flow of heat from the guides to the coolant in the cylinder heads.

Heat conductivity from pressed-in guides to the coolant is reduced by the joint between their outer circumference and the member in which they are installed. This joint acts as a "heat dam" to slow the flow of heat across it. The drop in valve temperature effected by integral guides isn't much but in combination with their apparently lower production cost it has caused them to find favor with a steadily increasing number of engine builders.

When integral guides become worn, the only way they can be reconditioned is by reaming them to the next standard oversize diameter. Valves with oversize stems must then be installed in them. Valves with several stem diameters are available for this purpose. Reaming integral guides is a precision operation that must be done correctly if the new bores are to be round, at the correct angles in the head, and of the correct diameter. Many automotive machine shops are now equipped to do this sort of work.

Installing new valves with oversize stems in integral guides that have been reamed could be an expensive procedure in cylinder heads that have been fitted with special valves. In some instances valves with the correct head and stem diameters might be practically impossible to obtain without having them made. About the only solution to this problem, and one that is receiving some attention from equipment manufacturers and builders of competition engines, would be to replace the integral guides with pressed-in guides that have the correct bore diameter for the valves to be used. This would require boring the guides completely out of the heads and then reaming the holes where they had been to the correct diameter to accommodate the pressed-in guides.

Worn pressed-in guides can be either pressed or driven out of the head or block. New guides are then installed in the same manner. Drivers for this purpose are available from many tool manufacturers. They consist of round lengths of steel, slightly smaller in diameter than the outer diameter of the guides, with a projection on one

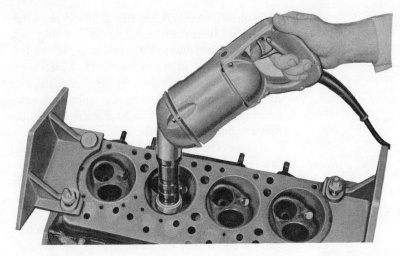

Valve seats are ground with special grinding wheels.

end that will fit in the guide bore. The projection acts as a pilot to hold the driver square on the end of the guide during the driving process. Before new guides are driven into place, their outer surface should be coated with a thin layer of white lead. White lead acts as a lubricant and will make the installation easier.

If definite guide installation information isn't available, measurements should be made before the old guides are removed to determine exactly how far they extend out of the heads. New guides should extend out of the heads the same amount as those they replace. This is important because guides are supposed to occupy a certain position in the valve ports. Guides for intake valves usually differ from those for exhausts; therefore, new guides must be installed in the correct ports. Also guides must be installed right side up so any special design features they may have will be in their proper positions in relation to the valve stems.

As a rule, new guides must be reamed with a special reamer after they have been driven into place. This is done to remove any burrs that might have been created at their ends by the driving or to open them up to size to correct for any undersize condition resulting from compression of the guides by the bores into which they were driven. Special reamers are available for this operation and care must be taken to use one of the correct size so the bores won't be reamed oversize. Reaming must be done carefully to provide straight, smooth bores.

Old guides found to be in serviceable condition can be cleaned by running a reamer of the correct size through their bores. This will re-

move deposits of carbon, gum, and varnish. After reaming operations have been finished, both old and new guides must be cleaned by running a brush soaked in kerosene or solvent through them. This will force chips left from the reaming out of new guides and force accumulations of foreign material out of old guides. Guide cleaning brushes are available from most parts supply houses, or brushes of the type used to clean pistol and rifle barrels can be used. Compressed air should be blown through all guides after they have been cleaned with a brush to dry them and finish the cleaning job. Clean guides are essential to a good seat grinding job — a grinder pilot cannot center itself correctly in a dirty guide.

Many types of valve seat grinders are available today and most of them do a satisfactory job in the hands of a competent operator. Var-

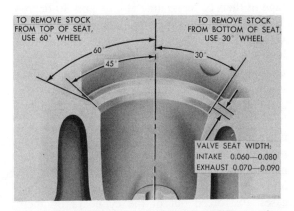

Ideal valve seats are narrow and ground at different angles.

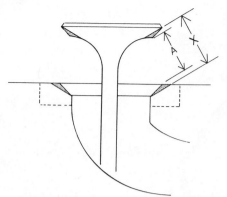

Larger opening is obtained around intake valve with 30°
seat (X) as compared to an intake with a 45° seat (A).

ious sizes and types of grinding stones are used for different seats and the stones must be dressed accurately to the desired angle.

When new valve guides have been installed it is absolutely essential that new seats be ground. The reason for this is that the center of the bore in new guides may not be in exactly the same position it occupied in the worn guides; therefore, original seats may not be absolutely concentric with new guides.

An engine's breathing ability is dependent to a certain extent on the angles of its valve seats. Theoretically, a seat that is perpendicular to the valve stem provides the best breathing between a valve head and its seat. However, a valve with a face of this type is not self-centering in its port, nor does it have the ability to seal as well as a valve with a tapered face. A tapered-face valve has a wedging action on its seat that increases its sealing ability.

Face angles of 45 to 30 degrees have been adopted by the automotive industry; 45-degree faces are used on exhaust valves, to take advantage of their better sealing ability, and 30-degree faces are used by some manufacturers for intake valves. The 30-degree angle is a compromise between a face perpendicular to the valve stem and one that provides maximum sealing. Sealing is not as difficult to attain with intake valves because they run at lower temperatures than exhausts but the breathing area they provide is important to the engine's volumetric efficiency. In most engines atmospheric pressure alone is depended upon to force fresh fuel and air mixture into the cylinders on intake strokes but exhaust gases are forced out of the cylinders by their own pressure and the pistons.

In most reworked engines a 30-degree angle is used on intake valves, regardless of the angle they had originally, to take advantage of the better breathing it provides and a 45-degree angle is used on exhaust valves to take advantage of its better sealing. Changing the angles of valve faces and seats from 45 to 30 degrees is a simple matter and well worth the effort involved.

At one time valve seats and faces were ground to exactly the same angles but now many manufacturers grind the valve faces one-half to one degree flatter than the seat angle so a line contact will be made between the face and the upper edge of the seat. Valves ground in this manner soon pound a seat for themselves in the head or block.

For a stock engine, valve seats should be ground to the widths specified by the engine manufacturer. These widths have become narrower in recent years for both intake and exhaust valves. Seats in reworked engines are usually made narrower than those in stock engines.

Narrow seats provide a tighter seal between the valves and their seats and they reduce some of the restriction between the valve heads and the seats when the valves are open. As most of the heat valve heads absorb is conducted to the engine's structure through their faces, narrow seats may reduce the rate of heat dissipation from the heads. However, this shouldn't cause any trouble if the valve and seat reconditioning is done correctly and the cylinders receive the proper air/fuel ratios.

Valve seats must be round and of uniform width throughout their circumferences. They are made this way by grinding their upper edge with a stone approximately 15 degrees flatter than the seat and grinding their lower edge with a stone approximately 15 degrees sharper than the seat. In other words, the upper stone for a 45-degree seat would have an angle of approximately 30 degrees, and the stone for the lower edge would have an angle of approximately 60 degrees.

Most engine manufacturers specify that the valve seat should contact the valve face midway between the face's upper and lower extremities. Seating a valve in this area reduces the effective diameter of its head and limits the breathing potential of its port. This is all right in a stock engine but the full diameter of the valve head should be utilized in an engine that has been reworked. This is accomplished by grinding the seats so they contact the upper portion of the valve faces. Only a slight clearance is left between the upper edge of the face and the upper limit of the seat contact area. The seat is then narrowed to its desired width by reaming or grinding its smaller diameter and then the valve port is enlarged to match the seat.

Perhaps the easiest way of checking valve seat diameters is with a pair of dividers. The dividers are adjusted so their points touch the faces of the valves at the point where the upper edge of the seat should be. Then they are used to check the larger diameter of the seats as the seats are ground. The smaller diameter of the seats can be checked by eye if one has had enough practice, or the dividers can be used for this purpose too. After a fellow has ground a few seats he can usually narrow them to the desired widths without the aid of measuring devices.

In any engine it is a good idea to make sure the valve seats aren't in recesses after the grinding has been finished. Quite often, after the top of the seat has been ground to make it round and of the correct diameter, it will be below the surface around it. This isn't a good condition because the flow of fresh mixture and exhaust gases past a valve head that is being lifted out of a recess is restricted until the smaller diameter of the valve's face is lifted past the surface of the combustion chamber around the recess. This gives the same effect as opening the valve later and closing it earlier, thereby shortening the time it is open.

It is sometimes possible to lower the combustion chamber surface around the valve seats to eliminate recesses by grinding it away with stones on a seat grinder. Stones used for this purpose must be flatter than those used for narrowing the seats. If sufficient material can't be removed in this manner it will be necessary to grind it away with a portable grinder. Any grinding done around the seats must be done with extreme care so the seats will not be scratched or gouged. Seats that have been scratched or gouged will have to be reground.

Installation of oversize valves after it has been decided that they are necessary and the correct sizes have been determined, is a fairly simple procedure. Oversize valves aren't necessary in an engine that hasn't been ported so it will be assumed that the valve ports have been enlarged by reaming or grinding to somewhere near their finished diameters. If possible, valve ports should be enlarged with piloted reamers of the correct diameter to match the oversize valves. Ports enlarged in this manner will be concentric with the valve guides and it will be easier to grind the seats and match the ports to them. It's important that the ports aren't enlarged too much because if they are there won't be any surface left for the valve seats.

After the valve guides have been replaced or reconditioned, a new seat of the correct angle is ground in the usual manner. The grinding is continued until the outer diameter of the seat is large enough to match the valve head. The top of the seat is then ground to make it round, as explained previously, and the seat is narrowed to the desired width by grinding its lower edge. The valve port is then enlarged and rounded as necessary

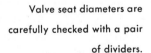

Valve seat diameters are carefully checked with a pair of dividers.

with a reamer or with grinding stones to match the lower edge of the seat.

After the seats in a reworked engine have been ground, the valves are fitted to them. This is done by putting a very light coat of Prussian Blue (available at most auto part stores and paint stores) on the seats and then lowering the valves faces onto them. Color transferred from the seats to the faces will indicate the areas of the faces contacted by the seats. As the larger diameter of the seats was determined by the diameters of the valve heads, it should be within a few thousandths of an inch of the upper edges of the faces; however, it is more than likely that the lower edges of the faces will extend too far below the seats. If this is the case, the underside of the heads should be ground in a refacing machine adjusted to an angle nearly perpendicular to the valve stem to narrow the faces until they extend the same distance below the seats as they do above them. This grinding must be done carefully and the valves must be kept cool while it is being done so their heads will not be distorted. It wouldn't be desirable to have to reface the valves again after their faces had been narrowed.

At one time it was considered necessary to lap all valves to their seats after the valves and seats had been ground. This practice is seldom recommended now and if the seats and faces were ground accurately it is definitely not needed. In cases where valve faces are ground with slightly flatter angles than those used for the seats lapping would be of no value. When faces and seats are of the same angles it is possible to check them for proper mating by making several lines across the faces with a pencil and then lowering each valve onto its seat and turning it about an eighth of a turn. Moderate pressure should be held on the valve head while it is being turned to force it against the seat. As the valve is rotated, the surface of the seat that contacts the face will wipe away the pencil marks. An examination of the marks after the valve has been removed from the guide will show how well the valve and seat are matched.

Valve springs are important to the way an engine will run, especially at high crankshaft speeds, and to the life of its valves and camshaft. Used springs being considered for reinstallation in the engine must be thoroughly cleaned and inspected to determine whether they will perform

satisfactorily. Cadmium-plated spring and springs without protective coatings may be cleaned in special cleaning solutions but painted springs must not be cleaned in any solution that will remove the paint. Springs are painted or plated to protect them from becoming rusted or corroded while they are in service. Rusted or corroded springs should be discarded.

Each spring should be checked first for a cocked condition. This is done by standing the springs, one at a time, on a flat surface alongside the blade of a machinist's square. Springs that aren't straight should be discarded. The free length of the springs is checked by standing them on a flat surface and measuring the length of each of them with a rule or some other type of measuring device. Springs that don't conform to the length specifications of the engine manufacturer should be discarded because they have taken a permanent set and will not exert the correct pressure on the valves when they are installed in the engine.

Pressure of the springs is checked next by compressing them to their factory specified lengths in a suitable testing machine. Springs that do not fall within the pressure tolerance listed by the engine manufacturer should be discarded. A pressure loss of 10 percent is often allowed for used springs and this is all right for a stock engine but any spring that does not meet the specifications for a new spring should not be used in a reworked engine. Valve springs are relatively inexpensive and it is easier to install them while the engine is apart than it is to install them at a later date. New springs, either stock or special, should be checked in the same manner as used springs.

If a reground camshaft is being installed in the engine it is possible that special valve springs should be installed. Check with the company that ground the cam to determine the type of springs that should be used. Their recommendations should be followed if maximum performance and satisfactory cam lobe and lifter life are to be expected.

Surfaces on the cylinder head or block or on special washers on which the springs seat should be inspected for wear. Worn surfaces on the head or block can be covered with steel shim washers to provide new seats for the springs. Worn seat washers can be replaced with new washers of the same type. Spring keeper washers and split locks must be inspected for worn surfaces, cracks, or other defects. Worn or defective parts must be discarded.

Valve lifters, pushrods, rocker arms, and rocker arm shafts must be thoroughly cleaned and inspected for wear or damage. If the bottom surface of any of the lifters is worn excessively, the camshaft should also be checked for wear. Lifters that are worn or cracked must be discarded. Adjustment screws in lifters of L-head engines must be reground or replaced if the ends of the valve springs have pounded depressions in them. It is impossible to make accurate lash settings when adjusting screws are worn in this manner because the thickness gauge blade used to check the lash clearance cannot be inserted between the end of the valve stem and the surface of the screw contacted by the stem. The blade will rest on the top of the screw, above the bottom of the depression.

Pushrods should be checked for straightness and wear. Bent or worn rods should not be reused. No attempt should be made to straighten bent pushrods because it is impossible to straighten a rod so it will remain straight.

Rocker arms wear at their valve contacting surfaces, at their pushrod seats or adjusting screws, as the case may be, and in their shaft bores. Worn valve contacting surfaces on rocker arms have the same effect on valve lash adjustments as worn tappet screws in L-head engines. The surfaces can be reground on valve refacing machines equipped with special attachments. One should not attempt to regrind these surfaces without the necessary equipment. Arms with worn pushrods seats must be replaced. Worn or damaged adjusting screws are easily replaced. Rocker arms with worn shaft bores must be replaced unless they are equipped with bushings; however, it is usually more satisfactory to also discard arms that have worn bushings rather than have new bushings installed in them. Worn rocker arm shafts must be discarded.

Valve and spring assemblies are installed in the cylinder heads or block in the same manner they were removed. All parts must, of course, be clean and the valve stems and guide bores should be coated with lubricating oil. In most overhead valve engines some sort of oil seal or deflector is required on the stems of the intake

The face of this valve lifter has been badly scored by action of the camshaft and the lifter must be replaced.

The lower end of this Chevrolet V8 rocker arm shows cracks and "cupping" of tip due to improper hardening operation.

valves and in some engines seals or deflectors are also used on exhaust valves. The purpose of these devices is to reduce the amount of oil that can flow down the stems and into the combustion chambers. Installation procedures for the seals vary as some of them are slipped over the stems before the spring and others after the spring has been compressed. Care must be taken to install the correct keeper washers on the intake valves because, in many engines, these washers differ from those for the exhaust valves. Springs with closed coils at one end must be installed so the closed coils are next to the cylinder head or block. Special devices designed to reduce spring surge must be installed according to the manufacturers directions.

After the springs are in place on the valves, their "installed length" must be measured. This is done by measuring the length of each spring, when its valve is resting on its seat, with a rule.

UNDERSIDE OF SPRING RETAINER

SURFACE OF SPRING PAD

The installed height of valve spring is measured with a pair
of calipers. Springs must never be longer than specified.

Measure only the spring — do not include the seat washer or washers under the spring in the spring length. Springs that measure longer than their specified length must be shortened by placing washers of the necessary thickness between their stationary end and the head or block. Special washers for this purpose are now available from most auto parts stores.

Establishing the specified installed valve spring length is important because the pressure a spring exerts on its valve is dependent on its length. Regrinding valve seats and faces allows the valves to seat lower in the head or block. This increases the distance between the spring seats in the head or block and the keeper washers on the valve stems by a corresponding amount. Increasing this distance allows the springs to assume a longer-than-specified length when they are installed and reduces their pressure accordingly. Although a spring may have its specified pressure at its recommended test length, it will not have its correct pressure in the engine unless its installed length is correct.

Installation of the valves and springs in flathead Ford and Mercury engines varies a little from that for other makes. These particular engines have non-adjustable valve lifters as stock equipment and it is necessary to make valve lash adjustment before the valves are installed in the cylinder block. To do this, each valve is installed in its respective port with a dummy guide and its clearance is checked with the blade of a thickness gauge. Special indicators that show which valve lifters are on the heel of their cams so their valves can be adjusted are available for this operation. Material is ground from the tappet end of the

valve stems to increase clearance or material is removed from the faces of the valves with a refacer to reduce clearance. An alternative method of obtaining the correct clearance is possible with some valve refacing machines that have gauges and special adjustable jigs to hold the valves while the tips of their stems are being ground. With this equipment the gauge is inserted in the block and then the valve-holding jig on the machine is adjusted so it will grind the stem to the correct length. Clearance is decreased by removing material from the valve face.

When adjustable tappets are installed in these engines the lash is adjusted by running the adjusting screws in or out of the tappets as necessary. This is done after the cylinder heads have been installed on the block. Installed valve spring length is checked after the valve guide locks have been installed. These locks position the guides in their bores and the spring length cannot be measured unless they are in place.

Cylinder head nuts and bolts on all types of engines must be torqued to factory specifications. They should be tightened gradually and evenly, preferably according to the tightening pattern specified by the engine manufacturer, in steps of 15 to 20 foot-pounds until the maximum tension is reached. Correct head nut or bolt torque is important to long gasket life and minimum cylinder head and block distortion.

Final valve lash adjustments on all engines except those that don't have an adjusting means are usually made when the engine is at its operating temperature but a preliminary adjustment must be made before the engine is started. This adjustment doesn't have to be done too carefully but the lash clearances should be fairly close to those specified so there will be no danger of the valves being held open during the warm up period.

After first starting an overhead valve engine, oil should be squirted on its valves and rocker arms so they won't run dry while the overhead valve portion of the engine's lubrication system is filling itself. When oil is flowing freely from the rocker arms, the rocker arm covers are bolted temporarily in place to help retain the heat around the valve assemblies while the engine is warming up. The level of the water in the radiator must be checked after the engine has reached its normal temperature because occasionally air will be trapped in the cooling system the first time it is filled and it will need more water after the engine has been run for a while.

Cylinder head bolts or nuts must be retorqued after the engine has reached its normal operating temperature. If the engine has cast-iron heads this should be done while the engine is still hot; if it has aluminum heads the bolts or nuts must not be retorqued until the engine has been allowed to cool. After the heads have been retorqued, the final valve lash adjustments should be made while the engine is at its operating temperature. This time the lash should be adjusted as closely as possible to specifications.

From this point on the service delivered by the valves will depend in part on the man who takes care of the engine. It's up to him to see that only high quality fuel and lubricating oil are used in the engine, that it is kept tuned for top performance at all times, and that its valve lash is maintained at factory specifications. Using high quality fuel and oil reduces valve troubles by minimizing lead and other deposits on the faces and stems of the valves. Deposits on the faces can induce valve burning by holding the heads off their seats during combustion. Seating is not affected if the deposit is uniform around the face but if a portion of the deposit should flake off, a path for hot combustion gases would be created between the face and its seat. This would cause the head to overheat and burn.

Deposits of gum and varnish from inferior grades of gasoline and oil can collect on valve stems to the extent that movement of the valves in the guides is seriously impaired or stopped altogether. This is the valve ailment commonly referred to as "sticking valves."

Keeping the engine tuned for top performance will eliminate incorrect fuel mixtures and ignition timing that might cause the valves to be damaged. Maintaining valve lash adjustments at factory specifications, or to the specifications of whoever ground the cam, allows the valves to remain on their seats the correct number of degrees of crankshaft rotation each cycle. This gives the heads their required length of time to dissipate heat to the cylinder block or head.

Valves operating with insufficient lash may, in extreme cases, be held partially open during the

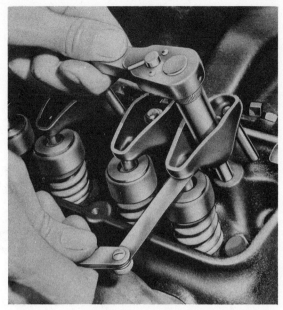

Valve lash is adjusted with a special wrench and thickness gauge. This operation is typical for Chevrolet and Pontiac.

power stroke, causing them to become overheated and burned. Insufficient lash can also cause poor engine idling and loss of power.

Excessive lash clearances can be the cause of broken valves. Valves breakage of this type is the result of higher than normal stresses created in the valve stems by the springs when the valves are allowed to seat before their tappets contact the closing ramps on the cams. The purpose of these ramps is to slow the valves from their high closing speed and lower them comparatively gently onto their seats. If valve lash should become so great that the valve head contacted the seat before the valve lifter was slowed by the closing ramp, the high pressure on the stem and the speed of the valve's movement could jerk the stem off the head. Failures of this type are comparatively rare but they do happen.

About all that remains is to drive the car within the operating range of its valve actuating mechanism so the valves won't be floated. Valve float causes a drastic drop in horsepower output and in some engines it is possible for the piston heads to hit the heads of floating valves. When this happens, the valves or pistons, or both, can be broken. Valve float can also break valve lifters. It should be avoided.

CHAPTER SIX

The Complete Story of Engine Carburetion

Single, dual, triple, quad. The problems of progressive linkage. Maintenance and service for better starting, idling, acceleration, speed, and economy.

AN ENGINE'S CARBURETION SYSTEM has a pronounced influence on how the engine will run and the amount of horsepower it can develop. Carburetion systems on most stock engines are built to compromise specifications and their most important requirement is that the engine be capable of idling well and running smoothly with good torque output at low engine speeds. Performance at high speeds is given some consideration but it is secondary to low-speed performance.

The reasons a carburetion system can affect the way an engine runs are directly attributable to the principle on which carburetors function. A modern carburetor is a complex mechanism but its principle of operation is identical to that used in carburetors on the engines of cars that had fringe on their tops.

A carburetor is a device for mixing a liquid fuel, usually gasoline, with air to form a combustible mixture. Gasoline, by itself, will not burn but when it is vaporized and mixed with the correct proportions of air it will burn with such speed that its combustion becomes almost an explosion. The proportion of air in a mixture delivered by a carburetor to the fuel in the mixture is the mixture's "air/fuel" ratio. This ratio is determined by the weight of the air and the weight of the fuel. An air/fuel mixture in which the weight of the air is low in comparison to the weight of the fuel is a "rich" mixture, and one in which the weight of air is high in comparison to the weight of the fuel is a "lean" mixture. Limits of combustion for air/fuel mixtures are roughly 8 to 1 on the rich side, which means that the weight of the air is 8 times that of the weight of the fuel, and 15 or 16 to 1 on the lean side.

Air/fuel mixtures required by the average automobile engine vary according to the demands made on the engine. For good idling, a fairly rich mixture is required. This is usually somewhere between 11 and 12 to 1. One reason the idling mixture must be rich is because gases remaining in the cylinders at the end of exhaust strokes limit the quantity of mixture that can be inducted into the cylinders when the engine is running with closed throttle, and they dilute the fresh mixture. Therefore, the fresh mixture must be rich if its air/fuel ratio after it has been diluted with exhaust gases is to be within the limits of combustion. At higher engine speeds the fresh mixture is still diluted by exhaust gases but the amount of dilution is much lower due to the greater quantities of mixture allowed to flow into the cylinders past the open throttle valve in the carburetor.

The air/fuel ratio required by an engine running in its cruising range, which is above the speed at which the idle system in the carburetor ceases to function, varies for different engines but the ideal approximately 15 to 1. A ratio as lean as the ideal is seldom achieved in a multi-cylinder engine. There are many reasons for this, one of the more important being the poor distribution of mixture to the cylinders. Poor distribution is the result of poor manifolding and it causes some cylinders to receive comparatively rich mixtures and for others to receive lean mixtures. The ratio supplied by the carburetor at any engine speed must be rich enough that the leanest mixture received by any cylinder will be below the upper limit of combustion. Some engines will cruise on a ratio as lean as 14.5 to 1 but others will require a ratio as rich as 13.9 or 14.0 to 1.

When an engine is called on to deliver its maximum horsepower under full throttle conditions it requires a richer mixture than for light-load cruising. This ratio is usually around 12 to 1 but it is not unusual for it to be richer than this, especially if the engine has been reworked for greater power. Reasons for the greater percentage of fuel in power mixtures are to provide more fuel for its primary purpose as a source of energy and to use the fuel as a coolant to help maintain temperatures of the piston head and other combustion chamber surfaces within safe limits.

A carburetor's primary duty is to supply the correct air/fuel ratio to its engine for the conditions under which the engine is running at any given time. This is far from a simple task, but the thing about a carburetor that affects engine performance is not the way it decides which air/fuel ratio to deliver, but its air flow capacity. This is determined by the diameter of the carburetor's "venturi." A venturi is a restricted area in a tube or passage through which air flows. Its purpose is to increase, at a given point, the rate of flow of the air passing through the tube. To achieve this purpose without creating too much of a restriction to the air flowing through the tube, the inlet and discharge sides of the venturi

are streamlined into the tube's walls. The inlet side is rounded but it is quite abrupt compared to the long taper of the discharge side.

Before the purpose of the venturi in a carburetor can be understood, one should know that fuel flow in a carburetor is dependent on "pressure differentials." Fuel in the bowl of the carburetor is maintained at a specified level by a float-actuated needle valve in the bowl's inlet. Fuel from the bowl enters the air stream passing through the carburetor by means of a discharge tube that extends into the air stream. When the engine isn't running, the level of the fuel in the discharge tube is at the same height as the level of the fuel in the bowl. This is because a liquid always seeks its own level. To get the fuel to flow into the air stream when the engine is running, it's necessary for the pressure on the fuel in the bowl to be higher than the pressure on the fuel in the tube. This is the reason for the venturi.

The opening in the end of the discharge tube is positioned in the venturi at the point where air velocity is highest and the end of the tube is shaped so that air passing it will create a low pressure, or vacuum, in the tube. Fuel in the float bowl is always under atmospheric pressure; therefore, when the engine is running with the throttle open enough to permit sufficient air to flow through the venturi to create a pressure lower than atmospheric at the end of the tube, the greater pressure on the fuel in the bowl causes fuel to flow from the tube and enter the air stream flowing to the engine's cylinders. So that the fuel will flow more readily from the tube and be more thoroughly atomized as it leaves the tube's tip, it is emulsified by mixing air with it as it passes through the tube. The degree to which the fuel is atomized determines how well it will be vaporized on its way to the cylinders.

The venturi's air flow capacity determines how much air can enter an engine when the throttle valve in the carburetor is wide-open. It also determines how much throttle opening is required before fuel will start to flow from the discharge tube. Fuel for idling is fed into the air stream through a port in the side of the carburetor throat near one edge of the throttle valve. Fuel flows from this port until the throttle valve is opened to a certain point. As the valve is opened beyond this point fuel must start to flow from the main discharge tube or there will be a gap be-

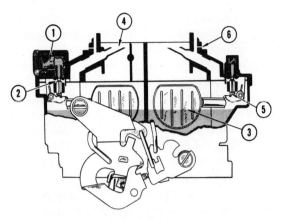

FLOAT SYSTEM

Fuel enters the four-barrel carburetor on the primary side (1) and passes through needle seats (2 and 5.) Bowl vents (4 and 6) equalize pressure between bowls and air horn.

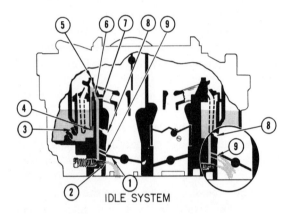

IDLE SYSTEM

Idle fuel is picked up through a calibrated tube (4) and mixed with air bled in (5, 7, 8, 9) to atomize fuel before it enters carburetor (2). Inset shows off-idle fuel flow (9).

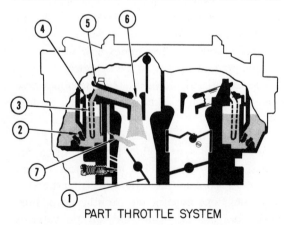

PART THROTTLE SYSTEM

At part throttle, air passage through boost venturi (6) forms a partial vacuum which pulls fuel through main well tubes (3). Primary jets (2) meter fuel flow to refill the main well.

tween the time when the idle system ceases to function and the main discharge tube takes over when there won't be any fuel flowing into the air stream passing through the carburetor. Such a gap in the fuel flow would result in a flat spot in the engine's acceleration.

A venturi must be small enough in diameter so that it will start fuel flowing from the main discharge tube before the idle system ceases to function and it should be large enough to pass sufficient air to supply the demands of the engine at high crankshaft speeds. Unfortunately, a venturi small enough to start the fuel flowing at the correct time isn't large enough to supply the engine's demands at high speeds. This is the reason compromises must be made in carburetor design.

Originally, automobile engines were fitted with carburetors that had one venturi and one main discharge tube. When engines began to require more air than could be supplied with a single venturi, carburetors were fitted with two venturis and two discharge tubes and idle systems. Throttle valves for the two venturis were synchronized to open simultaneously but the venturis were small enough that at low engine speeds ample air flowed through both of them to cause fuel to flow correctly from the carburetor's fuel discharge systems. Comparatively small venturis had the additional advantage of providing better fuel atomization and vaporization than was possible with larger venturis.

As engine displacement continued to grow, two-throat carburetors became inadequate at high crankshaft speeds. The industry's next move was to incorporate four carburetor throats and venturis in a single carburetor. Two of the throats have idle and acceleration systems and all four have main discharge tubes. Each throat has its own throttle valve and those in the throats equipped with idle systems, which are the "primary" throats, are synchronized to open together, as are the two valves in the "secondary" throats. Throttle valves in the primary throats are used for all driving up to approximately 75 or 80 miles per hour and then the valves in the secondaries open. In some four-throat carburetors the secondary venturis are larger than the primaries, which seems to be the logical arrangement so that fuel vaporization and economy will be as good as possible when driving on the primaries, but in others primaries are larger than secondaries.

Secondary throttle valves are opened in one of two ways: by delaying their action with special throttle linkage, or by opening them with the primary valves and then controlling the flow of air through their throats with an additional pair of throttle valves that are actuated automatically by the pressure differential above and below them. Additional secondary throttle valves are either weighted or spring-loaded so they will remain closed until the specified pressure differential exists.

For a while, four-throat carburetors seemed to be the answer but competition eventually forced some automobile manufacturers to install two four-throats on their high-output engines. With some dual four-throat installations all four primary throttles are opened together but in others only the primaries in one carburetor are opened at low speeds and the primaries in the other carburetor are opened later, as are the secondaries. Venturi diameters of the carburetors are determined by the air requirements of the engine and the throttle arrangement.

For stock installations, dual four-throats are now in the minority. The trend is toward three two-throat carburetors. Three two-throats were first used by hot rodders many years ago. With this type of arrangement it is much easier to equalize mixture flow between an engine's cylinders and ample carburetion is available for any engine speed. Throttle linkage is arranged so that all normal driving up to 75 to 80 miles per hour is done on the middle (primary) carburetor only. When they are needed, the end (secondary) carburetors are brought into action by opening their throttle valves. On all stock setups made at the present time the secondary carburetors are controlled by vacuum. In General Motors installations the vacuum is created by a mechanically-driven pump and its flow to the diaphragms that open the throttle valves is controlled by a vacuum valve actuated by the primary carburetor. When this valve is open, the throttle valves in the secondary carburetors snap open, and when it closes, the throttle valves close. In the setup used on Mercury Super Marauder engines, vacuum for the secondary carburetors' throttle diaphragms is created by air flowing through the venturis in the primary carburetor. When this vacuum builds up to a specified valve, the valves in the secondary carburetors open.

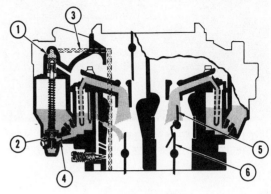

POWER SYSTEM

When the engine vacuum drops below pre-determined level, spring on power valve piston overcomes vacuum behind piston (1) and opens valve (2) to supply more fuel to main well and enrich primary. Velocity opens secondaries (5).

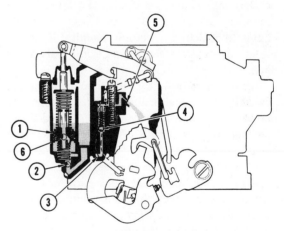

PUMP SYSTEM

Accelerating pump ball check (6) prevents fuel trapped in the pump well from vaporizing due to engine heat. Fuel enters well through check valve (2), is forced by pump (1) through passage (3), past check valve (4) to nozzles (5).

This is a modern four-barrel carburetor mounted in a typical overhaul stand, ready for disassembly and inspection.

Viewed from above, the four-barrel arrangement of Rochester carburetor is clearly visible. Note linkage at side.

Because they function only at high engine speeds, secondary carburetors used on production three-carburetor setups are usually fitted only with main discharge nozzles. As they don't function at idle and low speeds, secondary carburetors do not require idle circuits, power circuits, accelerating pumps, or chokes; however, some secondary carburetors are fitted with fixed idle circuits that deliver a certain quantity of fuel at all speeds except when their throttle valves are open.

Intake manifolds for multiple carburetors available as optional equipment from automobile manufacturers are usually of the "180-degree" type but lately manifolds of the "log" type have been released. Log manifolds seem to be favored by Chrysler Corporation engineers.

A 180-degree manifold for a two-throat carburetor is so designed that intake impulses from the engine's cylinders act on one of the carburetors throats and then the other, continually alternating so that at no time does one throat serve two consecutively firing cylinders. The purpose of this design is to equalize the air and fuel flow conditions in the carburetor throats and give the cylinders a chance to induct equal charges. When two or more carburetors are installed on a manifold of this type the throats in one side of the carburetors feed a common passage and the remaining throats feed another passage. These passages are divided in the same manner as they would be for a single two-throat so that intake impulses on them alternate.

A log manifold differs from a 180-degree type in that one of its sides serves all the cylinders in one bank of the engine and its other side serves the cylinders in the other bank. Intake impulses in a log manifold do not alternate evenly from one side of the manifold to the other; they alternate for part of the cylinders but not for all of them. Log manifolds are said to be all right if each log has adequate carburetion capacity so that the second of any pair of cylinders that might draw consecutively on one of its sides will receive a full charge of mixture.

To automotive engineers, log manifolds have several things in their favor. Among these are simplicity of construction due to the simplified routing of their passages, and that they can be made as low as possible because it isn't necessary to run their branches over each other. Manifold and carburetor height is becoming more of a problem each year as car height is reduced.

All standard production intake manifolds have one thing in common and that is that they are heated to improve vaporization of the fuel in the mixture passing through them. In all '58 engines except the large series of Ford product engines this heating is accomplished by routing exhaust gases through the manifold. This method of manifold heating is almost as old as the automobile itself. In the new larger Ford engines the manifolds are heated with water from the engine's cooling system. This isn't the first time this has been done but Ford is the first to try it in recent years. By using water it is said that the manifolds will heat quicker and a more even temperature will be maintained. In an engine used for normal driving, manifold heating is essential to smooth engine operation. Blocking the heat to the manifold will usually cause flat spots on acceleration and make it necessary to enrich the air/fuel mixture delivered by the carburetor to regain the original standard of performance. Heating the mixture has the disadvantage of lowering the engine's horsepower output because the heat expands the mixture as well as vaporizes the fuel, reducing the weight of mixture inducted into the cylinders on intake strokes. For competition engines that are not required to run smoothly at low speeds and that must deliver maximum power output without any consideration for fuel consumption, the intake manifold must be unheated.

Special intake manifolds for installation on stock or reworked engines are available in a large variety of types. Those for road use are heated in the same manner as stock manifolds but those for strictly competition use do not have heat passages. Manifolds without heat passages are called "cold" manifolds.

Special manifolds are made in both 180-degree and log types. Those for normal driving are usually of the 180-degree type and those for strictly competition may be of either 180-degree or log types. Log manifolds are becoming increasingly popular for competition.

Nearly all special manifolds are made for two-throat carburetors. Two-throat carburetors have the advantage over four-throat types of being much less complicated and therefore considerably lower in price. It is usually possible to buy three two-throats for the approximate price of one four-throat. When used in groups of two or more, two-throat carburetors provide the additional advantage of greater flexibility in manifold design, which allows better spacing of their throats in relation to the intake ports in the engine.

Special manifolds are made for three, four, six, and eight two-throat carburetors. An engine to be used for normal driving shouldn't require more than three two-throats. For competition use, or for a boat engine, four or more two-throats can be used satisfactorily, depending on the engine's displacement and the type of running it will be required to do. In addition to the air flow capacity they provide, multiple carburetors are definitely an advantage when special fuels are

used because of their fuel flow capacity. Fuel flow capacity is dependent on the quantity of fuel that can pass through a carburetor's needle and seat, main metering jets, and discharge nozzles. By doubling or tripling the number of carburetors on an engine, the carburetion system's fuel flow capacity is also doubled or tripled.

Some of the special log manifolds now being made are fitted with equalizer tubes that connect the logs so that carburetion for one cylinder bank will not be completely isolated from the other bank. The purpose of the equalizer tubes is to enable one log to draw mixture from the other and thereby reduce the possibility of any particular cylinders receiving a smaller charge of fresh mixture than that received by the other cylinders.

One type of eight-carburetor setup available is so arranged that both throats of a two-throat carburetor serve only one of an engine's intake ports. Each carburetor and its branch of the manifold is completely isolated from all the other carburetors and branches. This type of arrangement is good if the carburetor is mounted the correct distance from the intake valves so benefit can be taken of the ram effect of the mixture flowing through the carburetor, manifold, and intake passage in the cylinder head.

Special multiple-carburetor manifolds weren't too successful on engines used for normal driving until the introduction of progressive throttle linkage. Synchronizing the throttle valves in all three carburetors so they opened at the same time caused the same troubles at low engine speeds that are always experienced with too much ven-

This is a typical low-profile log-type manifold, used to mount six twin-throat carburetors for high-performance.

First and second steps of linkage installation are to replace old throttle shafts with new ones and attach arms to shaft.

open. This arrangement is much better than the vacuum-operated throttles used by automobile manufacturers. With vacuum throttles the driver has no control over the secondary carburetors; as a consequence, the car does not always react to throttle movement as the driver wants it to.

Progressive linkage was designed originally for three-carburetor manifolds but it is also available for some four-carburetor setups, and some car owners have adapted it to as many as six carburetors. There isn't any reason why progressive linkage can't be used on any number of carburetors but engines that have six or eight carburetors aren't used for normal driving and therefore don't require it. An engine used for competition

turi area. If the throttle pedals were moved too much to accelerate the car from rest, velocity of air through the carburetors was so low that fuel would not be forced from the discharge tubes. This would result in a faltering of the engine until crankshaft speed picked up enough for the air velocity through the venturis of the carburetors to reach the rate of flow that would cause fuel to flow from the discharge tubes. With progressive linkage this stumbling and faltering was eliminated by using only the primary carburetor at low speeds. Throttle valves in the secondary carburetors remain closed until the valves in the primary carburetor are either one-third or one-half open, depending on how the linkage is adjusted.

On engines equipped with automatic transmissions it is better to open the secondary throttles after one-half throttle movement. This gives the transmission control rod connected to the throttle linkage a longer range of movement before the secondaries open. This rod controls the oil pressure in the transmission's shifting mechanism and it must move far enough before the secondaries open to enable the pressure to rise to a value that will let the transmission handle the additional engine torque the secondaries make possible.

Progressive throttle linkage was the salvation of multiple carburetor manifolds for passenger cars. With it, the driver has complete control over the opening and closing times of the throttle valves in all the carburetors and he knows when the valves in the secondary carburetors start to

Slide bar is hooked up between front and center carburetors. Bar controls opening of end carburetors at set point.

will run satisfactorily with synchronized throttles because it never has to run at speeds so low that air velocity through the carburetors is below the minimum limit.

Installation procedures for progressive linkage depend primarily on the make of carburetors being used. In most instances installation is simple but it must be done carefully if the desired results are to be obtained. A fellow should follow, step-by-step, the instructions that came with the linkage and he should start with new, not used or rebuilt, carburetors. Used or rebuilt carburetors can have many things wrong with them that will make them unsatisfactory for multiple carburetor installations. The carburetor that came on a new engine and hasn't been used too long and is of the type that can be used for a multiple installation can, of course, be used if it is operating satisfactorily. Such a carburetor should be given a thorough cleaning to give it an even break with the new carburetors with which it will be used.

Before most carburetors can be used with progressive linkage it is necessary to change their throttle shafts. This must be done because the original shafts are too short for the installation of the arms used with the linkage. When longer shafts are needed they are supplied in the linkage kit. For this reason it is absolutely necessary that the make and model of the carburetors to be used be specified when the linkage is ordered. Also, the make of manifold should be specified.

Stock throttle shafts can be pulled out of their carburetors after the throttle valves have been removed. Before removing the throttle valves, their position in the throttle body, as indicated

Next, link between end carburetors is hooked up. Throttles should be set to reach wide open position at the same time.

by identifying marks, must be noted so they can be reinstalled correctly. These valves have beveled edges which make it necessary for them to be installed right side up and usually with a particular side next to the side of the throttle body that contains the idle discharge port. If the valves aren't marked it would be a good idea to mark them with a touch of layout dye or some other marking material that won't be readily wiped off while they are being handled.

Be sure there aren't any burrs on the shafts that will scratch the bores in the throttle bodies while the shafts are being removed. Scratches of this nature could result in air leaks that might make it difficult to make the engine idle as slowly as desired. Burrs can be flattened with a small

file. It will be necessary to grind or file the ends of some shafts so that arms on them can be removed. These arms are secured to the new shafts with screws supplied in the kits.

After the new shafts have been slipped into the throttle bodies, the throttle valves are reinstalled in their correct positions. New throttle valve screws will have to be used in some carburetors because the threaded ends of the original screws are riveted at the factory to prevent their coming loose and falling out. Once a screw that has been riveted has been removed from a shaft it is difficult to reuse it. The shafts must turn freely in the throttle bodies and the valves must be adjusted so they will close as completely as possible. This is absolutely essential to obtaining a slow idle speed.

Throttle valves are adjusted by tightening their screws so they are held snugly in the shaft but not so tightly so they can't be moved and then holding the upper end of the carburetor or throttle body up to a light while holding the throttle shaft in its closed position. With the carburetor in this position it is easy to determine how well the throttle valves are seating in their bores. By tapping on each of the valves with a screwdriver while holding the shaft in its closed position, the valves can be moved in the shaft as needed to make them seat as completely as possible. The importance of this operation cannot be overemphasized.

After both throttle valves have been seated, one end of the shaft and then the other should

Throttle rod is now connected to firewall arm. Automatic transmissions need an additional arm and link to finish job.

be tapped to move the shaft back and forth slightly to center the valves in the shaft. If one of the valves should be held in the shaft so that one of its sides dragged on the bore of the throttle body, it could cause the throttle to bind. All parts of the linkage must be perfectly free. After the valves have been seated in the bores and centered in the shaft and while the throttle shaft is being held in its closed position, all the throttle screws are tightened. Idle speed screws in the carburetors to be used as secondaries should then be adjusted to hold the valves just far enough open that they can't bind in the throats. Too much throttle opening will cause the idle speed to be high and if the valves can close far enough to bind they will make it impossible for the throttle linkage to operate smoothly.

Place new carburetor base gaskets on the flanges on the intake manifold and set the carburetors on the manifold in their correct positions. Tighten the nuts that hold the carburetors on the manifold tightly enough to hold the carburetors in place but leave them loose enough that the carburetors can be moved slightly, within the limitations allowed by the clearance between the studs and the sides of the holes in the carburetor bases. Throttle arms supplied in the kits are installed on the throttle shafts in the positions specified by the instruction sheet and then locked to the shafts by tightening the setscrews that contact the shafts.

Unless otherwise specified, the throttle arms must be positioned on the shafts so that when the shafts are in their full-open position the arms are an equal number of degrees from vertical as they are when they are in their closed position. In other words, when the throttle valves in any of the carburetors are midway between open and closed positions, the levers on their shafts will be vertical. The only thing that would change this condition would be some feature of the manifold that would not allow full movement of one or more of the levers while they were in this position on their shafts.

Throttle levers on the secondary carburetors are then connected with the rod supplied for this purpose and the rod is adjusted so that the throttle valves in both carburetors are completely closed at the same time. With the rod adjusted in this manner the throttle valves in both carburetors will be wipe open at the same time. Some carburetors have a stop that determines wide-open throttle position and if the carburetors are fitted with such a stop it may be necessary to adjust it so the throttle valves can open completely.

After it has been decided whether to open the secondary carburetors at one-third or one-half throttle, the rod that connects the primary carburetor to one of the secondaries can be installed and adjusted. This rod is adjusted so that it holds the secondary carburetors wide open when the throttle valves in the primary carburetor are wide open. A sliding stop on the rod is adjusted to hold the secondaries closed when the valves in the primary carburetor are in idle position. This stop is a safety device that will close the throttle valves in the secondaries in the event that the spring that is supposed to close them should break or become inoperative for some other reason. This spring should be connected to the linkage in such a manner that it will hold the throttle valves in the secondaries closed but it must not exert excessive tension on the linkage. In addition to holding the secondary carburetor throttle valves closed, the tension of the spring acts as a signal to the driver to let him know when the linkage is starting to open the secondary carburetors.

The linkage must be checked after the throttle rod from the accelerator pedal in the car has been connected to the primary carburetor to make sure the throttle valves in all the carburetors reach their wide-open position before the pedal touches the floor. Any adjustments that might be necessary to allow the pedal to fully open the carburetors must be made.

In addition to being adjustable to the extent that the secondary carburetors can be opened at one-third or one-half throttle, progressive linkage can easily be changed to synchronized linkage for competition use. It can also be installed to open the end carburetors first so they can be used as primary carburetors and then bring in the middle carburetor at either one-third or one-half throttle as a secondary carburetor. In some instances it might be better to use the two end carburetors for primaries but for most engines this might defeat the purpose of progressive linkage by giving too much carburetion at low speeds.

After the fuel lines have been installed and the engine has been started, the idle speed screw in the primary carburetor and the mixture adjustment screws in all three carburetors can be adjusted to obtain the best idle. On some installations it may be possible to screw the mixture screws in the secondary carburetors against their seats and idle the engine with the primary carburetor only but with others the screws in the secondaries must be backed out as much as a full turn each. This is something that must be worked out for each installation.

Fuel line kits consisting of copper tubing and the necessary fittings to connect the carburetors together are supplied with many three-carburetor manifolds. Fuel lines of this type are adequate for road driving and gasoline but lines with more capacity should be installed for competition use and for special fuels. The best fuel line arrangement for any multiple-carburetor manifold is a "fuel block" fitted with an individual line for each carburetor.

A fuel block is nothing more than a small chamber with drilled and tapped openings into which fittings for each of the carburetors and an inlet fitting from the fuel supply can be screwed. Fuel blocks are made from all sorts of material, the most popular being cast-aluminum, but their material and shape are of no importance as long as they have adequate capacity to distribute fuel from the source equally to the various carburetors.

A fuel block is usually mounted on a car's firewall or fender panel. Fittings are then screwed into its openings and into the fuel inlets on the carburetors and flexible hoses are installed between the block and the carburetors. Hose for this purpose varies from ¼ to ½-inch in inside diameter, depending on the type of fuel to be used. Hose with an inside diameter of ¼ or ⅜-inch is usually installed for alcohol or other special fuels. Actually, ⅜-inch hose between the fuel block and carburetors is adequate for alcohol and other special fuels but the hose between the fuel source and the fuel block should be ½-inch. Hose for fuel line installations is available in neoprene or plastic. Plastic is often used when appearance is a factor but for most installations neoprene is more practical and the safer of the two.

A standard mechanical fuel pump can be used as the source of fuel supply for a road engine but for competition a supply with a higher capacity is usually required. When a standard pump is used, its outlet is connected to the inlet on the fuel block with a length of flexible hose. Flexibility is required in this line because of the normal movement of the engine in relation to the firewall or fender panel on which the fuel block is mounted.

A car to be used for competition should be fitted with some type of pressure fuel system. This can be either permanently mounted in the car or it can be a temporary setup placed in the driver's compartment. Pressure systems are fitted with a hand pressure pump for building up air pressure in the fuel tank and with a gauge to show the pressure of the fuel being fed to the fuel block. A correctly installed pressure system has the advantage over a mechanically or electrically-driven fuel pump in that its fuel flow capacity is more than adequate for any converted automotive engine. It is, of course, important that the correct pressure be maintained in the tank when the engine is running.

Carburetors on an engine to be used for normal driving should be equipped with efficient air filters. Air filters will protect the engine's moving parts and keep the inside of the carburetor clean. Multiple-carburetor installations often pose a problem as far as air filter installation is concerned because for most of them the only filters available are of the wire-mesh type. These filters are extremely low in efficiency because they allow the finer particles of grit and foreign matter in the air to enter the carburetors and the engine.

The most efficient filters now available are those with corrugated paper filtering elements. These elements are standard equipment in practically all production automobiles and filters with them are available for some special applications. If filters with elements of this type can be installed on a multiple-carburetor setup, they should by all means be given preference over filters of any other type.

Maintenance of multiple-carburetor installations differs from that for single carburetors only in the number of carburetors involved and the method of making idle adjustments. The ideal way of measuring the air/fuel ratios delivered by one or more carburetors is with an exhaust gas analyzer while the car is running on the road or on a chassis dynamometer. A dynamometer has the advantage of convenience and more easily

Another method used successfully by some hot rodders to insure an adequate fuel supply is the special fuel pressure tank. This setup gives six pounds fuel flow pressure.

controlled conditions but it isn't always possible to find one of them.

Making idle adjustments on setups with progressive throttle linkage isn't too difficult because engine speed is controlled by the throttle valve adjusting screw on the primary carburetor. Mixture adjustments are then made on the primary carburetor, and possibly on the secondary carburetors until the engine idles smoothly and does not have any flat spots at speeds just above idle.

Idle adjustments are more difficult with multiple-carburetor setups that have synchronized throttles or with setups that have progressive linkage and two primary carburetors. For setups of this type there are several special gauges available that indicate the quantity of air flowing through a carburetor on an engine running at idle speed. To use a gauge of this type, it is placed over the air horn of each carburetor that

is functioning and the throttle valve adjusting screws on the carburetors are turned in or out until the reading on the gauge is the same for all the carburetors. This indicates that each carburetor is supplying the same amount of air to the engine. Idle mixture screws in the carburetors are then adjusted to make the engine idle smoothly.

The correct air/fuel ratio for the cruising range is more difficult to establish than the ratio for idling. The ratio required for cruising will depend on the engine and what has been done to it. For normal driving, cruising mixtures should be just rich enough to eliminate surge at 45 to 50 miles per hour on a level road and with steady throttle. Main metering jets determine the ratio of this range and progressively leaner jets can be installed until surge is encountered and then jets one or two sizes richer, as needed, should be about right.

When progressive throttle linkage is used, air/fuel ratios in the cruising range are usually determined by the primary carburetor; its main metering jets are the only ones that must be changed at this time. In multiple-carburetor setups with synchronized throttle valves, the main metering jets in all the carburetors will have to be changed at the same time.

Determining the correct air/fuel ratio for the power range is the most difficult of all. It is simplified immeasurably by the use of an exhaust gas analyzer. In the absence of an analyzer, about all one can do is go by the feel of the seat of his pants. Sometimes this isn't too positive. In most carburetors the air/fuel ratio for the power range is controlled by power jets that are opened by the throttle linkage when the throttle valves reach a certain position or by a spring when vacuum in the intake manifold drops to a specified value. The ratio is changed by installing a larger or smaller power jet.

In a setup with progressive throttle linkage power mixtures are usually controlled by the power jets in the primary carburetor and by the combined mixture supplied by the main metering and power jets in the secondary carburetors; however, it's not impossible for the primary carburetor to still be in its cruising range when the secondaries open.

The many different throttle positions possible with progressive linkage make it difficult to establish any set rules for adjusting fuel mixtures. About all one can do is work out a satisfactory adjustment for each particular setup. For setups with synchronized throttles the problem is somewhat simpler in that the transition from cruising to power will occur at the same time in all the carburetors and they can all be fitted with the same size main metering jets and the same size power jets.

Three carburetors with progressive throttle linkage are ideal for the fellow interested in gasoline mileage for normal driving but who occasionally wants good performance too. The primary carburetor can be jetted so the engine will get good mileage at normal speeds and the secondaries can be jetted to bring in the correct mixture for power when their throttles are opened. It would be possible to use a carburetor of a different type or size for the primary carburetor. Some makes of carburetors are much more effi-

cient than others as far as fuel mileage is concerned and small venturis are often more economical than larger ones because of the better fuel atomization and vaporization they provide. A primary carburetor with small venturis would provide just as good or possibly better engine performance at low speeds than a carburetor with large venturis. At the point where the small venturis began to become unable to supply sufficient air to the engine, secondary carburetors with venturis adequate for the engine could be cut in. Things that can be done along this line with three carburetors and progressive linkage are practically unlimited.

A problem usually brought on by multiple-carburetor installations is correct actuation of the vacuum advance mechanism in the ignition distributor. In most engines the vacuum for the distributor is taken from a fitting in the carburetor. Vacuum for this purpose can originate in the intake manifold or be created by the flow of air through the carburetor's venturis.

Distributors that use manifold vacuum are less of a problem than those that use venturi vacuum. If the primary carburetor of a multiple setup has a fitting for manifold vacuum, the distributor can usually be connected to it and be used satisfactorily. If the carburetor does not have such a fitting it will not be possible to use the distributor's vacuum advance mechanism. This wouldn't affect the engine's performance but it could lower its fuel mileage.

Ford distributors of the type that depend solely on vacuum for their advance are a problem with any type of multiple-carburetor setup. If used with a primary carburetor of the correct type, one of these distributors might function correctly while the engine was running on the primary carburetor, but when the secondaries opened there might not be enough velocity through the primary carburetor to advance the ignition timing the correct amount.

The ideal solution to the ignition distributor problem is to replace the stock distributor with one of the special two-coil makes available that do not require vacuum advance mechanisms. In addition to solving the advance problem, one of these distributors will provide the best possible ignition for all running conditions. Complete information on distributors of this type is given in the chapter on electrical systems.

CHAPTER SEVEN

Your Engine's Electrical System

High-Performance ignition, magnetos, distributors, coils, condensers, spark plugs, batteries, generators, regulators. How to get better performance through ignition conversions.

An AUTOMOBILE'S ELECTRICAL SYSTEM has many things to do. Among these are to supply illumination inside and outside the car, crank its engine to start it, and fire the compressed fuel and air mixture in the engine's cylinders. Of these duties, the one that is of the most importance to a hot rodder is the firing of the mixture in the cylinders. This is the function of the engine's ignition system.

For many years the electrical systems of automobiles built in the United States operated on six volts. Six volts were adequate until engine displacement and compression ratios rose to the point where they couldn't crank the engines briskly enough for starting nor fire the mixture in the cylinders efficiently. The solution to these problems was to switch to twelve volts. Starting motors wound for twelve volts have ample power to crank any modern engine and ignition coils used in twelve-volt systems can efficiently fire any stock engine.

A car will run without lights and it can be pushed to start its engine but its ignition system must be functioning efficiently if the engine is to run well at high speeds and deliver its maximum torque and horsepower outputs. An ignition system includes many parts. These are the battery, battery cables, the ignition switch, ignition coil, ignition coil resistor, condenser, ignition distributor, spark plugs, spark plug cables, engine ground strap, generator, generator regulator, and the wires that connect some of these components.

The battery is the very heart of an electrical system. It must be in good condition and fully charged if the rest of the components in the system are to be expected to function as they should. An ignition system cannot create a spark of full intensity at the spark plugs if the battery voltage isn't up to specifications. If the battery is in good condition its voltage is dependent on the generator and the generator's regulator. The generator maintains the battery in a fully charged condition by converting mechanical energy to electrical energy. This electrical energy is stored in the battery. The amount of electrical energy the generator supplies to the battery is determined by the generator's regulator; therefore, the regulator must be in good working order and correctly adjusted if the battery is to be maintained at the correct voltage.

Cables and wires that connect the battery to the electrical system must be in good condition and have connections that are electrically as well as mechanically tight so the full voltage of the battery will be conducted to the system's components. Switches in the system must be in good condition so they too will conduct full voltage.

Something that is often overlooked in an electrical system is the engine ground strap. In many cars the engine and driveline are insulated from the frame by rubber motor mounts and rubber or fabric bushings in the rear springs. In a car in which the engine and rear axle assembly are mounted in this manner current flow from the engine to the battery would be restricted if the battery were grounded to the car's frame, as it is in many older cars and some that have been reworked in different ways. There is usually some metallic connection between the engine and the frame but more often than not such a connection doesn't have sufficient electrical conductivity to carry the amperage required by the engine's starting motor and it is often inadequate for the small amount of current required by the ignition system. To complete the circuit between the

engine and the frame for such installations, a ground strap, which usually is a braided strap with an eye on each end, is bolted to the engine and to the frame. In late model cars the possibility of a poor electrical connection between the engine and the battery is eliminated by grounding the battery to the engine. A ground strap is then used between the engine and the car's body so the light circuits can receive full voltage.

An ignition system's main duty is to create charges of sufficient voltage to jump the gap between the electrodes of the spark plugs in the engine when the gap is exposed to the compressed fuel and air mixture in the cylinders. While jumping the gap, the voltage creates a spark that ignites the mixture. With a standard ignition system the voltage for this purpose is created by a single ignition coil that boosts the battery's voltage to several thousand volts.

An ignition system has two electrical circuits. One of these is the primary circuit and the other is the secondary. The primary circuit is the one that creates the high voltage current in the secondary circuit. Current for the primary circuit originates at the battery and when the ignition switch is on it travels from the battery, through the ignition switch, through the ignition coil resistor, through the primary winding in the ignition coil, through the breaker points in the distributor, and then to ground, completing the

DELCO-REMY...12 VOLT ELECTRICAL SYSTEM

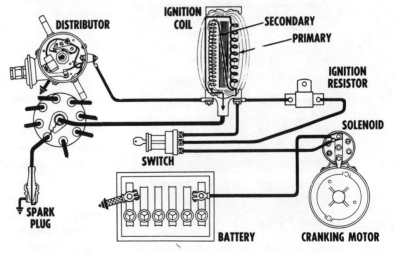

This schematic diagram is typical of stock, single-coil, engine electrical systems.

circuit back to the battery. Current for the secondary circuit originates in the ignition coil and it travels through circuits in the distributor cap and on the distributor rotor, to the spark plugs, across the gap between the spark plug's electrodes, then to ground, completing the circuit.

An ignition coil has two sets of windings and a soft iron core in a common case. One of the windings is the primary and the other is the secondary. Ends of the primary winding are connected to posts on the top of the coil, and one end of the secondary winding is connected to a socket, usually on one end of the coil. Ignition coils of different makes vary in their construction but all of them contain the same essential parts and use the same principle to create secondary charges.

When the ignition switch is in its ON position and the breaker points in the distributor are closed, current from the battery flows through the primary winding in the coil and to ground. As the current passes through the winding it creates a magnetic field around the coil's soft iron core. The lines of magnetism that form the magnetic field move out from the core and cross the wires, or conductors, in the primary and secondary windings, inducting a voltage in the conductors. In the primary winding this voltage creates a force called "self-induction" that opposes the flow of battery current through the winding.

Self-induction causes the magnetic field to build up comparatively slowly when current first

High-grade ignition coil (left) and condenser. Note the electrical resistor at the top of the coil on the right.

starts to flow through the primary winding. This prevents a voltage of any consequence from being created in the coil's secondary winding. But when the flow of current through the primary winding is interrupted by opening the breaker points in the distributor, the magnetic field collapses rapidly and the lines of magnetism cross the conductors in the secondary winding with such velocity as they return to the coil's core that a high voltage current is induced in the secondary winding. This current flows to the center terminal of the distributor cap and then to one of the engine's spark plugs.

When the breaker points open, the rapidly collapsing magnetic field creates a self-induced voltage in the coil's primary winding as well as in the secondary. This voltage tries to continue to force current through the primary circuit in the direction it was moving when the points were closed. If this current were not controlled in some manner it would arc from one of the distributor point contacts to the other, causing the contacts to be burned and preventing the magnetic field in the coil from collapsing quickly enough to create sufficient voltage to jump the gap in the spark plugs. This current is controlled by the condenser in the primary circuit.

A condenser for an automobile engine's ignition system consists of two long, narrow strips of lead or aluminum foil that are insulated from each other with special condenser paper. These strips are rolled to form a winding and are placed in a metal case of tubular shape. One of the strips is connected electrically to the case and the other is connected to an insulated terminal on the case or to a wire that projects out of the case's cover and has a terminal on its free end. When the condenser is installed in the ignition system its case is connected to ground, which grounds one of the strips, and the terminal or wire from the other strip is connected to the ignition coil side of the breaker points. In other words, the condenser is connected across the breaker points, or in parallel with them.

When the breaker points open, the condenser offers less resistance than the gap across the points to the induced current in the primary winding that tries to flow across the gap, so the current flows into the condenser, charging it. As the current flows into the condenser it is slowed and finally stopped and then it oscillates back and forth, into the primary circuit and then back into the condenser, until it diminishes to a voltage equal to that of the battery. As the current is dissipating it is speeding the collapse of the magnetic field in the coil and bringing the primary circuit back into equilibrium for the next cycle. All this is happening while the high-voltage current induced in the secondary winding is being discharged across the gap between the spark plug electrodes.

It would seem as though it would take some time for the ignition system to complete one of its cycles but in actuality the time involved is only a fraction of a second. An eight-cylinder engine running at 6500 revolutions per minute requires 433 secondary charges per second. However, creating secondary charges of sufficient voltage to fire the spark plugs in a high compression engine at this frequency requires an ignition system that is an excellent condition both mechanically and electrically. Engine speeds over 4500 to 4700 rpm are beyond the capabilities of the average stock ignition distributor.

Another duty of the ignition system is to deliver the secondary voltage to the spark plugs in the correct sequence according to the engine's firing order and at the correct time in relation to the position of the pistons in the cylinders. The timing is dependent on the initial spark lead, which is determined by the position of the distributor in the engine, and on automatically controlled mechanisms in the distributor that advance and retard the timing according to engine speed and the load on the engine.

In one type of distributor the automatic timing control consists of governor weights that rotate the distributor's breaker cam on its shaft to open the points earlier or later in relation to the shaft's position. Movement of the governor weights is determined by the shaft's speed of rotation. The faster the shaft rotates, the more the weights expand to move the breaker cam ahead of the shaft. In other distributors the spark is advanced by a vacuum-actuated diaphragm that rotates the breaker plate on which the points are mounted so they will be opened earlier or later by the breaker cam. Vacuum for the advance diaphragms of distributors of this type is created in carburetors by air passing through their venturis.

Most distributors that have governor weights also have a vacuum diaphragm that rotates the

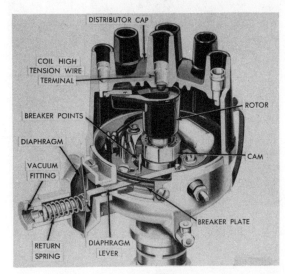

Components of the distributor head include distributor cap, rotor, breaker points, and vacuum advance mechanism.

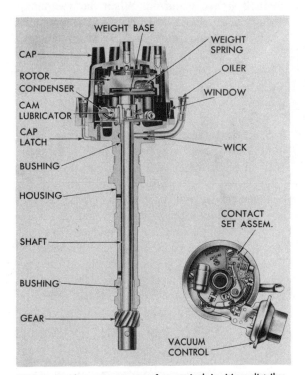

These are the components of a typical ignition distributor including the driveshaft, driven off the camshaft.

This is external view of vacuum advance mechanism. Note 'advance' and 'retard' adjustment scale below bolt head.

breaker plate to provide additional advance over that supplied by the governor. Diaphragms for additional advance are actuated by vacuum in the engine's intake manifold. When the vacuum is high, the diaphragm advances the timing, and when the vacuum drops, such as when the engine is running under load during periods of acceleration or when climbing a hill, the timing is retarded. The theory of this additional timing is to improve the fuel mileage delivered by the engine.

As far as the intensity of its secondary voltage is concerned, the efficiency of an ignition system is dependent on the period of time current can flow through the primary winding of the coil. This period is determined by the point "dwell," or "cam angle," which is the number of degrees of breaker cam rotation during which the points remain closed. Dwell is the same at all engine speeds but as the speed increases, the period of time during which the points are closed becomes shorter; however, increasing the number of degrees of dwell lengthens the time the points remain closed at any given speed.

With an eight-cylinder engine, which requires an eight-lobe breaker cam when a single coil is used, it's a common occurrence for the time during which the points remain closed to become so short at high speeds that a magnetic field large enough to create sufficient voltage to fire the spark plugs cannot be built up in the coil. When this happens, engine horsepower falls off and car performance suffers.

Ignition system modifications designed to make it possible for a system to function properly at high speeds so its coil can create a satisfactory spark are many and varied. They include minor and major modifications to stock ignition distributors, and special distributors that use two coils instead of only one.

Two of the faults common to most stock ignition distributors when they are forced to operate at speeds higher than that for which they were designed are point "bounce" and "float." Bounce describes the action of the movable point arm when its contact bounces off the stationary contact after the points have closed, and float is the action of the points when the rubbing block on the arm fails to follow the surface of the breaker cam as it should. Either of these actions reduces the period of time the points remain closed as the breaker cam rotates.

One of the original ignition system modifications was "double-springing" the point arm in the distributor to eliminate bounce and float. Double-springing won't cure all of a stock distributor's shortcomings but it will make it possible for the distributor points to function as they should at high engine speeds.

Points are double-sprung by installing the spring from another arm of the same type on the arm in the distributor along with the original spring so that the arm has two springs instead of one. The comparatively high pressure exerted on the arm by the two springs forces the arm's rubbing block to follow the breaker cam at all times and holds the point's contacts together when the points close. Distributor manufacturers frown on double-springing because the additional tension on the arm causes its rubbing block to wear faster than it would normally. When the block wears, the gap between the open points is reduced. It's possible for the block to wear so much that the points will fail to open as the breaker cam rotates; however, rapid rubbing block wear is of little consequence when good engine performance at high crankshaft speeds is concerned.

Although double-springing will make the point arm function as it should, point dwell, and the period of time the points remain closed, is still determined by the distributor's design. A modification that will increase dwell is the installation of a "dual-point plate." A distributor fitted with a dual-point plate still uses an eight-lobe cam and one condenser.

Dual points were stock equipment in distributors used on Ford V8 and Mercury engines built prior to 1949. At the present time they are used in the distributors on some of the industry's optional high-performance engines. The principal that enables dual points to increase point dwell, and therefore the time current can flow through the primary winding of the ignition coil at any given engine speed, is easily understood.

Both sets of points on a dual-point plate are mounted on the same breaker plate in such positions that it is possible for either set to be open when the other is closed and also for both sets to be open at the same time. The sets are connected electrically so they are in parallel with the primary circuit through the distributor. As the distributor shaft rotates the breaker cam, one set, which is called the "make" set, is opened by one of the cam's lobes while the other set, which is called the "break" set, is still closed. As the cam continues to rotate, the make set is held open and another lobe on the cam opens the break set. When the break set opens, both sets are open and the flow of current through the primary winding of the ignition coil is interrupted and the voltage for the spark plug is created in the coil's secondary winding. As the breaker cam continues to rotate, the break set is held open but the make set closes so that current can again flow through the coil. Further rotation of the cam allows the break set to close so that again both sets are closed.

By overlapping the open and closed times of the points as described it is possible for both sets to be adjusted so they open far enough to reduce arcing from one of their contacts to the other to the minimum but at the same time increase their total point dwell. It would be possible to attain the same dwell with a single set of points but to do so it would be necessary to reduce the gap between the points when they were open to such a degree that arcing would soon cause them to become burned beyond further use. Another advantage of dual points is that the make set doesn't open the primary circuit; therefore there is never any arcing of current across its contacts to burn and corrode them. This means that the contacts are always clean and capable of making a good circuit for the primary current.

Bounce and float are just as apt to occur with the points on a dual-point plate as they are with stock points. If these conditions are encountered, they can be corrected by double-springing the points. Double-springing is common practice in early Ford dual-point distributors. It has enabled many road engines with otherwise stock ignition systems to run extremely well.

Dual-point plates for many of the more popular V8 engines are available from several manufacturers. A plate of this kind is simple to install because it is made to replace a stock plate without any alterations to the distributor, but as the sole purpose of dual points is to increase dwell, it is essential that the points be adjusted correctly. This should be done on a distributor machine. Each of the point sets is adjusted individually so that together they give the specified number of degrees of dwell.

A dual-point plate is a definite improvement in any stock distributor fitted originally with a single set of points but an ignition system with a single coil is limited in its ability to fire the cylinders of a high compression engine that is running at high crankshaft speeds. Only one battery ignition system modification can correct this shortcoming and it is the installation of a distributor designed to operate with two coils and condensors. Two-coil distributors fall into two categories. One of these includes converted stock distributors and the other includes special distributors that are made specifically for two coils.

A two-coil distributor is, in effect, two four-cylinder distributors in a common housing. It has two sets of breaker points that are isolated from each other, a four-lobe breaker cam, and two secondary circuits on its rotor. The advantage of such an arrangement is that it enables the engine's cylinders to be fired by two coils instead of only one. Each coil fires half the cylinders and the coils discharge alternately. Because the breaker points are opened by a four-lobe cam, they can have as much as twice the dwell of the single points in a stock distributor. This makes it possible for current to flow through the primary winding of the coils twice as long at any given engine speed as it could otherwise, enabling the coils to become completely saturated with magnetic flux for each of their discharge cycles. A coil in a two-coil system on an engine running at 6000 rpm is creating high-voltage secondary discharges at the same frequency as the coil in a single-coil system on the same engine running at 3000 rpm.

Converting a stock ignition distributor to two-coil operation is an involved project. An extra set of breaker points must be mounted on the distributor's breaker plate, four of the eight lobes must be ground off its breaker cam, and its rotor and cap must be converted to accommodate the second coil. The cap and rotor are usually the most difficult parts of the conversion because of the material of which they are made and the high electrical voltage that must be accommodated. The rotor must have two secondary pickups and the cap must have an additional secondary socket for the cable from the second coil.

Two or three types of caps and rotors that were made years ago for two-coil distributors are still available and sometimes it is possible to adapt one of these caps and its rotor to a stock distributor housing. When ready-made caps and rotors are used it is generally necessary to alter the distributor housing and the upper end of the distributor shaft to enable them to be installed. When a stock cap is used, a brass ring is usually fitted to it so the ring is between the center terminal in the cap and the terminals for the spark plug cables. A contact that will pick up the voltage from the ring and conduct it to the spark plug cable pickups in the cap is then attached to the rotor.

Stock distributors reworked for two-coil operation are, at best, makeshift affairs when compared to the special two-coil distributors available. There isn't anything makeshift about the special distributors because they are made specifically for two-coil use. They are precision-built of the finest materials and to exact specifications to provide faultless ignition at all engine speeds. Breaker camshafts in the better two-coil distributors are supported by ball bearings that hold the shaft and breaker cam in their correct positions in relation to the points. Their breaker cams are precision ground to guarantee that their lobes are exactly 90 degrees apart. Lobes on a breaker cam must be equally spaced so each of of the engine's cylinders will receive its spark at the correct time in relation to the other cylinders. This is important to a smooth-running engine and maximum horsepower output. Lobes on cams for stock distributors are often out of position one way or the other in relation to each other.

Breaker plates in special distributors that are fitted with vacuum diaphragms are mounted on a ball bearing that holds them in their correct position in relation to the cam when they are rotated to advance or retard the timing. Another special very important feature of distributors is their advance mechanisms that can be adjusted for best performance from either stock or reworked engines. For a reworked engine, the advance rate is usually speeded up at low engine speeds, in comparison to that provided by a stock distributor, and the total degrees of advance is increased to suit the engine. The exact advance curve would depend on the engine for which the distributor was made.

Regardless of the type of distributor used in an ignition system, the system cannot be any better than its coils. Stock coils, especially twelve-volt types, are entirely adequate for stock engines but they may not have the ability to create secondary voltage of sufficient intensity to fire the mixture in a reworked engine that has an extremely high compression ratio. Using coils of this type in pairs with two-coil distributors doesn't make them any more suitable for high compression engines because each coil must still be capable of creating sufficient voltage to jump the gap between the electrodes in the spark plugs.

There are some stock coils that are suitable for any engine when used with a two-coil distributor. Among these are those used as stock equipment (not replacement coils made by another manufacturer) on 1942 through '48 Fords and on '55 Fords. These are for six-volt current. For twelve-volt current the '56 Ford coil with the resistor made for it can be used. Special coils, designed to create exceptionally high secondary voltage, are available. The most popular of these is the Mallory "Voltmaster." Voltmaster coils are made in both six and twelve-volt types and they are sufficiently strong for any single or two-coil installation. Special condensers are made for use with Voltmaster coils and it would be advisable to install one of them with each coil.

An important part of any twelve-volt and some six-volt ignition systems is the resistor between the ignition switch and the primary terminal of the ignition coil. The purpose of this resistor is to reduce the voltage of the current that flows through the coil's winding. Resistors for twelve-volt systems cut the current to between 8 and 9 volts. Resistors in six-volt systems usually drop the current to approximately four volts.

Although twelve-volt ignition systems were adopted for their better ability to fire the mixture in the cylinders of high compression engines, the full twelve volts is not used in the ignition coil. This is because a coil with a primary winding that could take the full twelve volts with an amperage flow low enough that it wouldn't burn the breaker points in the distributor would be too sluggish for high engine speeds. Such a coil would require too much time to create its secondary charges. But with between 8 and 9 volts in the primary winding, the coil's reaction time is fast enough for any engine and the amperage flow in the primary circuit is low enough that it won't burn the breaker points.

Whenever a coil is installed on an engine it is important that the correct resistor be installed with it. It is equally important that there be only one resistor between the ignition switch and the primary terminal of coils that require a resistor and that a resistor not be installed with six-volt or special coils that do not require them—some six-volt coils need a resistor but others do not. Resistors on special coils that require them will be built into the coil. If there should happen to be two resistors between a coil and its ignition switch, voltage delivered to the coil would be abnormally low and the coil's secondary output would be restricted.

Factory-installed resistors for twelve-volt coils are usually in the engine compartment but in the past it was popular to install resistors for six-volt coils on the passenger side of the firewall. A resistor inside the passenger compartment is out of sight and could be easily overlooked when a special coil or ignition system is being installed. When installing any coil other than a stock replacement it is a good idea to run a new wire from the ignition switch to the coil or its resistor. This eliminates the possibility of a hidden resistor's reducing the voltage received by the coil and also guarantees that current from the switch to the coil or resistor will not encounter any resistance that might be in the old wire or its terminals. Terminals on the new wire should be either soldered or securely crimped to the wire's conductor.

Installation of a stock ignition distributor on an engine is a simple matter of turning the engine's crankshaft until the piston in its number one cylinder is at the specified number of degrees before top center on its compression stroke, turning the distributor shaft so the contact on its rotor is pointing at the terminal inside the cap for the cap's number one spark plug wire socket, and then inserting the lower end of the distributor in the cylinder block so its gear meshes with the drive gear on the cam shaft and the end of the shaft meshes with the oil pump drive gear. Usually, before the distributor is inserted in the cylinder block, its shaft has to be rotated one way or the other from the position it should be in when it is in the engine. This is because the angles of the teeth on the gears on the shaft and camshaft will cause the distributor shaft to be rotated a few degrees as the gears mesh.

Spark plug cables are installed in the distributor cap by inserting the wire from cylinder number one in the cap's number one socket and then moving around the cap in the direction the rotor rotates and according to the engine's firing order. The primary wire from the coil is then connected to the primary terminal on the distributor and the secondary wire from the coil is inserted in the tower in the center of the distributor cap. After the engine has been started the timing is adjusted to factory specifications with the aid of a timing light. This is done by rotating the distributor housing in the engine while watching the timing marks on the engine's crankshaft pulley or flywheel with the light. When the light shows number one cylinder to be firing at the specified number of degrees before top center, the capscrew that holds the distributor in the engine is tightened.

Installation of a converted stock two-coil ignition distributor or a special two-coil distributor is basically the same as that for a stock distributor but there are important differences. In most two-coil distributors the set of points that fires number one cylinder and the lobe on the breaker cam that opens the points are marked. If a distributor that isn't marked in this manner is being installed it will be necessary to determine the position the distributor will occupy in the engine so the distributor cap socket most convenient to cylinder number one can be located and marked. The distributor's shaft is then rotated until the

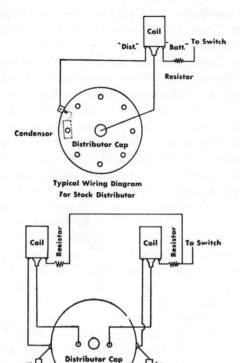

Typical Wiring Diagram
For Stock Distributor

These schematic diagrams show the differences between a single-coil ignition system and a dual-coil ignition system.

cam reaches a position where it is holding one of the sets of points open and one of the contacts on the rotor is pointing at the terminal inside the cap for the marked socket. The points that are open and the cam lobe that is holding them open are then marked.

With the piston in cylinder number one the specified number of degrees before top center position on its compression stroke, and the distributor's shaft positioned so the marked lobe on the breaker cam is just starting to open the marked points, the distributor housing is positioned in relation to the engine and lowered into the cylinder block. As with a stock distributor, it may be necessary to rotate the distributor shaft one way or the other a few degrees so it will be in the correct position after its gear has meshed with the gear on the camshaft.

Spark plug cable installation in the distributor will vary for different types of distributors but the first thing to do before installing the cables is to determine the kind of conductor they have. If the cables are of the comparatively new TVRS

type used as stock equipment on most late model engines they will have non-metallic conductors and they must be replaced with cables that have copper conductors. Non-metallic conductors have a built-in resistance to reduce radio and television noise caused by automotive ignition systems. This resistance might reduce the voltage of the secondary current delivered to the spark plugs.

Most converted stock distributors and some special two-coil units have single caps but there are some special units that have two caps. Sockets in single caps are sometimes marked after the distributor has been converted to two-coil use to indicate which cylinders they serve. Sockets in other single caps may not be numbered, or the socket for cylinder number one may be the only one that is numbered or marked. If the sockets in a single cap are numbered according to the cylinders they serve, it is a simple matter to install the cables from the spark plugs in them by matching the numbers of the cylinders to the numbers on the sockets. If none of the sockets are numbered, the socket for cylinder number one is determined by the position of the rotor and the cable from cylinder number one is inserted in this socket. After determining the direction the rotor rotates when the engine is running, and starting the count from socket number one, the cable for the third cylinder in the engine's firing order is inserted in the third socket in the direction of rotor rotation, the cable for the fifth cylinder in the firing order is inserted in the fifth socket, and the cable for the seventh cylinder in the firing order is inserted in the seventh socket. The cable for the second cylinder in the firing order goes in the sixth socket, the cable for the fourth cylinder in the firing order goes in the eighth socket, the cable for the sixth cylinder in the firing order goes in the second socket, and the cable for the eighth cylinder in the firing order goes in the fourth socket. The cables must be mixed in this manner because secondary charges from the rotor alternate between its two terminals. After cylinder number one has been fired, the rotor rotates one-eighth of a turn and delivers its next charge from its other terminal.

Sockets in caps of special distributors that have two caps may be numbered to match the numbers of the cylinders in the engine but more likely they will be numbered in the order in which they receive current from the rotor. Sockets numbered according to cylinder numbers pose no problem because all that must be done is install cables from the cylinders in the sockets with the same number. For sockets that are numbered according to the order in which they receive voltage from the rotor, a chart is made by writing numbers one through eight on a piece of paper and then, starting with number one, writing the engine's firing order so each number in the order is below one of the numbers written previously. Then the cable from cylinder number one is inserted in socket number one, the cable from the cylinder whose number is below the number two in the upper row is inserted in socket number two, the cable from the cylinder whose number is below number three is inserted in socket number three, and so on.

To wire the primary circuits of any two-coil distributor, connect the wire from the ignition switch to the "Bat." post on one of the coils and then run a wire from this post to the "Bat." post on the second coil. If the coils require resistors, run a wire from the switch to the "Bat." terminal of one of the resistors and then another wire from this terminal to the "Bat." terminal of the other resistor. Then run a wire from the "Coil" terminal of the first resistor to the "Bat." terminal of the first coil and connect the "Coil" terminal of the second resistor to the "Bat." terminal of the second coil with another length of wire. The "Dist." terminal of the first coil is then connected to one of the primary terminals on the distributor and the "Dist." terminal of the second coil is connected to the remaining primary terminal on the distributor.

At this time it doesn't matter which coil is connected to which distributor terminal although the secondary and primary wires from the coils must be connected to the correct terminals on the distributor or the engine won't start. The easiest way to determine the correct wiring order is by trying to start the engine. If the engine doesn't start readily, switch the secondary cables in the coils or in the distributor sockets, or switch the primary wires on the coil "Dist." terminals or on the terminals on the distributor. It is necessary to switch only one end of either the secondary or primary wires. This will correct the condition if the coils weren't wired correctly. After the engine has been started, the timing can be adjusted with a timing light.

Another type of ignition system that is very popular for competition engines and also entirely satisfactory for road machines is a magneto. The respective merits of battery ignition systems and magnetos have always been highly controversial subjects among hot rodders but the answer to the question as to which of the systems is the better for high-performance competition engines is slowly resolving itself in favor of the magneto. Battery ignition systems utilizing special two-coil ignition distributors are found on some competition engines but most engines of this type are now using one or the other of two magnetos.

As far as their construction and the quality of the materials used in them are concerned, there is no doubt that the two most popular magnetos now available are far superior to stock battery ignition distributors or to stock distributors that have been reworked for two-coil use. The construction and materials in special two-coil distributors, such as the Kong "Roto Faze" or Spaulding "Flamethrower," are equal to those in the magnetos but these are probably the only

To obtain better ignition of fuel, special electrical components are often used by hot rodders. This is a Spaulding 'Flamethrower' dual-coil ignition distributor; excellent unit.

Cap Socket Numbers	①	②	③	④	⑤	⑥	⑦	⑧
Firing Orders								
● Olds	1	8	7	3	6	5	4	2
● Buick	1	2	7	8	4	5	6	3
● Ford ● Mercury ● Lincoln ● Continental	1	5	4	8	6	3	7	2
● Chevy ● Chrysler ● Pontiac ● Studebaker ● Cadillac ● Nash ● Dodge ● Hudson ● Plymouth ● Packard ● De Soto	1	8	4	3	6	5	7	2

Chart shows relationship of distributor cap socket numbers to firing order of various engines.

two ignition distributors now popular of which this can be said.

In addition to being fully capable of firing the compressed fuel and air mixture in the cylinders of a high-performance engine running at high crankshaft speeds, magnetos have the advantage of being self-contained ignition systems. They generate their own primary current, which means that they don't require a battery or external coil. In many competition cars, especially dragsters, the weight of a battery would be highly unwanted excess baggage. Drag cars are built as light as practical to keep their horsepower-to-weight ratio as high as possible.

The two most popular magnetos now available are the Swiss-built Scintilla Vertex and the Harman & Collins. Vertex magnetos are made for all popular makes of engines. They are, by far, the most popular of all magnetos. One of the things that adds to their versatility is that they are designed to replace stock battery ignition distributors. All that must be done to install a Vertex is remove the battery distributor and insert the

Vertex in the cylinder block in the distributor's place. Spark plug cable sockets in the mag's cap are numbered in the order in which they receive secondary charges from the rotor. Installation of cables in the sockets is simplified by making a chart as described for the installation of cables in caps of battery ignition distributors that have sockets numbered in the order they receive secondary voltage.

Vertex mags have generator-type spark advance mechanisms and they do not require any vacuum. The advance mechanisms are fully adjustable, enabling them to be adjusted to provide the desired rate of advance and the correct number of degrees of advance for stock engines that have been extensively reworked or fitted with a supercharger of some type. Complete engine specifications must be supplied to the company from whom a Vertex is ordered so that the magneto received will have the correct advance curve.

Harman & Collins magnetos were made originally for Ford V8 and Mercury flathead engines. They have a three-bolt mounting flange that bolts to the engine's timing gear cover so they can be driven directly by the engine's camshaft. Since ohv V8 engines became popular, these mags have been adapted to many of them that are used strictly for competition. This is done by installing a special front cover on the engine or by using an adaptor that is inserted in the ignition distributor opening in the cylinder block. Most of the adaptors made to be inserted in distributor openings have a flange to drive a Hilborn fuel injector fuel pump. It is necessary to reverse the rotation direction of the magneto's shaft for some of these installations.

As Harman & Collins mags do not have an automatic advance mechanism, they are not suitable for road engines. With a mag of this type the number of degrees of advance for best engine performance in the speed range in which the engine is to be run is determined by trial and error and then the mag is adjusted to deliver the desired advance.

A special ignition switch is required for any magneto because magnetos do not require battery current, as does a battery ignition system. A magneto is operative when it is not fitted with a switch of any type and a switch must be fitted to it so it can be made inoperative to stop the engine. Switches for this purpose complete the circuit between the magneto's primary circuit and ground when they are in their "Off" position. When the switch is in its "On" position, the circuit between the mag's primary post and ground is open.

Special relays that can be used between a stock ignition switch and a magneto to open and close the magneto primary circuit correctly for On and Off positions of the ignition switch are available. A relay of this type makes a nice installation.

The Scintilla Vertex magneto (right) is popular with hot rodders.

The Harman & Collins magneto (below) is mounted on a typical hot-rod powerplant.

CHAPTER EIGHT

Engine Balancing

*Hot rodders have learned that in order to get
top high performance the rotating parts of an engine
must be in perfect balance. Here's how.*

ONE OF THE MOST IMPORTANT STEPS in any
engine rebuilding job is the complete rebalancing of the rotating and reciprocating parts of
the engine's crankshaft and rod and piston assemblies. All engines are balanced when they are
built but the balance of a V8 is upset when parts
with different weights than those of the original
parts are substituted for worn parts in its internal
assembly during the rebuilding process.

Rebalancing is often considered essential only
to completion or converted engines but such
is definitely not the case. Many factory-built
engines, regardless of their type or number of
cylinders, can often be improved by precision
balancing. But, to be entirely satisfactory, balancing must be done on precision equipment by a
trained operator.

Due to the design of V-type engines, their
balance is much more sensitive to changes in the
weights of their rotating and reciprocating parts
than is the balance of in-line engines. At one
time rebalancing was considered by many hot
rodders to be a luxury they could do without,
although it was essential if their engines were to

run smoothly and attain the crankshaft speeds of
which they were capable, but now that crankshaft
stroking is so popular it is a rare reworked V-type
engine that can be assembled without first being
rebalanced. A stroked crankshaft that wasn't rebalanced could shake its engine apart in only a
few miles of running.

The theory of engine balancing can be reduced
to its simplest terms by saying that all parts of
an engine directly related to its piston assemblies
and crankshaft must be of the same weight if they
move in a straight line and have equal distribution of weight about their axis if they revolve.
Parts that move in a straight line are called
"reciprocating" parts. Included in this group
are pistons, piston pins, pin locks, piston rings,
and the upper ends of the connecting rods. Parts
that revolve are called "rotating" parts and they
are the crankshaft, connecting rod bearings, the
lower ends of the connecting rods, rod nut locks,
flywheel, and clutch pressure plate assembly.
Most balancing formulas for V8 engines designate
two-thirds of the total weight of a connecting
rod as rotating weight and the remaining one-

third as reciprocating weight; however, the ratio used for the actual balancing operation is generally arrived at by experimentation.

Reciprocating parts are balanced by equalizing the weights of individual parts or combinations of parts. Because connecting rods contribute to both rotating and reciprocating weight, they present a particular problem. The rods in a set should be balanced so that their lower ends weigh the same and their upper ends weigh the same. When these conditions exist, all the rods have the same total weight.

Rotating parts are subject to two types of balance: "static," which refers to balance at rest, and "dynamic" which is balance in motion. Static balance requires the total weight of an object to be disposed about its axis in such a manner that a heavy point on one side of the axis is balanced by an equally heavy point on the opposite side. The balancing point can be located anywhere along the length of the object as long as it is on the opposite side of the axis from the portion it is balancing. In other words, a heavy point at one end of an object may be

statically balanced by another heavy point on the opposite side of the axis but at the other end of the object. A crankshaft supported in such manner that is is free to rotate with a minimum of friction is in static balance when it will remain in any position in which it is placed. Adding weight at any point on its surface will cause the shaft to rotate until that point is as low as it can possibly be.

Dynamic balance becomes more important as an object's axis becomes longer. A flywheel, for instance, requires only static balancing because it has a short axis but a crankshaft must be in dynamic balance if it is to operate satisfactorily. Dynamic balance requires the mass of an object to be equally disposed about the object's axis in such a manner that any portion of the object on one side of its axis is balanced by another portion on the other side of the axis and approximately the same distance from the object's end. If an object that is in dynamic balance is divided into sections by cutting through it at right angles to its axis, each section will be in both static and dynamic balance because each portion of the

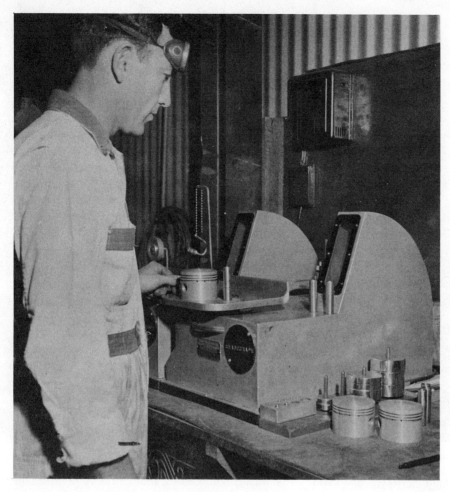

One of the first balancing operations is the checking of pistons and their matching pins on a sensitive balance to find the lightest combination.

sections is balanced by another portion on the opposite side of the axis. If a shaft in static balance only is divided in the same manner, it is more than likely that none of the sections will be in either static or dynamic balance because the counterbalancing point for a specific heavy portion on one of the sections may now be on another section. Therefore, a shaft that is in static balance is not necessarily in dynamic balance.

Although a shaft that is in static balance but not in dynamic balance will remain in any position in which it is placed when it is supported so it is free to rotate, centrifugal force created when it is rotated will pull the heavy portions of its individual unbalanced sections out of their normal paths. This will cause the shaft's axis to try to move in a rotary path as it follows the heavy portions. Movement of the shaft is restricted by the main bearings in the cylinder block, but as the shaft pounds against the bearings

a vibration is created in the engine structure. This continual pounding shortens the life of the bearings and the journals on the shaft and the vibration it creates is detrimental to driving enjoyment.

Reciprocating parts for most engines are balanced at the factory on a "tolerance" scale. The usual tolerance is one-half ounce, and a part is considered usable as long as its weight is within the tolerance. Rotating parts are usually held to a tolerance of one ounce-inch, which is equal to the force of one once acting on a lever one inch long.

When such wide tolerances are used for the individual parts in an assembly, the degree of balance of the completed engine depends on the weight of the individual parts in relation to each other. If a group of parts that happen to be of the correct weight are assembled together, the engine will be smooth-running and vibration-free.

If a group of parts which weighed high or low on the tolerance scale are assembled together, or high and low parts are used in combinations, the engine will be comparatively rough-running.

Parts that a company must have before they can completely balance a V8 engine are all its pistons, piston pins, and connecting rods; sufficient pin locks, piston rings, rod nut locks, and connecting rod inserts for one cylinder; and the crankshaft. For an in-line engine the same parts, with the exception of the pin locks, piston rings, rod nut locks, and connecting rod inserts, must be on hand. Additional parts that should be balanced to make either job complete are the crankshaft pulley, or the pulley-damper assembly; and the flywheel and the clutch pressure plate assembly, or torque converter or housing. If any of these parts is out of balance when it is installed on the crankshaft of a balanced assembly it will throw the assembly out of balance. In most balancing shops weights of reciprocating parts are held to a tolerance of one-half gram (one ounce equals 28.25 grams) and rotating parts are held to a tolerance of one gram-inch.

An assembly for an in-line engine is balanced by equalizing the weights of its reciprocating parts and dynamically balancing its bare crankshaft. An assembly for a V8 engine is balanced by equalizing the weight of its reciprocating parts and dynamically balancing its crankshaft while "bob-weights" are attached to the shafts' crankpins. Bob-weights are equal in weight to a certain percentage of the total weight of the pistons, connecting rods, and bearing assemblies that will be attached to the crankpins. Changing a crankshaft's stroke doesn't affect the weight of the bob-weights that must be used to balance the shaft; however, by changing the length of the crank throws, stroking increases or decreases, depending on whether the stroke was lengthened or shortened, the effect of the bob-weights by lengthening or shortening the leverage through which their weight is applied to the shaft.

Bob-weights are not used on shafts for in-line engines or on the comparatively rare single-plane shafts for V engines. Single-plane shafts for V engines are similar to shafts for four-cylinder engines and they differ from two-plane shafts used in modern V8's in that their crankpins are 180 instead of 90 degrees apart.

When the parts for a V8 engine are being balanced it is necessary for the rod and piston assemblies to be balanced first. Each piston and its pin is balanced as a unit because it is difficult and impractical to change the weight of individual pins to compensate for variations often found between the pins in a set. The assemblies are checked against each other on a sensitive scale until the lightest is found. Then the weight of the heavier assemblies is reduced to that of the lightest by chucking the pistons in a lathe and removing material from the inner circumference of the lower web in their skirts. In most pistons this web is left heavy for balancing purposes. It provides a place where material can be removed from the pistons without creating a weak spot.

Connecting rods are balanced next. Methods of doing this vary in different shops but where the balancing is done correctly the end result is the same. One at a time each of the rods in the set is supported in such a manner that its ends can be weighed individually. In some shops the ends are weighed one at a time and in others they are both weighed at once. After the weight of the lightest big-end has been determined, each of the big-ends is reduced to that weight. This is done by grinding material from the balancing bosses on the heavy big-ends. After all big-ends have been equalized, material is removed from the small-ends to make the total weight of all the rods the same.

Sometimes it is necessary to remove material from the sides of the rod ends instead of from balancing bosses. When this happens all grinding is done parallel instead of at a right angle to the shank of the rod to prevent creating scratches that might be starting places for cracks that could result in eventual breakage. It is wise to fit piston pins to rods fitted with bushings after the rods have been balanced because grinding may distort the small ends. If this should happen after the pins had been fitted, it would be necessary to refit them. The amount of material removed during normal pin fitting operations is not enough to affect the balance of the engine. Connecting rod alignment should be checked after the rods have been balanced so that any misalignment resulting from the grinding can be corrected.

Preparation of the bob-weights for the crankshaft is next. This is done by recording rotating

Removing material to reduce weight for balancing purposes is taken from the lower web in piston skirts in a lathe.

and reciprocating weights of the rod and piston assemblies in grams and applying the weights to a formula from which the weight of the bob-weights is computed.

Bob-weights are usually made of bronze and they are split so they can be easily installed on a crankshaft's crankpins. The two halves of the weights are held together by capscrews. At several points around their circumference the weights are drilled and tapped for quarter-inch diameter bolts. Their weight is increased or decreased by adding or removing washers or nuts to or from bolts screwed into these holes. After the bob-weights have been installed on the crankpins, the shaft is ready to be balanced.

Machines used to check the balance of crankshafts are complicated and quite sensitive. One machine made for this purpose consists of two sets of ball bearing rollers arranged to support round objects so they may be rotated with a minimum of friction; an electric motor-driven rubber belt which runs on pulleys attached to a lever pivoted at the rear of the machine; sensitive electronic units beneath the rollers which pick up and transmit the vertical movement of the rollers as an object supported by them is rotated; an electronic unit with numerous switches and controls for changing the characteristics of the machine and easily read meters showing the degree of unbalance and the speed of rotation of an object mounted on the rollers; and a portable stroboscopic lamp actuated by movement of the rollers.

To an operator who has complete knowledge of the machine being used and the problems of

balancing, the actual procedure of balancing a crankshaft is comparatively simple. The shaft is placed on the rollers so it is supported by its end main bearing journals and a heavy chalk mark is made on one of the counterweights or crank arms at each of its ends. These marks are placed so they are both in the same position in relation to the shaft's axis. A pulley is attached to the front snout of the crankshaft to be used as a friction surface for the motor-driven belt. As the belt is rotated by its motor it is held in contact with the pulley. The speed of rotation of the shaft is determined by the length of time the belt is held on the pulley.

High speeds of rotation aren't necessary because the average shaft usually reaches its critical speed of primary vibration at less than 1000 rpm. This speed is indicated by the machine before the balancing is begun so that all guesswork on the part of the operator is eliminated. If the shaft is in balance at its critical speed of primary vibration, it will be in balance at all other speeds. At speeds above or below the critical speed the degree of vibration is correspondingly lower.

Observations and readings to determine the points and amount of unbalance are taken after the driving belt has been lifted from the crankshaft and its motor has stopped to prevent vibration from the motor and belt from being transmitted to the machine. The shaft is always accelerated to a speed higher than its speed of critical vibration so that after it ceases to be rotated by the drive belt it passes through its critical speed again as it decelerates. During the period of deceleration the positions of the chalk marks on the ends of the shaft are observed with the stroboscopic lamp and the amount of unbalance, as indicated by the meter, is noted.

With the machine described, the location and amount of static unbalance, as well as dynamic unbalance, present in the shaft can be observed while the shaft is being rotated. This is accomplished by flipping one of the switches on the instrument panel. When a shaft is rotating, static balance becomes "kinetic" balance. Locating static unbalance while an object is being rotated is much more accurate than by supporting the object on knife edges and allowing its heaviest side to settle to its lowest point. Rotation exaggerates the amount of unbalance so it is more easily located.

Connecting rods are checked on the sensitive balance so they may be matched in weight.

Kinetic balance has a lower critical speed of rotation than dynamic balance so therefore both dynamic and kinetic balance can be checked on the same spin of the shaft by merely changing the position of the switch on the instrument panel. When the switch is in position for kinetic balance the stroboscopic lamp flashes when the heavy side of each end of the shaft is in its lowest position, and when the switch is in position for dynamic balance the lamp flashes when the heavy side at one end of the shaft is up and the heavy side at the other end is down.

By knowing whether the heavy side of the shaft is up or down at the instant the lamp flashes, the operator of the machine can easily locate the heavy side by observing the location of the chalk mark on the shaft as it is indicated by the lamp. If the machine is set for kinetic balance and the light from the lamp shows the chalk mark to be above the axis of the shaft and in a vertical position, the operator knows that the heavy side at that end of the shaft is

directly opposite the chalk mark. Locating the heavy side for any other position of the chalk mark as it is shown by the light is merely a matter of comparing the mark's position to the position the heavy side must be in to flash the light.

After the heavy side of one end of the shaft has been located, weight is removed from it by

Bob-weights for crankshaft balancing are checked to match a percentage of the weights of rod and piston assemblies which they temporarily replace on balancing.

Bob-weights are installed on crankshaft crankpins with capscrews, washers, and nuts of proper weight to do job.

Crankshaft is rotated in balancing machine by temporary contact with a motor-driven belt in machine operation.

Chalk marks on crankshaft in balancing machine indicate points of unbalance when illuminated by stroboscopic light.

either grinding the shaft's surface with a portable grinder or drilling holes in its counterweights, depending on where the weight must be removed. After the operator has removed what he considers to be sufficient weight, all chips and grindings are wiped or blown from the shaft and its balance is rechecked. This procedure is repeated until the machine's unbalance meter shows the shaft to be in balance.

Crankshaft stroking has advanced to such a degree that it has become necessary to add weight instead of removing it from most stroked shafts to bring them into balance. This is because of the exceptionally long stroke increases now popular and the additional weight of oversize pistons and heavy-duty piston pins. Weight for this purpose is added to the shaft's counterweights. Plates of sheet steel, which are cut to conform to the shape of the counterweights and are of adequate thickness to add the desired weight to the shaft, are welded to the counterweights. Usually the weight of the plates is such that after they have been added to the shaft the counter-

Removal of metal from the crankshaft for balancing purposes is sometimes done by drilling the counterweights.

Flywheels are often mounted on a special mandrel before being placed in the balancing wheel for operations.

weights are just a little heavier than they should be. The shaft is then brought into balance by drilling shallow holes in the counterweights.

After the crankshaft has been balanced, the crankshaft pulley, or pulley-balancer assembly, is installed on the shaft to enable its balance to be checked. Material is removed from the heavy side of the pulley or assembly to bring it into balance.

Flywheels are balanced on the same machine and in the same manner as crankshafts. They are mounted on special mandrels consisting of a center shaft with a mounting flange so they can be supported and rotated in the machine. Flywheels can also be balanced while they are bolted to their crankshafts. When this is done the crankshaft is balanced first so it will be known that any unbalance shown in the crankshaft and flywheel assembly will be in the flywheel. After the flywheel's heavy side has been found with the stroboscopic lamp and chalk mark method, sufficient weight is removed from it to bring it into balance. All flywheels, and especially those

The stroboscopic lamp and chalk method is also used to balance flywheels. This shows a typical setup in shop.

To balance a flywheel, metal is removed by drilling shallow holes near edge. Balancing operations require skill.

Clutch pressure plate and cover assemblies are balanced after being mounted on flywheel on which they are used.

that have been "chopped" or machined in any way, should be rebalanced before they are used. Their large diameter makes them especially sensitive to balance.

Clutch pressure plate and cover assemblies are balanced while they are mounted on the flywheel with which they are to be used. After the flywheel has been balanced it becomes, in effect, a mandrel for the pressure plate assembly. After the heavy side of the assembly has been located, weight is removed from the pressure plate itself by inserting a drill through openings in the cover and drilling the bosses that extend up through the pressure plate springs. These bosses are provided for balancing purposes but quite often a plate that has been rebuilt and rebalanced several times will not have any bosses left. In a

case such as this the weight of the light side of the assembly is increased by applying sufficient solder to the cover to balance the assembly. An important part of clutch balancing is the marking of the cover and flywheel before the pressure plate assembly is removed from the wheel. These marks should always be in line when the pressure plate assembly is bolted to the flywheel.

Mounting the pressure plate assembly on the flywheel in the same position it was in when it was balanced prevents a possible unbalanced condition resulting from misalignment of the center of the pressure plate assembly with the center of the flywheel. Misalignment of this type is the result of incorrectly positioned pressure plate mounting holes in the flywheel. Slight pressure plate misalignment has no detrimental effect when the flywheel and pressure plate are balanced as a unit but should the pressure plate assembly be bolted to the flywheel in another position, the flywheel and pressure plate assembly, as a unit, would be thrown out of balance. Pressure plate retaining capscrews should be of equal length and have the same type lock washers. Most flywheels require special shoulder-type capscrews for pressure plate mounting.

If an engine is to be bolted to an automatic transmission instead of to a stick-shift box, the torque converter or converter housing that will be bolted to its flywheel should be balanced. This operation is complicated somewhat in that factory specifications usually state that converters or converter housings contain a certain quantity of automatic transmission fluid while they are being balanced. The reason for this is that any dents or irregularities in the shape of the housing will affect the distribution of the oil in the housing when the unit is in operation in the automobile. It the unit were balanced dry, its balance could be upset when oil was added to it and the oil had become distributed by centrifugal force as the housing was rotated by the operation of the crankshaft.

To balance a clutch pressure plate, metal is removed by drilling the bosses that extend through the pressure plate springs.

CHAPTER NINE

Facts on Higher Compression

How to get better performance
through higher compression ratios.
The importance of high octane fuels.

ONE OF AN ENGINE'S MOST IMPORTANT FEA-
TURES is its compression ratio. Compression
ratio has a definite influence on the torque and
power an engine can develop because the amount
of pressure exerted on the engine's pistons by the
burning fuel and air mixture in its cylinders is
dependent on the pressure of the mixture at the
instant it is ignited by the spark plug. The pressure
rise after combustion is four to five times the
pressure at the time of combustion; therefore,
the higher the initial pressure, the greater the
pressure on the pistons during power strokes.

Compression ratio is purely mechanical. Once
it is established, it never varies. It is the ratio
of the total volume of a cylinder and its combustion chamber to the volume of the combustion
chamber. It is computed by adding the volume
of the cylinder to the volume of the combustion
chamber and dividing the total by the volume of
the combustion chamber.

For instance, if a cylinder and its combustion
chamber have a total volume of 50 cubic inches,
and the combustion chamber has a volume of
five cubic inches, 50 divided by five gives a compression ratio of 10 to 1.

Compression ratio is important in that it is
the feature of the engine on which compression
pressure is dependent. Theoretically speaking, a
high compression ratio means high compression
pressures but in this case things that go on in
any engine may not conform to theory. An engine
cannot have high compression pressures unless it
has a high compression ratio but it is entirely
possible for it to have a high compression ratio
and low compression pressures. This is because
compression pressures are dependent on the
quantity of mixture in the cylinders at the end of
intake strokes and the ability of the valves and
piston rings to retain these pressures.

Things that control the quantity of mixture in
cylinders at the end of intake strokes are the
engine's breathing ability and its valve timing. If
the engine does not breathe well it won't be
possible for its cylinders to induct the volumes
of fresh mixture they should. Valve timing affects
the volume because the opening time of intake
valves and the closing time of exhaust valves determine when mixture can start to flow into the
cylinders and the closing times of the intake
valves determines how much of the mixture will

be trapped in the cylinders at the beginning of power strokes.

Losses of compression pressure past valves and piston rings are the results of either poor workmanship or worn parts and such losses will lower the torque and horsepower outputs of a high-performance engine. When a reground camshaft is used to improve engine performance at high speeds, losses of compression pressure resulting from valve timing are more pronounced at low engine speeds than at high speeds. This often provides an additional asset to engine performance in that it enables an engine to have compression ratio higher than it could use at low speeds if its compression pressure wasn't reduced by valve timing. At high speeds, where compression pressures are always lower due to an engine's normally lower breathing ability, the high compression ratio is used to advantage because the lower breathing ability holds the compression pressures within usable limits.

Because of the influence compression ratio has on engine performance, it is imperative for a high-performance engine to have a high compression ratio. However, the maximum compression ratio any engine can use is limited by "detonation."

Detonation is an abnormal combustion process and it can be caused by many things. It is the cause of the sound usually defined as "ping," or as a "sharp crack." In an engine tuned to specifications, detonation is the result of trying to use a fuel that has too low an octane rating for the engine. A fuel's octane rating is its ability to resist detonation; the higher the rating, the greater the resistance.

During normal combustion in a cylinder, the compressed fuel and air mixture is ignited by the spark plug as the piston nears the end of its compression stroke. When the mixture is ignited it starts to burn at the spark plug and a flame front moves out from the plug like a ripple caused by a stone dropped into a pond. This flame front moves steadily across the combustion chamber until all the mixture is consumed.

As the flame front moves out from the spark plug, the expansion of the burnt mixture behind it compresses the unburned mixture ahead of it (this unburned portion of the mixture is called "end-gas") compressing it even more tightly against the surfaces of the cylinder head and piston head and raising its temperature. Compared to the temperature of the end-gas, these

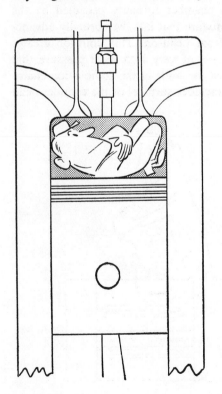

Compression ratio is the ratio of the volume of the cylinder and combustion chamber at the bottom of the stroke to the volume at the top of the stroke.

Reducing combustion chamber volume by milling cylinder heads is one way to increase the compression ratio.

surfaces are comparatively cool and the end-gas dissipates some of its heat to them. The end-gas is eventually consumed as the flame front continues to move across the chamber. As the mixture burns, it expands and exerts pressure on the piston to force it down the cylinder.

The mixture's slow burning rate is the thing that makes it necessary for the spark to occur in the cylinder before the piston reaches the end of its compression stroke. By igniting the mixture early, the maximum pressure created by the burning mixture is exerted on the piston before the piston has traveled too far down the cylinder on its power stroke. The actual time of ignition of the mixture in relation to piston position varies in different makes of engines and according to crankshaft speed and the load on the engine. In stock engines it usually occurs somewhere between six and eight degrees before top dead center at idle speeds, and as much as 45 degrees before top dead center when the engine is running under light load at normal highway cruising speeds. For other conditions of speed and load the spark occurs at times between these.

When detonation occurs because the engine's compression ratio is too high for the fuel being used, a different set of conditions exists in the combustion chamber during the combustion period. Combustion of the mixture is started by the spark plug in the normal manner but as the flame front moves out from the spark plug, compressing the end-gas ahead of it, the end-gas becomes

heated to the point where it "autoignites." When this happens, the entire volume of the end-gas is consumed instantaneously instead of at the comparatively slow rate of the normal combustion process. This instantaneous combustion causes an extremely high pressure in the portion of the combustion chamber formerly occupied by the unburned mixture that hits the normally advancing flame front head-on. This collision creates pressure waves of very high local pressure that break against the walls of the combustion chamber, which includes surfaces of the cylinder head

Another method commonly employed by hot rodders to increase compression ratio is to bore out the cylinders.

and piston head, and cause them to vibrate. This vibration is the source of the sound heard outside the engine; however, detonation is not always audible to a car's driver or passengers. Detonation of an extremely destructive nature can be going on in an engine without being audible above the normal sounds made by a car in motion. Accompanying detonation are high temperatures of the combustion chamber surfaces in the areas in which it occurs.

Detonation can be triggered by several things other than a high compression ratio. A fuel might have an octane rating more than adequate for an engine's compression ratio but it is entirely possible for some abnormal condition in the combustion chamber to cause the end-gas to be compressed and heated above its point of autoignition. Features of a combustion chamber that influence the tendency of a mixture compressed in it to detonate include the distance from the spark plug to the farthest point in the chamber, the chamber's "squish area," and the amount of turbulence the shape of the chamber creates in the mixture as the mixture is compressed.

The distance from the spark plug to the most remote point of a combustion chamber influences detonation because it determines the amount of end-gas in the chambers during combustion. The greater the distance, the greater will be the quantity of end-gas and its tendency to detonate. Also, it is important that the end-gas be compressed in an area that is free of hot spots, such as the exhaust valve head, that might tend to raise its temperature.

It's common practice to have combustion end in the squish area, which is the narrow space between the head of the piston and the surface of the cylinder head. In most engines the clearance between these surfaces when the piston is at top dead center in the cylinder is maintained at less than .060-inch. Mixture trapped in the squish area is easily cooled because none of it is over half the width of the clearance from the relatively cool surfaces of the cylinder head or piston head. This renders the squish area practically non-existent as far as the length of the combustion chamber is concerned.

The squish area serves another purpose in addition to helping suppress detonation by shortening the effective length of the combustion chamber. As the piston reaches the top of its compres-

sion stroke, mixture in the squish area is forced at great speed into the combustion chamber's main area. This rapid movement of the mixture creates a turbulence, or motion, in the combustion chamber. This turbulence mixes the stagnate mixture clinging to the comparatively cool surfaces of the combustion chamber walls with the rest of the mixture and helps spread the flame through the mixture after the spark occurs at the spark plug. Compressed mixture that wasn't turbulent would burn so slowly that combustion wouldn't be completed with sufficient rapidity to enable the engine to run at high crankshaft speeds. However, if turbulence is too great, it is possible for combustion to be too rapid, with resultant engine roughness. Turbulence is also dependent on the velocity of the mixture as it enters the cylinder. These things are dependent on intake port size and contour.

Included in the list of terms that have come into being down through the years to describe the causes of detonation are spark knock, preignition, and surface ignition. Each of these terms describes a method by which detonation is instigated but they become confusing because in some instances they are related. Spark knock is often used synonymously with detonation because normal detonation can be controlled by retarding the ignition timing so the spark occurs at a later time in relation to piston position in the cylinder. This reduces the pressure on the end-gas, allowing it to remain below its temperature of autoignition. As a rule, unless a fuel with a high octane rating

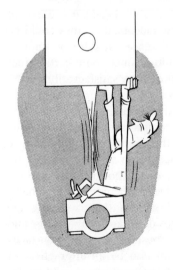

Lengthening the crankshaft stroke is another way of increasing the compression ratio.

This piston was destroyed by prolonged and severe detonation, caused by very high temperatures and pressures.

is used, an engine's initial ignition timing will have to be retarded to prevent detonation as its compression ratio is raised. Therefore, the actual amount of spark advance any engine that has a normally high compression ratio can use is dependent on the octane rating of its fuel. However, another point of confusion exists here because a fuel that would operate satisfactorily in one make of engine that has a 10 to 1 compression ratio might detonate furiously in another make of engine that also has a 10 to 1 ratio. Differences of this nature are often due to the design of the combustion chambers in the engines. Another factor that enters into the initial ignition timing requirement is that the spark advance curve of the distributors of two identical engines could be within the factory tolerance but still vary enough that one engine would detonate on a certain fuel but the other would operate satisfactorily on the same fuel.

Preignition is a term generally used to describe the ignition of the compressed mixture by some source other than the spark plug. This can be caused by hot surfaces, such as the electrodes on spark plugs that are of too hot a heat range for the engine; sharp edges in the combustion chambers, such as head gaskets that overhang the cylinders; sharp edges of exhaust valve heads; and corners where combustion chamber surfaces meet. Preignition can also be an after effect of detonation. The high temperatures created by detonation can heat the surfaces of the cylinder

head and piston in the areas where it occurs to the point where they will preignite the mixture on subsequent compression strokes. As the surfaces can't cool as long as detonation and preignition continue, this action and reaction will go on until the load on the engine is reduced.

Other sources of preignition are the deposits of carbon and other matter that collect in combustion chambers. Some of these deposits will become so hot during normal combustion that they will glow and remain glowing through the following compression stroke. Near the end of the stroke they will ignite the compressed mixture in the cylinder. Preignition from this source is called "surface ignition."

All surface ignition is not necessarily preignition. It can occur either before or after normal ignition by the spark plug and it is possible for it to occur without causing detonation; detonation results only when the surface ignition causes the end-gas to be autoignited. Surface ignition is also the cause of a type of detonation called "wild ping." Wild ping doesn't follow any pattern because it is caused by both stationary and floating deposits.

Prolonged detonation of a severe nature can destroy an engine by breaking its pistons and other mechanical parts. Broken parts from this cause are the result of the higher than normal pressures and temperatures detonation creates in the combustion chambers. Lesser evils of detonation are blown head gaskets, stuck piston rings, and high-temperature corrosion of pistons and valves. Stuck rings are caused by decomposition of the oil in the ring grooves into a gummy substance that traps free carbon and causes the rings to become bound tightly in the grooves. Decomposition of the oil is the result of high pressures and temperatures. Corrosion of piston and valve surfaces is the result of high local temperatures.

Detonation is detrimental to engine performance because an engine loses power as soon as detonation begins. Also, detonation causes fuel consumption to be increased because the portion of the mixture consumed by autoignition doesn't contribute as much effort toward turning the crankshaft as it should.

As the primary factor that determines the highest compression ratio an engine can use without detonation is the octane rating of the fuel available, the compression ratios of stock engines have been limited by the fuel available at the time they were released to the public. From year to year, octane ratings of commercially available gasolines have been steadily rising, and to take advantage of these higher ratings, the compression ratios of stock engines have also been going up. Not too long ago compression ratios of 7 and 8 to 1 were considered extremely high but in 1958 some stock engines had ratios as high as 10½ to 1, with the lowest in those of modern design being approximately 9½ to 1. Any engine with a ratio over 9½ to 1 requires premium gasoline, and some of the '58 models that have a 10½ to 1 ratio detonate quite badly on some premium fuels available in many parts of the country when they are tuned to factory specifications. Detonation of this nature can usually be eliminated by tuning the engine for the fuel available. This involves changing fuel mixtures and altering the ignition distributor's spark advance characteristics.

A fuel's actual octane rating doesn't mean too much to a hot rodder because two fuels with identical ratings might show altogether different detonation characteristics in the same engine. It is usually safe to assume that the compression ratio of an engine that is mechanically strong enough to stand the higher combustion pressures can be raised to equal the ratio of current production engines of the same make. The engine could undoubtedly be rated satisfactorily on at least one brand of premium gasoline available at that time. To find this particular brand of gasoline might require a few days of trial and error but the time would be well spent.

For an engine to be run on alcohol, compression ratios as high as 15 to 1 are generally satisfactory as far as the detonation characteristics of the fuel are concerned. For blended fuels that contain high percentages of nitromethane, best results are obtained with compression ratios lower than those that can be used for gasoline. Depending on the type of combustion chamber in the engine and the percentage of nitromethane in the fuel, the best compression ratio for such fuels is usually between 7½ and 9 to 1.

It is important that an engine that has been reworked to enable it to develop greater torque and horsepower outputs have the highest compression ratio it can use without causing the fuel that will be burned in it to detonate. This means that the ratio of an engine that isn't of a current model will have to be increased by one means or another. At one time it was considered mechanically safe to raise an engine's compression ratio only one ratio, such as from 7 to 1 to 8 to 1, but most of the overhead valve V8 engines built since 1949 are designed to withstand normal combustion pressures of ratios as high as 12 to 1. It is reasonable to assume that for gasoline the ratio of any of these engines can be raised to equal that of the current models of the same make, and up to approximately 12 to 1 for alcohol, without fear of overstressing their internal parts. For all-out competition conversions and for special fuels the ratios of such engines are often raised considerably higher that 12 to 1; however, when this is done it is not unusual to experience an occasional broken crankshaft or similar failure in the engine's internal assembly. Many of these failures are due to detonation but this is only natural

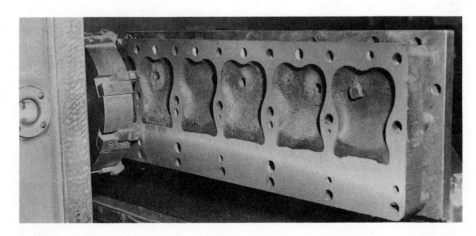

An L-head being milled on a milling machine to increase the compression ratio.

TABLE OF RECOMMENDATIONS FOR HEAD MILLING

CAR	YR.	MODEL	TRANS. TYPE	CU. IN. DISPL.	STD. RATIO	AMOUNT REMOVED	NEW RATIO
Buick V8	'54	Spec.	Sync.	264	7.20	.030	7.6 (1)
		Spec.	Dyna.	264	8.10	.030	8.5 (1)
		Sup., Cen.	Sync.	322	8.00	.030	8.6 (1)
		Sup., Cen., Road.	Dyna.	322	8.50	.030	9.0 (1)
	'55	Spec.	Sync.	264	7.50	.030	7.9 (1)
		Spec.	Dyna.	264	8.40	.030	9.0 (1)
		Sup., Cen.	Sync.	322	8.40	.030	8.9 (1)
		Sup., Cen., Road.	Dyna.	322	9.00	.030	9.6 (1)
	'56	Spec.	Sync.	322	7.60	.030	8.0 (1)
		Spec.	Dyna.	322	8.90	.030	9.5 (1)
		Sup., Cen., Road.	Sync.	322	9.50	.025	10.0
	'57	Spec. Sup., Cen., Road.	Dyna.	364	9.50	.020	10.0
		Sup., Cen., Road.	Dyna.	364	10.00		OK as is
Cadillac V8	'54	All	HM	331	8.25	.070	9.2
	'55	All	HM	331	9.00	.070	10.0
	'56	All	HM	365	9.75	.025	10.0
	'57	All	HM	365	10.00		OK as is
Chev 6	54-'55	All		235.5	8.00	.090	8.4 (2)
6		All		235.5	8.00	.060	9.0 (2)
V8	'55	All Corvette		235.5	8.00	.090	9.0 (3)
6	'56	All		235.5	8.00	.090	9.0 (2)
V8	'56	All		265.0	8.00	.060	9.0 (3)
6		All P.P., Corvette	Sync.	265.0	9.25	.045	10.0 (3)
6	'57	All		235.5	8.00	.090	9.0 (2)
V8		All		283.0	8.00	.060	9.0 (3)
V8		All		283.0	8.50	.060	9.6 (3)
V8		All		283.0	9.50	.030	10.0 (3)
V8		Fuel Injection		283.0	10.50		OK as is
Chrysler 6	'54	Windsor		264.5	7.00	.100	7.8
V8		All		331	7.50	.050	8.2 (1)
V8	'55	Windsor		301.0	8.00	.050	8.8 (1)
V8		All except Windsor		331.0	8.50	.040	9.2 (1)
V8	'56	Windsor		331.0	8.50	.040	9.2 (1)
V8		All except Windsor		354.0	9.00	.020	9.3 (1)
V8	'57	Windsor, Saratoga		354.0	9.25		OK as is
V8		New Yorker		392.0	9.25		OK as is
V8		300C		392.0	10.00		OK as is
DeSoto 6	'54	All		250.6	7.00	.065	7.7
V8	'54	All		276.1	7.50	.050	8.1 (1)
V8	'55	All		291.0	8.00	.050	8.2 (1)
V8	'56	All		330.0	8.50	.040	8.3
V8		All		325.0	8.50	.040	8.4 (1)
V8		All		341.0	9.25		OK as is
Dodge 6	'54	All	Sync.	230.2	7.25	.070	8.1
			Auto.	241.3	7.10	.050	7.8 (1)
V8	'54	All		241.3	7.50	.050	8.3 (1)
V8		All		230.2	7.40	.070	8.4
6	'55	All		270.0	7.60	.070	8.5
6	'56	All		270.0	8.00	.050	8.8
V8		All		315.0	8.00	.050	8.9
Lincoln V8	'54	All		317.0	8.00	.060	9.1
	'55	All		341.0	8.50	.060	9.7
	'56	All		368.0	9.00	.045	10.0
	'57	All		368.0	10.00		OK as is
Mercury V8	'54	All		256.0	7.50	.060	8.4
	'55	Custom, Monterey		292.0	7.60	.060	8.6
		Montclair		292.0	8.50	.060	9.7
	'56	All	Sync.	312.0	8.00	.060	9.1
		All	Auto.	312.0	8.40	.060	9.7
		Optional	Auto.	312.0	9.25	.040	10.0
	'57	All		312.0	9.70	.025	10.0
		Optional		368.0	9.70	.025	10.0
Nash 6	'54	Ambassador		252.6	7.60	.090	8.6
6		Ambassador		252.6	8.00	.060	9.2
6		Rambler		184.0	7.25	.060	7.9
6		Rambler	Sync.	184.0	7.50	.060	8.3
6		Rambler	Sync.	195.6	7.30	.060	8.2
6		Rambler	Auto.	195.6	7.50	.040	8.4
6		Statesman		195.6	7.8	.090	9.0
V8	'55	Ambassador		252.6	7.6	.090	8.6
V8		Ambassador		320.0	7.8		8.8
6		Statesman		195.6	7.45	.060	8.3
6		Statesman		195.6	8.00	.060	9.0
4		Metro		73.2	7.20	.060	7.9
6		Rambler		195.6	7.30	.060	8.2
6		Rambler		195.6	7.50	.060	8.4
6	'56	Ambassador		252.6	7.60	.090	8.6
V8		Ambassador		352.0	9.55	.030	10.0
4		Metro		90.9	7.20	.060	8.0
6	'57	Rambler		195.6	7.47	.075	8.5
V8		Ambassador		327.0	8.25	.050	10.0
6		Rambler		195.6	8.25	.060	9.3
6-		Rambler		250.0	8.25	.060	9.0
Olds V8	'54	All		324.3	8.25	.080	9.4
V8	'55	All		324.3	8.50	.050	9.8
V8	'56	All		324.3	9.25	.050	10.0
V8	'57	All		370.7	9.50	.035	10.0
Packard 8	'54	Clipper		288.0	7.70	.060	8.2
		Cavalier & Clipper		327.0	8.00	.060	8.6
		Packard		359.0	8.70	.030	9.0
	'55	Clipper Deluxe, Super	V8	320.0	8.50	.060	9.5
		Clipper Custom, Packard		352.0	8.50	.060	9.7
	'56	Clipper	V8	352.0	9.50	.030	10.0
		Packard, Caribbean		374.0	10.00		OK as is
Plymouth 6	'54	All		217.8	7.10	.050	7.7
6		All		230.2	7.25	.050	7.9
6	'55	All		230.2	7.40	.050	8.1
V8	'56	All		241.0	7.60	.050	8.3
V8		All		260.0	7.60	.050	8.4

Make / Cyl.	Year	Model	Trans.	CID	CR	Shim	New CR
Ford							
V8		D500		315.0	9.25	—	OK as is
6	'57	All		230.2	8.00	.060	8.8
V8		All		325.0	8.50	.035	9.2
V8		D500		325.0	9.25	—	OK as is
6	'54	All		239.0	7.20	.080	8.3
V8		All		223.0	7.50	.060	8.1
6	'55	All		223.0	7.60	.080	8.6
V8		All		272.0	8.50	.060	8.5
V8		All	Sync.	272.0	8.50	.060	9.6
V8		Bird	Auto.	292.0	8.10	.060	9.1
V8		Bird	Sync.	292.0	8.50	.080	9.7
V8	'56	All	Auto.	223.0	8.00	.060	9.3
V8		All	Sync.	272.0	8.00	.060	9.0
V8		All	Auto.	272.0	8.40	.060	9.5
V8		All	Sync.	292.0	8.00	.060	9.0
V8		Bird	Auto.	292.0	8.40	.060	9.6
V8		Bird	Sync.	292.0	8.40	.060	9.6
V8		Bird	O.D.	312.0	8.40	.060	9.7
V8		Bird	Auto.	312.0	9.00	.040	10.0
6	'57			223.0	8.60	.050	9.5
V8		Custom 300		272.0	8.60	.060	9.7
V8		Fairlane 500		292.0	9.10	.045	10.0
V8		Power Option		312.0	9.70	.030	10.0
V8		Bird	Sync.	292	9.10	.045	10.0
V8		Bird	Auto., OD	312	9.70	.030	10.0
Henry J 4	'54	All		134.2	7.00	.060	7.7
Hudson 6	'54	All		202.0	7.50	.060	7.4
6		Jet		202.0	8.00	.060	8.0
6		Wasp	Sync.	232.0	7.50	.070	8.6
6		Wasp	Auto.	232.0	7.00	.070	7.8
6		Super Wasp		262.0	7.50	.070	7.9
6		Hornet		308.0	7.50	.060	8.0
6	'55	Wasp		202.0	7.50	.060	8.0
6		Wasp		202.0	8.00	.060	8.6
6		Hornet		308.0	7.50	.060	8.0
6	'56	Wasp		320.0	7.80	.060	8.8
6		Wasp		202.0	8.00	.060	8.0
6		Hornet		202.0	7.50	.060	8.6
6		Hornet		308.0	8.00	.060	8.0
V8	'57	Hornet		352.0	9.55	.030	10.0
Kaiser 6	'54	All		327.0	7.30	.050	7.9
				226.2		.060	

Make / Cyl.	Year	Model	Trans.	CID	CR	Shim	New CR
6	'56	All		230.2	7.60	.050	8.3
V8		All		270.0	8.00	.050	8.8
V8		All		301.0	9.25	.050	OK as is
V8		Fury		230.2	7.6	.050	8.3
6	'57	All		277.0	8.0	.050	8.8
V8		All		301.0	8.50	.040	9.2
V8		All		318.0	9.25	—	OK as is
V8		Fury					
Pontiac 6	'54	All	Sync.	239.2	7.00	.060	7.7
V8		All	HM	239.2	7.70	.060	8.4
8		All	Sync.	268.4	6.80	.070	7.6
8		All	HM	268.4	7.70	.070	8.5
V8	'55	All		287.2	7.40	.060	8.3
V8		All	Sync.	287.2	8.00	.060	9.0
V8	'56	All	HM	316.6	7.90	.060	9.0
V8		All	Sync.	316.6	8.90	.060	10.0
V8	'57	All	HM	347.0	8.50	.060	9.6
V8		All		347.0	10.00	—	OK as is
Stude 6	'54	Champion		169.6	7.50	.070	8.3
V8		Commander		232.6	7.50	.090	8.7
6	'55	Champion		185.6	7.50	.070	8.4
V8		Commander (early)		224.3	7.50	.090	8.7
V8		Commander (late), Pres.		259.2	7.50	.090	8.8
6	'56	All		185.6	7.50	.070	8.4
6		All		185.6	7.80	.070	8.7
V8		Comm., Pwr. Hawk, Parkvw.		259.2	7.80	.090	9.1
V8		Comm., Pwr. Hawk, Parkvw.		259.2	8.30	.090	9.6
V8		Pres., Sky Hawk, Pinehurst		289.0	7.80	.090	9.3
V8		Pres., Sky Hawk, Pinehurst		289.0	8.30	.090	9.8
V8		Golden Hawk		352.0	9.50	.030	10.0
6	'57	Champion	Sync.	185.6	7.80	.070	8.7
V8		Comm., Parkview, Prov.		259.2	7.80	.090	9.1
V8		Comm., Parkview, Prov.		259.2	8.30	.090	9.6
V8		Pres., Classic, Sil. Hawk, Broadmoor		289.0	7.00	.090	8.5
V8		Pres., Classic, Sil. Hawk, Broadmoor		289.0	7.50	.090	9.0
V8		Pres., Classic, Sil. Hawk, Golden Hawk		289.0	8.30	.090	9.8
V8		Golden Hawk		289.0	7.00	.040	7.5 (4)
V8		Golden Hawk		289.0	7.50	—	OK as is (4)
Willys 6		'54 Ace, Eagle		226.2	7.30	.060	8.0
6		Lark		161.0	7.6	.060	8.5
		'55 All		226.2	7.3	.060	8.0

NOTES:

(1) It is recommended that high compression pistons be installed instead of milling the heads.

(2) On Chev sixes, place shims equal to one half the amount removed from the heads beneath all rocker arm stands. Intake valves must be seated deeper into the head so that valve heads are flush with cylinder head surface to provide sufficient piston-to-valve clearance.

(3) On all Chev V8's equipped with flat top pistons, piston head must be notched for sufficient piston-to-valve clearance. Notches must be between 3/64 and 1/16 inch deep.

(4) Supercharged.

The effect of lack of clearance between pistons and valves is evident here on the heads of pistons.

as detonation is more apt to occur with high compression ratios. Detonation is more dangerous to an engine's parts when the engine is developing a high power output because more than likely the parts are already overstressed at this time by just normal combustion pressures. When the higher temperatures and pressures of detonation are exerted on them, some of the parts might let go.

Changing an engine's compression ratio to bring it up to current standards, or even higher for special fuels, can present problems. When flat-head Ford V8 and Mercury engines were popular their compression ratios were raised by either installing special aluminum cylinder heads on them or by milling their stock heads. When an extremely high ratio was desired it was necessary to use special heads because the contour of the chambers in stock heads was such that the volume of the chambers couldn't be reduced enough to provide a high ratio. But even with special heads it was difficult to obtain a ratio of over 9½ or 10 to 1 because of limitations to the combustion chamber shape and size dictated by the placement of the valves alongside the cylinders.

Special cylinder heads aren't available for modern overhead valve V8 engines. This leaves no alternative but to use stock heads and to establish the desired ratio by utilizing one or more of several methods that might be applicable. Engines of this type in which it would be desirable to raise the compression ratio can be divided into two classifications. One of these includes engines that have their standard base and stroke, and the other includes engines that have been reworked by boring, stroking, or combinations of both.

It's possible to raise the compression ratio of an engine that has its standard bore and stroke by either milling its heads, installing heads from a later model engine of the same make, installing thinner head gaskets, installing special pistons in its cylinders, or by using combinations of these things.

Head milling is entirely satisfactory for some engines but for others it creates complications that make it undesirable. It isn't recommended at all for Chrysler product engines that have hemispherical combustion chambers. When the heads of these engines are milled, the diameter of their combustion chambers is reduced to a smaller diameter that doesn't match the cylinders as it should, and in some of them the lower edges of the chambers are moved much too close to the valve seats. The compression ratio of engines of this type should be raised by installing special pistons that have domed heads in their cylinders.

The theory of head milling is to reduce the volume of the combustion chambers in the heads. The more the volume is reduced, the higher the compression ratio will be raised. As the amount the volume of any combustion chamber can be reduced by head milling is limited, this method is satisfactory if it isn't necessary to raise the ratio too high.

Some of the things in an engine that can be affected by head milling are alignment of the ports in the intake manifold with the ports in the heads, sealing of the valve lifter chamber in engines that use the intake manifold as the chamber cover, clearances between valve heads and the pistons and other surfaces of the combustion chambers, pushrod length, and the depth of oil channels in the head's gasket surface. The most important of these are valve clearance and intake port alignment.

Valve head to piston clearance is critical in only a few engines, among these being '55 and later 265- and 283-cubic-inch Chevrolets. The period during which interference will occur is when the piston is at the end of its exhaust stroke and the valves are in their overlap period. In engines in which this clearance is critical it is possible for the pistons to hit the valves if the valves are floated at high engine speeds; therefore, if the clearance is reduced by milling the heads so that the valve heads are moved closer to the piston heads, it is almost certain that interference will occur between the pistons and valves. This can result in bent valves, broken pistons, or both. It is possible to sink the valves into some heads the same amount the heads were milled to restore valve to piston clearance to stock specifications but this is a makeshift arrangement that brings on other problems. For one thing, it causes the rocker arm ends of the valve stems to be moved farther away from the cylinder heads making it necessary to shim the valve springs the same amount the valves were recessed and to either shorten the stems or raise the rocker arm stands so the arms will contact the stems at the same angle they did originally.

In one or two makes of engines it is possible for the valve heads to hit the upper edges of the cylinders after heads have been milled. This is the result of moving the valve heads closer to the surface of the cylinder block by removing material from the gasket surface of the cylinder heads. The only corrections for this are to either sink the valves into the heads the same amount the heads were milled or grind reliefs in the block for the valve heads.

Another thing that reduces the clearance between valves and the pistons and cylinder block is the installation of a reground camshaft. Reground cams open the intake valves earlier and

close the exhaust valves later. This brings the valve heads closer to the piston heads during the overlap period. Reground cams also open the valves farther, which moves the valve heads closer to the edges of the cylinders when the valves are in their open positions. Therefore, in engines that have valve clearance problems, consideration of the clearance when the heads are milled becomes even more important when the engine is equipped with a reground camshaft.

Alignment of the ports in the intake manifold with those in the cylinder heads is changed when heads are milled. This is due to the angle of the cylinder banks in relation to each other, and the angles of the mating surfaces of the manifold and cylinder heads. Two types of intake manifolds are in use now and they differ in that one of them acts as the cover for the tappet chamber in the cylinder block whereas the other does not touch the block at any point. However, despite this difference, the angularities that exist in the engines and manifolds cause either type of manifold to remain in its same position in relation to the cylinder block regardless of the amount of material milled from the gasket surfaces of the cylinder heads. A manifold that acts as the cover for the tappet chamber cannot possibly move in relation to the block and a manifold of the other type is just as inflexibly supported by the cylinder heads.

When heads are milled, their intake ports are moved closer to the cylinder block. This lowers the ports in relation to those in the intake manifold. If the head and manifold ports were in line originally, they won't be in alignment after the heads have been milled; however, it's not impossible that the ports were not in alignment originally and that milling the heads will bring them closer to alignment than they were. The only way this can be determined is by checking the original alignment. This can be done by examining the gaskets used between the manifold and the heads.

Manifolds that do not act as covers on the cylinder block can be lowered the same amount in relation to the block that the heads were lowered by machining either the manifold flanges on the heads or the flanges on the manifold. There is a definite relationship between the amount of material that must be removed from the flanges and the amount the heads were milled but this relationship varies for different engines because

Special high-compression pistons are available for several makes of engines.

of the different angles of their manifold mounting flanges. Most companies that mill cylinder heads have charts that state how much material should be removed from the manifold flanges for certain amounts of head milling.

Manifolds that serve as covers for the block can also be fitted to milled heads by machining their flanges but they present an additional problem in that their surfaces that seat on the cylinder block must also be machined. In most engines with manifolds of this type another problem arises in that their ignition distributor seats on a flange on the manifold. Lowering the manifold changes the distributor's position in the engine. This might or might not cause trouble, depending on the amount the manifold was lowered.

Pushrod length in engines that don't have adjusting screws in their rocker arms or some other means of adjusting valve lash becomes a problem because milling the heads has the same effect as lengthening the pushrods the same amount. Engines with rocker arms of this type would have to have hydraulic valve lifters, and hydraulic lifters are critical as far as the position of their pushrod seats is concerned. This means that pushrods must be the correct length. The only satisfactory method of correcting this condition is with shorter rods, which might possibly be available, or adjustable pushrods that could be shortened to the correct length. Attempts are sometimes made to correct this condition by placing shims equal in thickness to approximately one-half the amount the heads were milled between the heads and the rocker arm stands but there is little to recommend this procedure. It is a compromise affair that destroys the original angularity between the rocker arms and the valve stems and even then does not allow the pistons in the valve lifters to return all the way to their normal positions.

Other things that must be checked and corrected when cylinder heads are milled are the squish area clearance, the depth of oil channels in the gasket surface of the heads, and the length of head bolts or studs. Squish area clearance is not affected by head milling if the heads of the pistons are flat. If the piston heads have domes to match corresponding areas on the heads it is possible that the pistons might hit the heads after the milling. The original clearance between the pistons and the heads should be restored by machining the surfaces on the heads to the correct contour.

Oil channels in the gasket surface are used in Oldsmobile heads to connect the passages in the cylinder block through which oil flows to the rocker arm assemblies to passages in the cylinder heads. When the heads are milled these channels are made shallower and they should be restored to their original depth to guarantee ample flow of oil to the rocker arms and valve assemblies. This can be done with small grinding stones or rotary files.

Cylinder head bolt or stud length should be checked carefully with the cylinder heads and gaskets of the correct type on the cylinder banks to determine whether heads on bolts, or nuts on studs, will tighten against the heads as they should. If the bolts or nuts do not tighten against the heads it will be necessary to use hardened steel washers of adequate thickness between them and the heads. It is important that the bolts or nuts exert their required pressure on the heads if the head gaskets are to be prevented from blowing.

Another thing that must be considered when a head of any type is being milled is the thickness of the material on its gasket surface. If the thickness of this surface is reduced beyond practical limits, the strength of the surface will be lowered to the point where it will be unable to hold gaskets.

In many instances it is possible to install a pair of cylinder heads made for a later model engine of the same make on an early engine and effect an increase in compression ratio. When such a change is being contemplated care must be taken to insure that the heads to be used fit the block as they should and that they will actually raise the ratio. A set of heads may be rated at 9 to 1 on the engine for which they were made but still provide a ratio of only 7 to 1 or so on an earlier engine. The reason for this is that the displacement of the later engine is greater than that of the earlier engine; therefore, the heads would not raise the ratio of the smaller displacement early engine as much as one would think. The factor that determines the ratio any heads will provide on a specific engine is the actual volume of their combustion chambers in relation to the displacement of the cylinders in the engine. To be on the safe side it would be wise to actually measure the volumes of the chambers.

Raising a compression ratio by installing thinner head gaskets is a satisfactory method if the gaskets used are of good design and quality. Installing thinner head gaskets has the same effect on compression ratio and the mechanical alignment and clearances in the engine as milling the cylinder heads the same amount the new gaskets are thinner than those they replace. Some engine manufacturers make head gaskets of different thicknesses for their engines and these gaskets will give good service. Many of the special "compression raiser" gaskets sold by hot rod shops are inferior in design and shouldn't be used. Gaskets of this type are cut from sheets of copper or steel. Sometimes it is hard to tell a good special gasket from one that isn't good but one rule to follow is to not use one that doesn't have raised rings similar to the rings on stock single-layer gaskets around its openings. These rings form areas of high pressure between the cylinder head and the block to prevent compression and combustion gases, water, and oil from leaking past them.

Pistons made for the purpose of raising compression ratios are available for the more popular makes of engines. They effect an increase in a compression ratio by having special domes on their heads that reduce the volume of the engine's combustion chambers when the pistons are at top dead center in the cylinders. When valve head clearance is a problem in an engine,

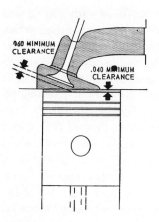

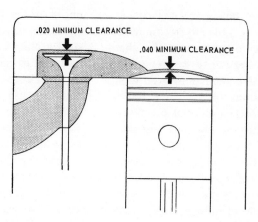

.020 MINIMUM CLEARANCE

.040 MINIMUM CLEARANCE

.060 MINIMUM CLEARANCE

.040 MINIMUM CLEARANCE

Minimum clearance between heads, pistons, and valves for both L-head and overhead-valve engines is shown here.

special pistons of this type have notches in their heads to provide adequate clearance for any condition. If it were desirable or necessary to use pistons of this type with milled heads, it would be wise to check with the piston manufacturer before ordering them to determine whether they could be used with the smaller combustion chambers. After the pistons were installed with either stock or milled heads, the squish area clearance and valve head clearance should be checked with modeling clay.

Modeling clay can be used to measure squish area clearances by laying narrow strips of the clay on the tops of the pistons in the squish area and placing the cylinder heads and the gaskets to be used with them on the cylinder banks. If the heads are to be held in place with capscrews, a couple of the capscrews can be started in the block to hold each of the heads in alignment with the cylinders but they shouldn't be tightened against the heads, nor should nuts be installed on head studs. The heads can be held against the block by hand while someone rotates the crankshaft at least one full turn in its normal direction of rotation. The heads should be held tightly against the block to compress the modeling clay if the clay touches them but not so tightly that actual contact between the head and the pistons will damage anything.

After the crankshaft has been rotated, the heads are removed from the block and any of the strips of clay that were compressed are carefully removed from the surface to which they are adhering and their thickness is measured. This measuring can be done with an outside micrometer if one is careful. Sometimes it is advantageous to cut the clay through the middle

of its compressed area with a razor blade while it is still in place on its member so a visual determination of its thickness can be made. Any area that doesn't have sufficient clearance will have to be machined to provide the clearance, or different pistons will have to be installed.

Clearances between valves and pistons, or valves and the edge of the cylinder block, can often be computed by comparing the amount the valves will open with the distance from the valve heads when the valves are on their seats, to the possible point of interference. The head gasket thickness must be taken into consideration when this computation is being made. To check the clearances with clay, it will be necessary to install the heads and all their valve actuating mechanism of the cylinder banks and adjust the valve lash. Then the crankshaft is rotated at least two full turns and the compressed thickness of the clay measured as explained previously. If the crankshaft seems to lock-up at any time while it is being rotated, it shouldn't be forced because a piston may be against the valve head.

Clearances in combustion chambers shouldn't be less than the following: .040-inch between the heads of the pistons and the cylinder heads, and .060-inch between heads of valves and the pistons at the end of exhaust strokes. The clearance between piston heads and cylinder heads in the squish area should not be more than .060-inch. When the clearance becomes greater than this the ability of the squish area to control detonation is reduced. As this factor is important in a high-compression engine, it is imperative that the clearance be correct.

Establishing the desired compression ratio in an engine that has been bored and stroked is sometimes easier than in one that has a stock bore and stroke. This is because boring and stroking increase an engine's displacement, and, therefore raise its compression ratio even when stock heads are used. It is usually wise before assembling a bored and stroked engine to compute the compression ratio it will have. By doing this it will be easier to make necessary changes to the parts to raise or lower the ratio as needed. If the increased displacement is going to make the ratio too high it might be possible to get another pair of cylinder heads that have larger combustion chambers, or, in extreme cases, to use pistons with lower compression height. When pistons with a lower compression height are to be used it is important that the squish area clearance be maintained at somewhere near .060-inch so that the area can function as it should.

To compute the compression ratio it is necessary to compare the volume of the cylinders with the volume of the combustion chambers. Cylinder volume can be determined mathematically but combustion chamber volume will have to be measured with a liquid. To determine cylinder volume, use the following formula: $V =$ bore x bore x .7854 x stroke. This gives displacement of one cylinder. If the bore and stroke measurements are in inches, the displacement will be in cubic inches.

To measure the volume of one of the combustion chambers in the cylinder head, the valves and spark plugs must be installed in the chamber and the head must be supported so its head gasket surface is level. Then water or light oil is poured from a graduated beaker into the chamber. Only enough liquid should be poured into the chamber to fill it to its gasket surface. The surface tension of water and some other liquids will allow the liquid to build up above the surface so that the chamber can actually be overfilled. The amount of liquid poured into the chamber is determined by subtracting the quantity still in the beaker from the original quantity. Most beakers are graduated in cubic centimeters (cc) making it necessary to convert the result to cubic inches.

Cubic inches are converted to cubic centimeters by multiplying them by 16.387, and cubic centimeters are converted to cubic inches by dividing them by 16.387. The volume of the opening in the head gasket must be computed by multiplying its area in square inches by its thickness in thousandths of an inch. Sometimes it is necessary to roughly calculate the square-inch area of the opening but the calculation can usually be made with sufficient accuracy that it won't affect the final computation. If the volume of the head gasket opening is computed in cubic inches, and it is necessary to convert it to cubic centimeters, this is done in the same manner the cylinder displacement was converted. The volume of the head gasket opening is added to the combustion chamber volume.

Another thing that must be taken into consideration is the volume of the area between the top of the piston and the top of the cylinder block. This is computed by measuring the distance as accurately as possible with a depth micrometer or some other measuring device and then multiplying the area of the cylinder by the depth. The formula for this is $V =$ bore x bore x .7854 x Distance from the top of the piston to the top of the cylinder block. This volume is added to the volume of the combustion chamber and head gasket opening. This total is then considered as the final combustion chamber volume.

To use these figures to compute the compression ratio, the final combustion chamber volume is added to the cylinder volume and the total is divided by the final combustion chamber volume. The answer is the compression ratio the engine will have when it is assembled.

This method of computing compression ratio can be used only in engines that have pistons with flat heads. If the piston heads are domed or have projections of any type it will be impossible within practical means to determine the volume displaced in the combustion chambers by the domes or projections. The compression ratio of an engine that has domed pistons can be determined after is has been assembled by measuring the actual capacity of one of its combustion chambers with a liquid. This is done by turning the crankshaft so the piston in the cylinder to be checked is at exactly top dead center and both valves are closed and then rotating the cylinder block so the chamber can be filled by pouring the liquid through its spark plug opening. When the chamber is being filled it is absolutely necessary that all air in it be allowed to escape so it will be completely filled. It is usually necessary to move the engine from side to side during the filling to allow the air to escape. Once the chamber capacity has been measured, the capacity of the cylinder can be determined mathematically, as explained previously, and the compression ratio can be computed in the same manner described for engine with flat top pistons.

A fellow that wanted to be sure his engine was going to be as right as he could make it should check the volumes of all the combustion chambers in the cylinder heads because quite often the volumes will vary, even in stock heads, and it is practically certain that they will vary if they have been machined for valve head clearance or any other purpose. Sometimes when a head is milled it is accidentally set up at a slight angle in the machine so that more material is removed from one of its ends than from the other. This causes variances in the capacities of the head's chambers.

Chamber capacities that don't vary too much can be equalized by grinding material from the surfaces of the smaller ones; however, this shouldn't be done until some other things in the engine are checked. These are the stroke length for the individual pistons and the distance between the top of each piston head when it is in its top dead center position and the top of the cylinder block. It is rare that the stroke lengths of the throws on a crankshaft that has been stroked by one of the better companies will vary but it might be possible to find variances in a stock shaft. All the stroke lengths are equal but since the distance between the tops of the pistons and the top of the cylinder block vary, it would be wise to measure the center-to-center distance of the connecting rods, which is the distance between the center of the big-end bore and the center of their piston pin bore, and the compression height of the pistons, which is the distance from the center of the piston pin bore to the top of the head.

Rod length and piston compression height should be measured before the pistons are installed on the rods. Any discrepancies found could be corrected before any further work was done on the parts. Measuring connecting rod length might be a problem for the average fellow who doesn't have a full complement of precision measuring devices but usually a method can be devised that is accurate enough for the purpose. Compression heights of the pistons can be compared by inserting a piston pin in each piston so it extends out from the side of the piston and then measuring the distance from the surface of measurements but if found it would be wise to rare that any variation will be found in these the pin to the surface of the piston head. It is exchange the pistons before going any further.

If slight variations in stroke length and piston height in the cylinders are uncorrectable for any reason, some compensation for the differences they cause in cylinder and combustion chamber volumes can be made by varying the volumes of the combustion chambers in the cylinder heads. This will help to equalize the compression ratios between the cylinders.

When installing milled or special heads on L-head engines the clearances between the valve heads and the roofs of the combustion chambers, the squish area clearances, and the head bolt or stud length must be checked. Clearances in the combustion chambers can be checked in the same manner described for ohv engines. They should be .040-inch between the heads of the pistons and the cylinder heads, and .020-inch between the heads of fully opened valves and the roofs of the combustion chambers. As far as detonation is concerned, squish area clearances are just as critical in an L-head engine as they are in ohv engines.

If any of the clearances are less than those specified, they can be increased by machining the areas over the pistons and valves. Machining areas over valves is called "flycutting" and machining areas over piston heads is called "doming." Many automotive machine shops that do head milling and other types of special parts reworking are equipped to do these jobs. Doming must be done with the correct tool so the machined areas will have the same radius as the piston heads.

CHAPTER TEN

The Pros and Cons of Fuel Injection

The latest developments in the field of

fuel injection systems. Power and economy

aspects versus carburetor-type fuel systems

AUTOMOBILE ENGINES have always depended on carburetors to mix the fuel they consume with air but in the last two or three years engineers of automobile companies and manufacturers of carburetors and other automotive accessories have been displaying the results of years of development work on fuel injectors. Some automobile manufacturers have even gone so far as to actually introduce fuel injectors for public consumption but for some reason or another none of these units, with the exception of a very few on Chevrolet automobiles, have fallen into the hands of average drivers.

Carburetors, despite the many years they have been used and the amount of development work that has been done on them, are far from perfect fuel metering devices. The reason carburetors aren't as efficient as they might be is that the air/fuel ratios required by an engine vary so much for different conditions of crankshaft speed and load. Attaining the correct fuel flows for these conditions is an extremely difficult task. The task is made even more difficult by performance demands that require an engine to be ca-

pable of developing the maximum horsepower its design will permit and still deliver good torque output at low speeds, and to do these things without using excessive quantities of fuel. It isn't any secret that carburetion systems don't meet these demands because of compromises in them that favor low speed performance at the sacrifice of maximum horsepower output.

An engine's maximum power output is dependent on the amount of air/fuel mixture its cylinders can induct on intake strokes. This, in turn, is dependent on the areas of the air passages through the carburetor and intake manifold. For maximum power, the passages must have large areas. However, after the fuel has been mixed with the air flowing through the carburetor it must be held in suspension in the air flowing through the passages. This isn't any problem at high engine speeds but at low speeds the velocity of the mixture through large passages is so low that some of the fuel drops out the air and collects on the floors of the passages. As this is detrimental to good low-speed performance, manifold passages are made small enough that

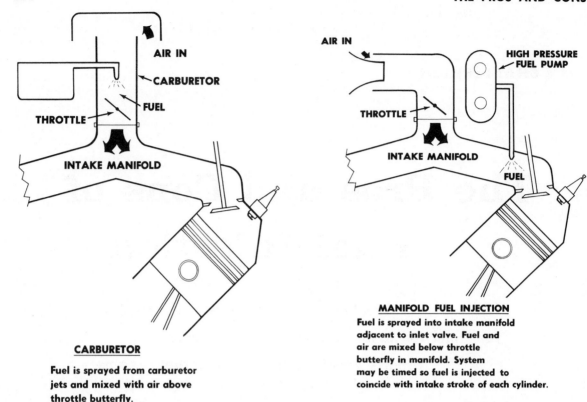

CARBURETOR

Fuel is sprayed from carburetor
jets and mixed with air above
throttle butterfly.

MANIFOLD FUEL INJECTION

Fuel is sprayed into intake manifold
adjacent to inlet valve. Fuel and
air are mixed below throttle
butterfly in manifold. System
may be timed so fuel is injected to
coincide with intake stroke of each cylinder.

These diagrams illustrate the principles of carburetion and fuel injection. Note that
the center diagram represents both constant-flow and timed injection systems.

the velocity through them is sufficiently high at
low engine speeds to hold the desired percentage
of fuel in suspension. Passages of this size restrict the flow of air to the cylinders at high
speeds.

A necessary part of an intake manifold is the
hot spot under or around its carburetor risers
that heats the air/fuel mixture as it flows into
the manifold from the carburetor. This heat is
necessary to help vaporize the fuel so it will mix
more thoroughly with the air. Heating the mixture in this manner improves carburetion at low
engine speeds and increases the flexibility of the
engine but it expands the mixture, reducing the
weight of mixture inducted into the cylinders.
This restricts the engine's power output when it
is operating under wide-open throttle conditions.

The quantity of fuel consumed by a normally
carbureted engine is greater than that actually
required by the engine. There are several reasons
for this. One is that it is impossible to attain
even distribution of mixture to an engine's cylinders. Because of the different lengths and con-

figurations of the manifold branches through
which the mixture must flow from the risers to
reach the cylinders, mixture ratios received by
some cylinders are richer than those delivered
by the carburetor and mixtures received by some
of the other cylinders are leaner than those
the carburetor delivers. This uneven distribution
makes it necessary to enrich the mixture delivered by the carburetor so that the leanest mixture received by any cylinder has an ample
percentage of fuel for correct combustion.

The second reason a normally carbureted
engine uses more fuel than it should is that the
lack of fuel vaporization in the intake manifold
of a cold engine during the warm-up period is so
incomplete that the mixture delivered by the
carburetor at these times must be extra-rich. By
supplying additional fuel to the mixture, sufficient quantities of the more easily vaporized
light-ends of the fuel reach the cylinders to start
the engine and keep it running until it reaches
its normal operating temperatures.

The third reason for high fuel consumption

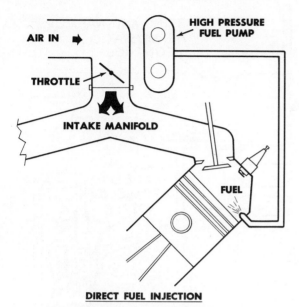

DIRECT FUEL INJECTION

Fuel is injected directly into each cylinder
and must be timed to coincide with
intake stroke. Fuel-air mixture takes
place in cylinder.

is the accelerating pump in the carburetor. Each time the throttle is opened the pump forces a charge of fuel into each of the carburetor's throats. The purpose of this extra fuel is to compensate for the additional air that enters the manifold at the time the throttle is opened but indications seem to prove that most of it is exhausted from the cylinders unburned.

Engineers working on fuel injection systems are trying to provide a fuel metering and distribution system that will eliminate the deficiencies of standard carburetion systems. This means that a fuel injection system must, to be completely successful, enable an engine to deliver a greater horsepower output, allow it to run efficiently with less fuel, and to operate at least as smoothly and flexibly, as it does with a standard carburetor and intake manifold setup.

Some automotive manufacturers claim that they have fuel injection systems now ready for public consumption that will achieve these ends but the mere fact that these systems don't seem

to be available would make one believe that they aren't as ready as their manufacturers would try to make us believe. What really happened was that one of the manufacturers (Chevrolet) announced its fuel injection system for its '57 models, although the system really wasn't ready for the public, to give it an advertising scoop over the rest of the industry. Other manufacturers, not to be outdone, immediately announced their systems, that weren't any more ready than the Chevy system, for public use. The result was a flurry among the car buying public that soon died when prices of the systems were announced, and then removal of the systems from the market when it was proved that they weren't sufficiently perfected to be ready for the public. Although they were advertised in 1958, it was practically impossible to buy one of the systems on a '58 automobile.

Passenger car fuel injection systems under present development vary considerably in design. They are made in two basic types, which are constant-flow and timed-injection. General Motors injectors, used on Chevrolet and Pontiac, are of the constant-flow type, and the Bendix Electrojector, advertised for Chrysler product cars and Rambler V8's, is of the timed-injection type. Several other injectors are under development, among them being one built by American Bosch Company, and another by Marvel-Schebler Division of Borg-Warner. With all the development work going on it seems inevitable that a practical injector that will replace carburetion systems as we know them today will eventually be built by one or more companies. However, until that time, the motoring public will have to be content with carburetors, which really aren't as bad as fuel injection men would have us believe.

Some of the things General Motors engineers learned during development work on the GM-Rochester fuel injector are interesting. Many of the conclusions made by these engineers have been questioned by engineers working on similar projects for other companies but this condition will be found when any project is being attacked by more than one company. However, results gained to date by General Motors engineers with their injector seem to bear out their findings.

Number one on the GM list of conclusions is that direct injection into combustion chambers

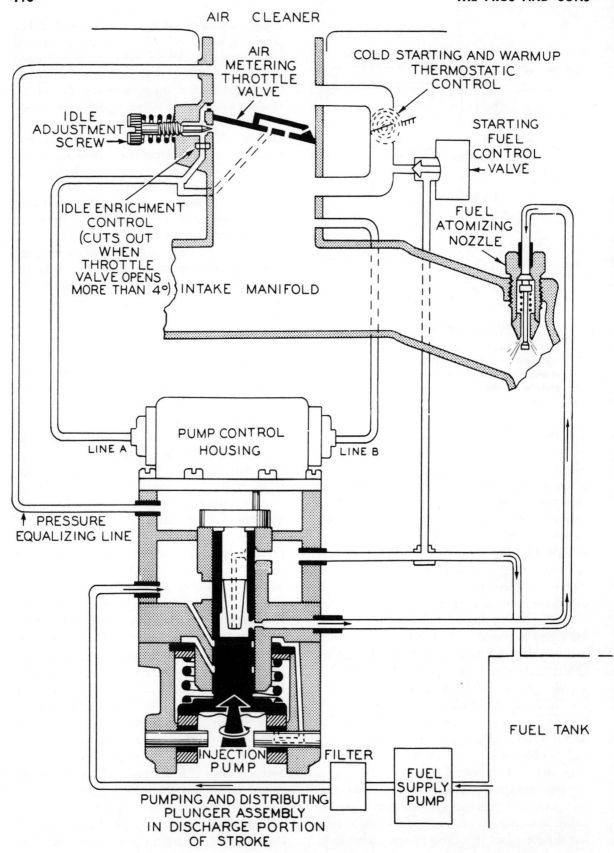

AIR   CLEANER

AIR
METERING
THROTTLE
VALVE

COLD STARTING AND WARMUP
THERMOSTATIC
CONTROL

IDLE
ADJUSTMENT
SCREW →

STARTING
FUEL
CONTROL
← VALVE

IDLE ENRICHMENT
CONTROL
(CUTS OUT
WHEN
THROTTLE
VALVE OPENS
MORE THAN 4°)

FUEL
ATOMIZING
NOZZLE

INTAKE   MANIFOLD

PUMP CONTROL
HOUSING

LINE A   LINE B

↑ PRESSURE
EQUALIZING LINE

FUEL TANK

INJECTION
PUMP   FILTER

PUMPING AND DISTRIBUTING
PLUNGER ASSEMBLY
IN DISCHARGE PORTION
OF STROKE

FUEL
SUPPLY
PUMP

The Marvel-Schebler timed-injection fuel injection system.

INJECTOR PUMPING AND
DISTRIBUTING PLUNGER
ASSEMBLY

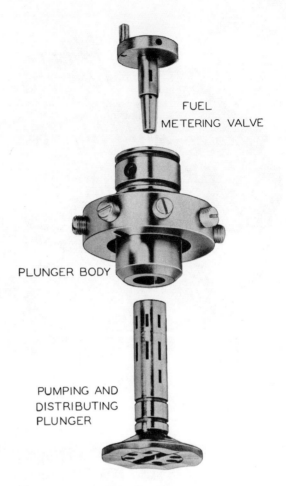

FUEL
METERING VALVE

PLUNGER BODY

PUMPING AND
DISTRIBUTING
PLUNGER

has no appreciable advantage over injection into intake ports. This would be concerned with the mixing of the fuel with the air.

Number two is that timed injection into the intake ports gives slightly less power and uses slightly more fuel than continuous injection. This is important from the standpoint of the cost of the unit because a constant-flow injector is considerably less expensive to build than one that uses timed-injection.

Number three is that injection directed toward the intake valve gives the most power, the best economy, the fastest warm up, and the best acceleration response.

Number four is that the greater the distance between the fuel nozzle and the intake port in the cylinder head, the more the injector will resemble a carburetor in dynamic operation. This is easy to understand because if the fuel nozzle were a considerable distance from the port, the air/fuel mixture would have to travel through the branch of a manifold, just as it must in normal carburetor setup. This would require that velocities through the branches feeding the cylinders be kept high, making it necessary to reduce the area of the branches and restrict their air flow capacity.

Number five is that with a fuel injector in which the fuel is injected into the air stream close to the intake ports in the cylinder heads, the individual air passages to the ports can be large enough for maximum power output without

having an adverse effect on the engine's idle and low speed operation. This is a definite advantage over standard carburetion systems. It is made possible by the fact that only air flows through the passages and therefore there isn't any fuel flowing through the passages that must be kept in suspension in the air by the air's velocity.

Number six is that engine performance in certain speed ranges can be improved by making the individual tubes for the ports of the correct cross-sectioned area and length. A combination of area and length that is most effective in the 40 to 65 mph range was incorporated in the final design for the Chevrolet injector.

Number seven is that 180-degree manifold design is not necessary with fuel injection as long as there is ample air capacity at the atmospheric end of each inlet tube so that each tube has an unrestricted supply of air regardless of

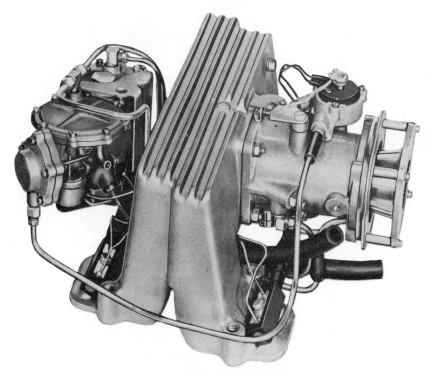

Externel view of the
GM-Rochester fuel injection
system.

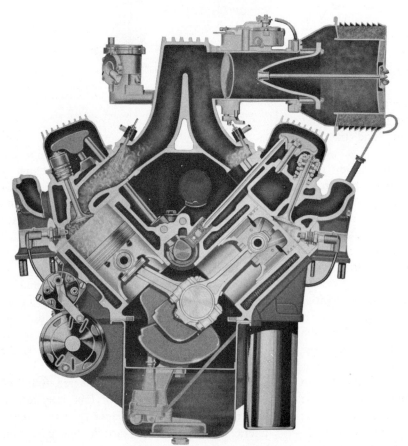

Cross-section diagram of
Chevrolet engine with fuel
injection. Note the fuel nozzles
in the intake manifold.

the order in which air flows through the tubes. This was accomplished in the GM injector by enclosing the atmospheric ends of the tubes in a common chamber that has adequate capacity and an air inlet of ample size to pass the amount of air required by the engine at high crankshaft speeds.

Power output of fuel-injected Chevrolet engines, when measured with an engine dynamometer, was found to be the same as that of engines equipped with four-throat carburetors, but on the road, acceleration with the fuel injector was considerably better than with the carburetor. This was due, apparently, to the more uniform rate the fuel was fed to the cylinders by the injector during acceleration. On a Pontiac, the engineers found that 0 to 60 mph acceleration was over ten percent better with the fuel injector than with a single four-throat.

On the economy side, Pontiac found that level road fuel mileage was the same with the injectors as with a four-throat but for cross-country mileage the injector was about five percent better. Under some conditions Chevrolets showed gains of the order of 15 percent in fuel savings; however, Chevrolet engineers are more conservative than this in most of their statements.

Although deficiencies in the fuel injection systems being built at the present time for standard passenger car use make the system unsuitable for the average driver, injectors have been used on all-out hot rod engines and professional racing engines for several years. On professional racing engines injectors have completely eliminated carburetors from the scene; however, as one highly successful race car builder and owner has said, the reason for this may be that at the present time no one is building a carburetor suitable for racing engines. Be this as it may, fuel injectors cannot help but be considered as highly satisfactory for competition engines.

In addition to the advantages fuel injectors would have for standard passenger cars, they have several other advantages of benefit to hot rod and racing engines. These additional advantages are the direct result of the elimination of deficiencies found in many of the carburetion systems used on competition engines; however, improved carburetion systems for competition hot rod engines that have eliminated some

deficiencies of previous systems have recently been made available. These improved systems consist of special intake manifolds designed to accommodate six or eight carburetors in such a manner that air flow conditions to each of the engine's intake ports are equalized. Most of these new systems were designed primarily for engines used in drag racing cars. Deficiencies that make carburetors unsuitable for track or boat racing still make some of the improved systems unsuitable for these uses.

First on the list of things that make carburetors unsuitable for competition hot rod and racing engines are the fluctuations in fuel flow through their metering orifices when a car's attitude changes suddenly. Sudden changes of attitude are common to competition and racing cars. They occur when a car is accelerating rapidly, turning, sliding, braking fast, and performing other gymnastics common to cars of this type. Fuel flow fluctuations during these periods are due to the method of controlling fuel flow into a carburetor with a float. When the car's attitude changes suddenly the float is apt to bounce around in its bowl, allowing fuel to enter the air stream flowing to the cylinders in an uncontrolled manner, or, in some instances, stopping the flow of fuel until the car regains its normal attitude.

Second is the reduction in volumetric efficiency resulting from the air flow restriction created by the venturi in each carburetor throat. A carburetor cannot function without a venturi; however, with some of the new manifolds it is possible to install enough carburetors on an engine to increase the total venturi area to the amount required for maximum performance.

Third is inferior acceleration resulting from inadequate fuel flow during periods of low manifold vacuum. This was borne out by the results obtained by GM engineers with Chevrolet and Pontiac engines. It is a condition that cannot be corrected by installing more carburetors. Time lost in this manner can make the difference between winning or losing a drag or track race.

Fourth is poor fuel vaporization, which causes erratic air/fuel ratios, low fuel mileage, and severe engine wear. Fuel mileage is of little consequence in the average hot rod engine but wear is an important factor in any engine. Wear caused by the carburetion system is the result

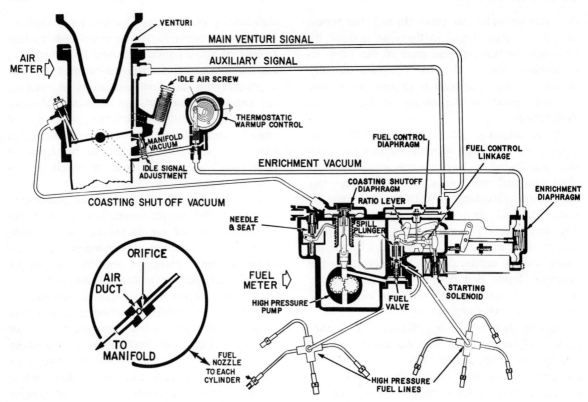

Schematic diagram of the GM-Rochester fuel injection system.

of dilution of the lubricating oil with unburned fuel. This condition is more pronounced when alcohol-base fuels are used. The reason for this is that approximately 2½ times as much alcohol as gasoline must be used for the same amount of air inducted into an engine; therefore, the chance of unburned fuel passing the piston rings and entering the crankcase is 2½ times greater.

Fifth is the limited fuel flow capacity of carburetors, unless many of them are used. Gasoline doesn't present too much of a problem in this respect but alcohol does. Properly modified, six or eight carburetors can supply adequate quantities of alcohol or blended fuel to an engine but fuel flow capacity might become a problem if fewer carburetors than this were used.

Sixth is the involved procedure required for most carburetors to make air/fuel ratio changes. Considerable time can be spent changing the main metering jets in six or eight carburetors. Also, a large selection of jets of different sizes is required.

The original and still most popular fuel injector for hot rods and the only one manufactured for professional racing engines is the Hilborn injector developed by Stuart Hilborn and now being manufactured by his company, Fuel Injection Engineering. Stuart began work on his injection system in 1945. At that time he was running a hot rod on Southern California's dry lakes. The original injector was designed for the hot rod's 1939 Ford V8 engine and this car and engine were used for much of the development work on the injector.

Before starting work on his injector, Hilborn studied the two basic injection principles, timed-injection and constant-flow—and he decided to concentrate on a type utilizing the constant-flow principle. This decision was made because the complicated design of a timed-injection unit would make its cost too high and such a unit would not be readily adaptable to engines already in use. That his choice was a wise one was borne out by the findings made more recently by GM engineers.

Hilborn's first injector was fabricated from steel plate and tubing. It was a meticulously constructed unit and a beautiful piece of workmanship. It consisted of a steel plate that was fitted with an air inlet for each port in the engine's cylinder block and that could be bolted to the intake port flanges on the block. The air inlets were quite short and each of them was fitted with a throttle valve. The throttle valves were mounted on two shafts, one for each cylinder bank, and they were connected at the rear of the unit by gears. A single throttle lever activated both shafts so all the valves opened and closed simultaneously.

Each air intake throat had its own fuel discharge nozzle that protruded into the air stream between the throttle valve and the port in the block. Fuel was delivered to the nozzles at a pressure of 35 psi by a pump driven by the engine. Flow of fuel to the nozzles was controlled by a metering valve linked to the throttle in such a manner that it opened and closed with the throttle valves. When the throttle valves were closed, the fuel valve allowed only the amount of fuel required by the engine to run at idle speed to flow to the nozzles. As the throttle valves were opened, the metering valve allowed additional quantities of fuel to flow to the nozzles to maintain the air/fuel ratio for maximum power output.

Many refinements were made in subsequent production injectors but to this date the principle of operation remains the same as that in the prototype. Two of the early refinements were a different type of fuel pump and a different method of controlling fuel pressure at the metering valve. Fuel pressure is now controlled by varying the size of an orifice inserted in a by-pass line that allows excess fuel delivered by the pump to the fuel valve to return to the fuel tank. In-

creasing the diameter of the orifice reduces the pressure on the metering valve and reducing the diameter of the orifice increases the pressure on the valve. This is a simple method of changing air/fuel ratios and it enables changes to be made in just a few minutes.

When Hilborn injectors were first made available to the hot rod and racing fraternities their foremost advantage over carburetors was the additional horsepower they provided. Horsepower increases of 10 to 34 percent were realized by merely replacing carburetors and their manifolds with an injector. However, the six and eight-carburetor intake manifolds now available have brought the horsepower output of hot rod engines fitted with them much closer to the output of injected engines.

Another advantage of an injector that is of importance to the owners of race cars that are run in long races is a reduction in fuel consumption. Reductions of 40 to 50 percent are realized by merely installing an injector in place of carburetors. This advantage holds little importance to hot rodders because of the short distances of their competition events.

The additional power output a Hilborn injector makes possible is the result of the unrestricted breathing area it provides between the cylinders and the atmosphere. Each intake throat is the same length and diameter, which equalizes the distance from the atmosphere to the cylinders, and there aren't venturis in the throats to restrict the flow of air through them. Better economy is the result of closer control of the fuel fed to the engine. The discharge nozzles are so constructed that a fine spray of fuel is fed into the air stream entering the cylinders. This provides a high degree of atomization and, consequently, very good vaporization of the fuel.

For several years Hilborn made injectors for

A Hilborn competition-type fuel injection system for a six-cylinder engine.

The Scott fuel injector can be more accurately described as an injector carburetor. Its aluminum flange, fitted with a fuel valve and discharge nozzles, is designed to bolt to a Stromberg 97 or 48 carburetor throttle body. Typical installation shown.

only alcohol and other special racing fuels but he now supplies injectors calibrated for gasoline that can be used on engines in sports cars and boats; they are not suitable for passenger car use.

Although Hilborn's injectors are covered by U.S. patents, similar versions have appeared on the market. More recently another device that is called an injector but that could be more accurately classified as an injector carburetor has been made available. This unit is built by Scott Engineering in Santa Monica, California, and it can be used in multiple installations or as secondary units in combination with a carburetor.

Scott injectors consist of an aluminum flange fitted with a fuel valve and discharge nozzles. The flange is designed to bolt to a Stromberg 97 or 48 carburetor throttle body. Linkage between the throttle shaft in the carburetor base and a lever on the fuel control valve opens and closes the valve as the throttles open and close.

Scott injectors function on the simple principle of spraying fuel under pressure into the air stream entering the intake manifold. This eliminates all problems of venturi restriction and fluctuation in fuel flow common to carburetors operating under competition conditions. The effectiveness of injectors of this type is dependent on the air flow capacity of the manifold on which they are used; however, maintaining the fuel they deliver in suspension in the air stream while the mixture is on its way to the cylinders should not present any problem. This is because when used as secondary units in combination with a standard carburetor, the injectors come into operation only at high engine speeds, when velocity through the branches of the manifold is high, and when used in groups of three to eight, without carburetors, they are installed only on competition engines that are not required to run well at low crankshaft speeds.

CHAPTER ELEVEN

Supercharging for Increased Performance

How much more power can you expect
from forcing greater quantities of fuel and air
into the cylinders? Superchargers available discussed.

SUPERCHARGING IS A METHOD OF HOPPING-UP an engine by providing a mechanical means to force greater quantities of fuel and air mixture into the engine's cylinders than the cylinders can induct normally. It is similar to normal engine conversion procedures in that it is a method of raising an engine's volumetric efficiency. Volumetric efficiency, as explained in another chapter, is the volume of fuel and air mixture, at atmospheric pressure and temperature, in a cylinder at the end of intake strokes. It is measured in percentages of cylinder volume.

Volumetric efficiency is dependent on an engine's speed, inlet valve opening area, valve timing, the temperature of the charges in the cylinders at the end of intake strokes, and other things. Mechanical things that limit volumetric efficiency do so by restricting the flow of fresh mixture into the cylinders. Temperature affects volumetric efficiency because it expands the mixture. Because of these things, the volumetric efficiency of a normally-aspirated engine is nearly always less than 1.00. Exceptions to this are possible in engines that are fitted with individual "tuned" induction and exhaust pipes for each cylinder but when induction and exhaust tuning are used, the range of engine speed over which the high volumetric efficiency occurs is very narrow and at other speeds the efficiency suffers in comparison to what it would be with normal induction and exhaust systems.

A supercharger (in hot rod lingo, a "blower") boosts volumetric efficiency by forcing fuel and air mixture into an engine's cylinders under a positive pressure—the task for atmospheric pres-

A supercharger is a blower, using power from the engine, which forces the fuel and air mixture into the cylinders.

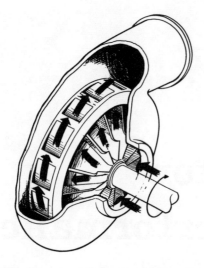

A centrifugal-type supercharger uses high rotational speed and high velocity to create "boost," or increased power.

sure is reduced to feeding air into the supercharger or carburetors. This positive pressure minimizes the detrimental effects of mechanical restrictions in the induction system, with the result that at the end of intake strokes the cylinders are filled with mixture that has a pressure greater than atmospheric. Increasing the quantity of mixture in the cylinders raises compression pressures and, consequently, combustion pressures. It is the higher combustion pressures that increase the pressure on the piston heads and enable the engine to deliver higher torque and horsepower outputs. The effect of supercharging is noticed most at high engine speeds where volumetric efficiency of a normally-aspirated engine usually drops off.

The pressure a supercharger creates is generally referred to as its "boost." Boost is measured in pounds pressure with an ordinary pressure gauge or with a gauge that indicates pressure in inches of mercury. The different types of gauges with which boost can be measured sometimes cause confusion among persons not familiar with the different units of measurement. A quick clarification might be in order at this time.

There are two standards of measurement for air pressure. One of these is "absolute pressure" and the other is "gauge pressure." Absolute pressure refers to pressure based on a zero pressure equal to that of a complete vacuum. Atmospheric pressures are examples of absolute pressures. Atmospheric pressure at sea level is approximately

14.7 pounds per square inch. If, for instance, the pressure indicated on a gauge tapped into a container were 50-psi absolute, the pressure would be 50 psi greater than it would be if there were a complete vacuum in the container. If the container were opened at sea level so the pressure could escape from it, the pressure in it would then be the same as atmospheric, or approximately 14.7-psi absolute. This is the pressure that would be registered by the gauge.

Gauge pressure is pressure over and above atmospheric pressure. If a different gauge on the same container used for the previous illustration indicated a pressure of 50-psi gauge, the pressure in the container would be 50 psi greater than the atmospheric pressure outside the container. If the container were opened at sea level and the pressure in it allowed to escape, the tank would contain air at atmospheric pressure but the pressure registered by the gauge would be zero pounds per square inch.

Supercharger boost is often measured in inches of mercury. One inch of mercury equals .49 pounds per square inch. Gauges calibrated to indicate inches of mercury can indicate either absolute pressures or pressures above atmospheric.

Many manifold pressure gauges made originally for airplanes and sold by surplus stores are used with supercharger installations. These gauges show absolute pressure. When the engine isn't running, the pressure they indicate is atmospheric pressure. Atmospheric pressure at sea level is equal to 29.92 inches of mercury. At altitudes above and below sea level atmospheric pressure will be lower or higher, respectively. When the engine is started, the gauge reading will drop according to the amount the pressure in the induction system is below atmospheric pressure, and as the engine is accelerated and the blower begins to function, the reading on the gauge will rise as the pressure in the manifold rises. With a gauge of this type, a reading of, for instance, 60 inches of mercury would indicate that the pressure in the induction system at the point where the gauge is connected would be 60 times .49, or 29.4 pounds per square inch absolute. At sea level this would be equivalent to a pressure of 15.7 pounds gauge. The pressure over the atmospheric pressure prevailing at the immediate time and altitude would be easily computed by subtracting the reading on the gauge when the engine wasn't running from the pressure indicated when the engine was running and multiplying the result by .49.

The point in the induction system of a supercharged engine at which the boost is measured is extremely important. To get a true indication of what the blower is doing for the engine, the place to tap a gauge into the system is as close as possible to one of the engine's intake ports. It's entirely possible for a blower to create a high boost at its outlet but for restrictions between the outlet and the ports in the engine to restrict the flow of air to the ports so badly that most or all of the benefit of the boost is lost as far as increasing pressures in the cylinders is concerned. This is the reason that blower installations that use stock intake manifolds often have little effect on engine performance. Included in supercharger kits of the better types are special intake manifolds that have ample capacity to conduct the full output of the blower to the ports in the engine. This is a point to consider whenever a supercharger is being purchased.

To get the most out of a blower installation it is necessary to install a reground camshaft in the engine. Valve timing requirements for a supercharged engine differ somewhat from those for a high-performance normally-aspirated engine. A blower can force the mixture into the cylinders but an intake valve that doesn't close at the correct time can allow much of the mixture to escape back into the intake port at the beginning of compression strokes. Also, improvements made to its valve actuating mechanism to enable a normally reworked engine to run at high crankshaft speeds must be made to a supercharged engine if it is to be expected to run at high speeds. Actually, a supercharged, all-out engine for competition can benefit from most of the reworking processes applied to unblown engines.

The lower end of most late model overhead valve V8 engines is sturdy enough to handle the greater horsepower output made possible by a blower but standard pistons sometimes present problems. Many pistons used in stock engines are too weak for the high combustion pressures in a blown engine, and they will either crack or break. Pistons of any type are sensitive to temperature, making it necessary for the power mixture in a blown engine to be extremely rich so

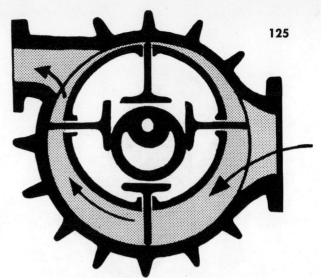

Vane-type supercharger is a positive-displacement type.

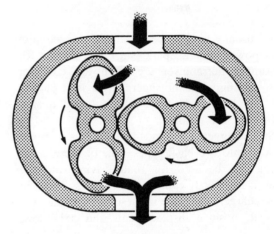

Roots-type unit is also a positive-displacement blower.

the heads of the pistons won't be burned or weakened by heat to the extent that they will collapse. The additional fuel in the rich mixture acts to cool the surfaces of the combustion chambers. Piston failure is often caused by the high pressures and temperatures of detonation that may or may not be audible above other sounds. Rich mixtures also help to suppress detonation.

Supercharging imposes additional loads on an engine's ignition system that many stock systems are not capable of handling. Many stock distributors and coils cannot create a spark of sufficient intensity to jump the gaps in the spark plugs of a supercharged engine when the blower is delivering its maximum output; the spark advance curve in stock distributors is seldom correct for a blown engine; and colder spark

McCulloch centrifugal supercharger.

The only centrifugal supercharger available at the present time is the McCulloch. Positive dislacement types include the popular GMC Roots blowers and Judson vane superchargers. There is only one axial-flow supercharger being manufactured for automotive use and it is the Latham.

McCulloch centrifugal superchargers are designed primarily for use on road cars, for which they enjoy some popularity, but they have been tried with varying degrees of success on many competition engines. Their big selling point is easy installation, and they are sold in kit form so that all the parts required for an installation are at hand. However, the problem is to get the engine to run correctly after the installation has been made.

The difficulties experienced with most McCulloch installations is the result of their principle of mounting the blower on the atmospheric side of the carburetor and blowing air through the carburetor and into the engine. In normal supercharger installations the blower is between the carburetors and the engine so the carburetor can function in a normal manner.

The operation of a carburetor depends on air pressure differentials. As air passes through a carburetor's throat on its way to an engine's cylinders, a low pressure is created at the carburetor's fuel discharge tubes. Atmospheric pres-

plugs usually have to be installed for maximum horsepower output. Spark plugs cold enough for maximum horsepower are often too cold for slow driving when the supercharger isn't putting out any boost and they will foul and misfire until they are cleaned.

Supercharger kits and installations can be divided into two basic types. One of these is for engines to be used for road driving and the other is for strictly competition engines. Types of superchargers available in these kits include centrifugal, positive displacement, and axial-flow.

This is a McCulloch blower in a '55 Ford Thunderbird. Note the carburetor enclosure on top of the engine.

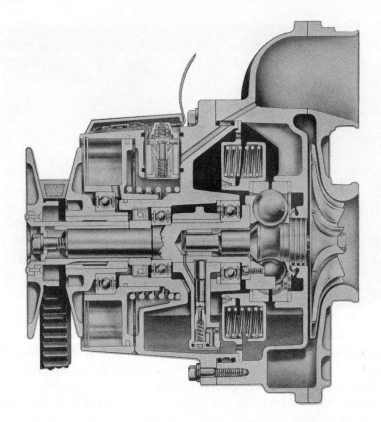

A cutaway view of McCulloch blower shows (left to right) drive pulley, speed actuating piston, ball and race speed multiplying device, and supercharger impeller.

sure on the fuel in the carburetor's bowl then forces fuel to flow from the tubes. When a McCulloch supercharger is installed, it blows air under a positive pressure through the carburetor and into the engine. This positive pressure in the carburetor's throat upsets the carburetor's pressure balance because it is higher than the pressure on the fuel in the bowl. Under this condition the carburetor cannot meter fuel as it should. To restore the pressure balance, the carburetor must be reworked, sometimes extensively, before it can function correctly. One thing that must be changed is the carburetor's fuel bowl vent so that the positive pressure in the carburetor's throat will also be exerted on the fuel in the bowl. Then, as air passes the end of the discharge tubes, a pressure lower than that on the fuel in the bowl is created at the ends of the tubes and fuel flows from the tubes, as it should. Changing the bowl vent in some carburetors is much harder to do than it sounds, and after the vent has been changed, the floats used in the bowls of some carburetors will be crushed by the blower pressure.

Increasing the pressure on the fuel in the bowl makes it necessary to raise the pressure of the fuel entering the carburetor. Sometimes this can be done by merely reworking the standard mechanical pump on the engine but for some installations one or more electric fuel pumps must be installed in combination with the mechanical pump. With some mechanical pumps it is possible to run a pressure line from the blower outlet to the atmospheric side of the fuel diaphragm to enable the blower pressure to assist the pump to deliver the correct pressure.

The only practical solution to the carburetor pressure balance problem when a McCulloch blower is used is to place the carburetor in an enclosure into which air from the supercharger can be blown. This restores the carburetor's original balance, as far as air and fuel flows are concerned. Factory installations made by the few automobile manufacturers who have tried McCulloch superchargers as standard equipment utilized enclosed carburetors, and McCulloch now supplies them for some installations. Enclosures for reworked engines were first manufactured by a company now out of business.

McCulloch superchargers are driven by a V belt of large cross section and they have a drive ratio of 4.4 to 1 (the blower drive shaft rotates

GMC blower is fed by two Stromberg carburetors and mounted on a Cadillac powerplant.

4.4 times crankshaft speed) but the ratio is controlled by a manifold vacuum so that the blower runs at a low ratio when it isn't needed. In their stock form the blowers are adjusted to deliver a maximum boost of 5 pounds per square inch gauge. It isn't stated where this boost is measured. Maximum boost is attained at approximately 3000 rpm when the drive is in hi-blower position. With this boost rate, a horsepower increase of 40 percent is claimed.

It's possible to render the speed-governing mechanism that governs the blower's boost inoperative so the blower will run at its 4.4 to 1 ratio at all times and deliver boost pressures higher than five pounds at high crankshaft speeds. However, when this is done, the balls and races of the speed multiplying device inside the blower that raises the rotational speed of the impeller in comparison to that of the driveshaft become overloaded and fail prematurely.

Installation kits for GMC blowers are available for both road and competition use. GMC blowers are well engineered and they are built with quality materials because they are designed for use on GMC two-stroke-cycle engines that are used in trucks and for other types of commercial service. Anything used on a truck must be of good quality because a truck that is off the road for service is costing its owner lots of money.

At the present time, three manufacturers are making the bulk of GMC blower installation kits. These are Cragar, which is a subsidiary of Bell Auto Parts; Potvin Engineering; and Tom Beatty Speed Equipment Co. Cragar and Beatty kits are similar in that they mount the blower on top of the engine and drive it with belts. Carburetors mount on the atmospheric side of the blower. Potvin kits mount the blower in front of the engine and drive it directly with the crankshaft.

Cragar kits now being manufactured are primarily for road use but it is said that they can be used for limited competition. The feature of an installation of this type that limits its use is the method of driving the blower. Blowers installed with present Cragar kits are driven by three narrow V belts. These belts can drive the blower satisfactorily at moderate engine speeds and blower output but they aren't able to transmit sufficient power to run the blower at the high speeds required for competition and to enable the blower to deliver high boost pressures. With this setup, Cragar installations are said to be able to deliver boost pressures of six to seven pounds per square inch gauge. For the average installation this is claimed to be good for a 40-percent horsepower increase.

Now in development at Cragar is an all-out competition kit which will have a drive belt of the timing belt type. Timing belts are flat with rectangular teeth on their drive side. The teeth mesh with recesses of the same shape in the drive and driven pulleys to provide positive power transmission. With this type of drive, Cragar says their blower installations will produce boost pressures of up to 15 pounds gauge. This would be adequate for any competition engine.

Beatty kits are similar to those built by Cragar with the exception that they have a competition drive assembly that uses six narrow V belts. Drive belts on a GMC blower used for competition must be in good condition; otherwise, they will slip and the blower will not put out the pressure it should. For this reason, usable belt life, even with six belts, is extremely short.

Kits that mount the blower on top of the engine include a special intake manifold to match the engine and blower, a crankshaft drive pulley, an idler arm and pulley assembly that maintains tension on the drive belts to keep them tight, the blower drive extension and shaft with ball bearings, a drive pulley, a rear cover plate for the blower, a carburetor adaptor flange, drive belts,

and necessary gaskets and other minor parts. These kits aren't inexpensive but their many parts are well made and only the best materials are used.

Cragar and Beatty manifolds are fitted with backfire valves. A backfire valve is necessary between the engine and a blower of the Roots type to relieve the pressure in the induction system in the event of a backfire in the engine. The pressure of a backfire could damage the blower beyond repair. Valves for this purpose are nothing more than spring-loaded covers over an opening in the manifold. Pressure of the spring or springs that hold the cover in its closed position is such that the blower boost cannot lift the cover off its seat but the higher pressure of a backfire can lift the cover easily and allow the pressure to escape to the atmosphere.

Kits are made for 3-71 and 4-71 blowers, depending on the engine on which they will be installed. The size of a GMC blower that should

This Potvin kit installation drives the GMC blower directly from the crankshaft. Fuel is fed by Hilborn fuel injectors.

This Latham supercharger is installed in a Ford Thunderbird.

be used on any engine is determined by the engine's displacement and the speed the blower is driven. Cragar considers a 3-71 to be adequate for 292-cubic-inch Fords and 265- and 283-cubic-inch Chevrolets. They recommend either a 3-71 or a 4-71 for 312-cubic-inch Mercurys, and a 4-71 for all models of Buick, Olds, Cadillac, and Chrysler V8 engines. Blowers are not included in the kits, although they can be supplied by the manufacturer of the kit for an additional charge.

Potvin kits eliminate the drive belt problem by driving the blower directly with the crankshaft but this necessitates mounting the blower ahead of the engine, making it impossible to use a kit of this type in a car to be used for normal road driving. The actual clearance needed ahead of the machined face on the front of the engine's cylinder block is 23 inches for 6-71 and 18 inches for a 4-71.

Driving a GMC blower at crankshaft speed limits its output to the point where a 3-71 becomes too small for engines with over 200 cubic inches of displacement. A 4-71 is capable of providing adequate boost for engines of 200 to 300 cubic inches and a 6-71 is required for engines larger than 300 inches. These limits are based on a desirable boost of approximately 15 pounds per square inch gauge at competition engine speeds. The actual boost the blower will produce will depend on the engine's exact displacement,

its compression ratio, its valve timing, the speed at which it is run, and many other variables that enter into an engine of this type. It is almost as important to not use a blower that is too large for an engine as it is to use one that is too small because the larger the blower, the more power required to drive it. If the job can be done with a 4-71, there is no need to add the extra torque load of 6-71 to the crankshaft. It is estimated that at least 25 horsepower is required to turn the rotors of a 6-71 at the speed and boost required by a competition engine.

Included in Potvin kits are an adaptor housing for the front of the engine, a pair of drive sprockets, a length of double-row chain to fit around the sprockets, a blower outlet chamber fitted with a backfire valve, the necessary parts for fabricating a pair of log-type intake manifolds, a pair of induction pipes, and the necessary hoses to connect the parts of the induction system together. When a Potvin kit is purchased it is necessary that Potvin have the blower that is to be used so he can check its parts for wear or damage, make a couple of minor alterations to it and fit the engine adaptor plate to it. The alterations consist of fitting an oil pressure inlet and an oil drain to the gear end of the blower's housing.

Nothing is included in the kit for the inlet side of the blower. If carburetors are to be used, the customer must make an adaptor to match the carburetors. If a Hilborn injector is to be used, it won't be necessary to make anything for the inlet, but the actual treatment of the inlet will depend on which of the two possible injector arrangements is to be installed. One of these is called an "open-face" and the other is a "closed-face." Both types are in use at the present time and neither seems to have any advantage over the other as far as performance is concerned.

The open-face setup is used mainly by purchasers who already have a standard Hilborn injector for their engine when they buy their blower kit. Manifolds supplied in a kit for an open-face installation are designed to match the inlet side of the injector throttle bodies. The original injector is used in its entirety, the only difference in the system being that the air that flows into the engine is forced into the injector by the blower instead of by atmospheric pressure. The inlet side of the blower is left open; nothing but air passes through the blower.

A closed-face setup requires an injector designed strictly for use with a blower. The customer must have injector nozzles fitted to the manifolds he received in the kit after he has assembled them and then he must obtain a fuel pump, a throttle body that bolts to the inlet side of the blower, and other miscellaneous parts needed for the injector.

When carburetors are used, Potvin recommends that at least 10 square inches of venturi area be provided for an engine of 400 cubic inches. This is roughly equivalent to the area provided by eight Stromberg 97's; however, downdraft carburetors shouldn't be used on a blower because of the possibility of fuel overflowing from the carburetor bowls and into the blower when the engine isn't running. If this should happen it would be possible for the blower to pump the fuel into the engine's cylinders when the engine was started. This could result in damage to the engine's internal parts. At present Potvin is recommending a single-throat updraft aircraft engine carburetor that has a 2⅛-inch venturi. Three of these carburetors provide a total venturi area of 10.62 square inches.

Potvin estimates that one of his blower kits will enable an engine of 400 cubic inches to develop in excess of 500 horsepower on gasoline, 600 horsepower on alcohol, and 700 horsepower on an alcohol-nitro blend containing 30 percent nitro.

Latham axial-flow superchargers are available for both road use and competition. These superchargers differ from conventional centrifugal and positive displacement types in that their only moving part is a long rotor encased in a tubular housing. The rotor runs on ball bearings and it is rotated by the crankshaft by means of a flat belt. The outer diameter of the rotor is fitted with a large number of blades, as is the inner diameter of the housing.

As the rotor is rotated, air moved in the housing by the blades on the rotor creates a low pressure at the front end of the housing and a high pressure at the rear end. Atmospheric pressure outside the blower forces air through carburetors bolted to the front of the housing to compensate for the low pressure. As the air passes through the carburetors, fuel is mixed with it and then the fuel/air mixture is forced to the rear of the housing and into the engine's intake manifold.

When Latham blowers were first made available they were designed to use the stock intake manifold on the engines on which they were installed. Performance with this setup wasn't too good because of the restriction to air flow created by the manifold but this condition was corrected at a later date by providing special manifolds with the blowers. These manifolds have adequate flow capacity to handle the air displaced by the supercharger, enabling the boost created by the blower to get into the engine. Good performance has been recorded at several competition events with this new setup.

Rotor and housing of a Latham axial-flow supercharger.

CHAPTER TWELVE

Engine Swapping for more Power

Savings in time and money can be made by installing a bigger engine. But, there are problems, including proper mounting and transmission hookup.

ENGINE SWAPPING, as a means of improving car performance, got its start shortly after Ford brought out their V8 and someone discovered that one of the new engines and its transmission could be installed in a Model A Ford without too much difficulty. Present day engine swaps are considerably different from those involving flathead V8's and A-bones but the reasons for making them haven't changed a bit.

Engine swapping came into its own as an important hopping-up procedure in 1949 when Oldsmobile and Cadillac brought out their new overhead valve V8's. Compared to other engines on the market at that time the new V8's were far superior in design and torque and horsepower outputs and their displacement was so much greater that they became highly desirable to the average hot rodder. Cadillac had displacement and horsepower advantages over the Olds, and as it was approximately the same size and weight as the Olds, it became the favorite for swaps.

For some reason or another, the name Ford can't be avoided when things of this nature are being discussed. Fords for 1949 and the subsequent years through '53 were good cars that rode nicely, looked good, were comfortable, easy to drive, and not too expensive, but they had the same old flathead V8 engine that had been all-right in the 30's but was definitely underpowered for cars built in the late 40's and early 50's. By installing a '49 or later Cadillac in one of these cars it became a "Fordillac." Fordillacs were the first of the engine swaps involving overhead valve V8's in earlier chassis and they undoubtedly will go down in hot rod history as the most famous of such swaps.

The advantages of installing a large-displacement V8 in a comparatively light chassis were, and are, so numerous that after the first Fordillac hit the street it seemed ridiculous for anyone to rework a Ford or Merc flathead engine for road use. Hundreds of dollars could be spent on a flathead to stroke its crankshaft, bore its cylinders, regrind its camshaft, add carburetion, and so forth, and when the work was finished, more than likely it would run second in a drag to a Fordillac that had a stock Caddy under its hood. And when flathead was down for repairs, the

This hopped-up 1954 Cadillac Eldorado engine powers a coupe built from 1932 to 1934 Ford components.

Cadillac engine would still be running nicely.

Cadillac installations in Fords weren't exactly inexpensive by the time a fellow had bought an engine and then made or bought the necessary equipment for the conversion and made the installation but in the long run it was considerably cheaper than trying to rework a flathead for comparable performance. For the guy who liked to hear an engine turning tight, the flathead was still the best deal because the Caddy gained its performance from the torque made possible by its displacement. But if a guy really wanted to go, he could rework the engine in his Fordillac and fly low.

The performance improvement gained by installing a Cadillac or other large displacement V8 in a Ford or other car of similar size is the result of lowering the car's weight-to-horsepower ratio. Using advertised horsepower ratings, a stock '49 or '50 Ford had 30 or 31 pounds of car weight per engine horsepower, and by merely installing a '49 Cadillac engine in the car, this was dropped to 21 or 22 pounds. As far as performance was concerned, this was quite a drop,

but nowadays 21 pounds per hp is heavy compared to some of the stock high-performance cars available. However, a '58 Caddy in a '49 or '50 Ford brings the ratio down to just over 11 pounds per horsepower!

In 1958 manufacturers of the industry's Big-Three killed much of the incentive for swapping engines by installing engines of large displacement in their passenger cars. There isn't too much to gain anymore by replacing a current model Ford, Chevrolet, or Plymouth with a Cadillac, Olds, or some other make of engine. However, all hot rodders don't drive 1958 automobiles. For this reason, the art of engine swapping is still very much alive.

A fellow with the courage to dive into an engine swap job in the early '50's was truly a pioneer. Unless he was building a Fordillac he found it necessary to design and fabricate the necessary special parts for adapting the new engine to his present transmission and chassis. In some instances this wasn't too difficult to do but in others the job became quite involved. It's a different story for the fellow who wants to make

Here, a much-modified Chrysler engine is squeezed into a 1932 Ford.

an engine swap today, unless he has a really odd-ball engine and chassis combination in mind. For most swaps it is possible to buy all the special parts needed over the counter of stores that sell speed equipment. For some combinations these parts are available in kit form. Included in the special parts are flywheel housings for adapting engines of different makes to several makes of transmissions, flywheels, clutch assemblies of all types, motormount brackets ready to weld or bolt to the frame, steering linkage parts, and special adaptor plates and parts for full-flow oil filters.

An engine swap job can be divided into five basic sections. In the order in which they are attacked, these are mechanical, lubrication, cooling, fuel, and electrical.

Included in the mechanical section are all the things that must be done to fit the new engine into the car's engine compartment and connect it to the car's transmission. The first step in this part of the job is comparing the outside measurements of the engine with those of the engine com-

partment. If similar installations have been made locally by others, this part of the job won't present any difficulty because benefit can be taken of the experience of the fellows who did the other jobs. If the job involves an untried engine-chassis combination, accurate comparisons of the engine's dimensions with those of the engine compartment will be necessary. It is surprising how much V8 engines of different makes vary in their external dimensions and it is equally surprising how well even the largest of them will fit in most chassis. In rare instances it might be necessary to widen the compartment by cutting into one of the fender panels at its sides to make room for the engine's generator, and to recess the firewall slightly so the special flywheel housing used to adapt the engine to the transmission will bolt to the transmission while the transmission is in its standard position. Usually all that is required for firewall clearance is a small depression for the ignition distributor; however, it isn't impossible that a section of the firewall might have to be moved as much as two or three inches toward the rear of the car for some odd-ball installations.

If a fellow is really ambitious and wants to improve the handling of his car by changing its weight distribution at the same time he is changing its engine, he can usually move a section of the firewall a few inches into the driver's compartment so the engine and transmission assembly can be moved closer to the rear of the car. This is something that is done only rarely because it adds a lot of work to the swap job. In addition to chopping the firewall, repositioning the engine in this manner also requires that the support for the transmission be relocated and the driveshaft shortened.

For some engine swaps the radiator must be moved toward the front of the car to provide adequate fan clearance. Usually this isn't too difficult but if it can be avoided by removing a spacer of the type used between many fans and their drive pulley, this should be done. In most instances it will be found that the fewer alterations made to a car and its many components to enable a different engine to be installed, the

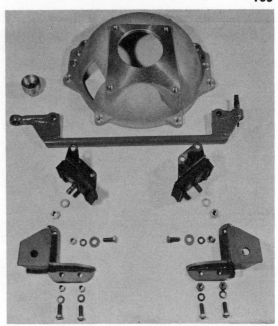

Parts required to install a Cad engine in 1949-53 Fords and 1952-53 Mercs are in this kit. Note dropped drag link below bell housing. Most speed shops have these kits.

Kit contains parts necessary to install Olds V8 in 1933-48 Fords and Mercs. Kit is complete to fuel pump cover.

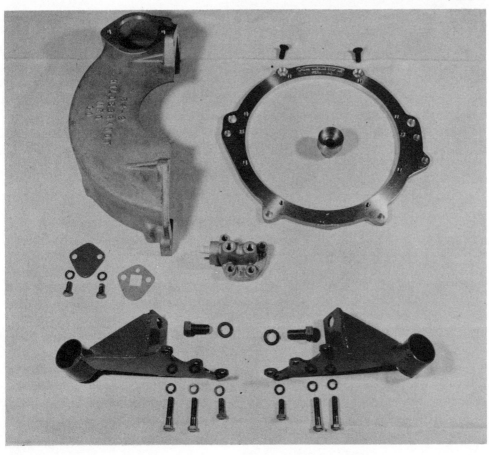

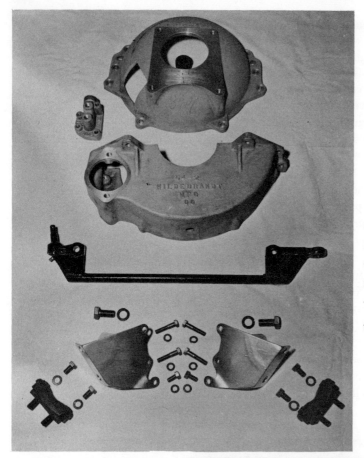

Oldsmobile V8's when installed in 1949-53 Fords require that the starter be transposed from the left to the right side to avoid interference with the steering gear. This and other essentials are provided for in this complete kit.

Typical of several kits is this one which joins an Oldsmobile engine with a 1949-51 Mercury, or a Cadillac engine with a 1933-48 Ford and 1939-51 Mercury. Neither starter switch-over plate or dropped drag link are necessary in these combinations.

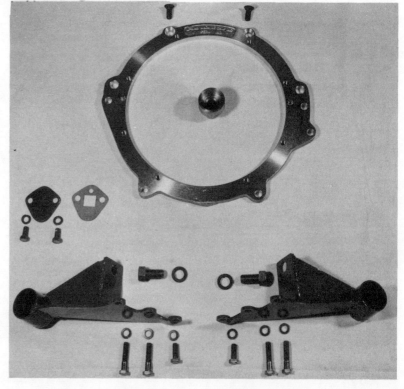

greater are the chances of the swap's being a success. Nothing can louse up an engine swap more thoroughly than two or three things done incorrectly, or left undone, so that something about the engine or the chassis doesn't function as it should. In this day and age a fellow can't have any excuse when a car with a larger, different make of engine under its hood doesn't drive as nicely as it did when it was stock, and perform much better.

When engine compartment measurements are being taken it may be found that the battery is smack in the way of one of the engine's accessories. The only correction for this is to move the battery to another location where the space isn't so valuable. This can be in some less crowded part of the engine compartment or in the car's luggage compartment. Automobile manufacturers put batteries in engine compartments to make them more accessible for servicing and also to make it unnecessary to use long cables between them and the engine.

There isn't anything wrong with placing the battery in the luggage compartment if the cross-sectional area of the cable between it and the starting motor control is compatible with the cable's length. Electrical resistance in a battery cable goes up as the cable's length increases and full battery voltage will not be delivered to the starting motor and the rest of the car's electrical components if the resistance of the cable is too high. The grounded terminal of the battery could be connected to the car's frame.

The point on a frame to which a ground cable is to be connected should be scraped or sanded until it is clean and bright so a good connection will be made between it and the cable. In some installations it has been found advisable to clean the frame and then apply a coating of soft solder to it. It is important that the solder have a good bond with the frame material. Then, after the solder has cooled, the cable is bolted to the frame so its terminal rests on the solder. This guarantees a good electrical connection between the cable and the frame.

When a battery carried in any location in a car is grounded to the car's frame, one end of a suitable ground strap must be bolted to a clean spot on the engine and the other end of the strap must be connected to the frame as explained for the battery ground strap. This will complete the electrical circuit between the frame and the engine. Another strap should be installed between the engine or frame and the car's body so that electrical circuits in the body will receive full battery voltage. Without these ground straps, flow of current from the engine and the body to the battery could be resisted by rubber and fabric engine and body mounts.

In most engine swaps it will be found that some part of the engine's oil pan or its starting motor will interfere with the chassis' steering linkage. When this happens it is far more satisfactory to make changes to the engine rather than to the steering linkage to gain the necessary clearance; however, sometimes the required changes can't be made to the engine and it becomes necessary to alter the linkage.

Steering linkage interference caused by the engine's pan can be the result of the location of the pan's sump or the pan's width. Sump problems for some engines can be corrected in a number of ways but for others the location of the oil pump makes it impossible to alter the sump. When a sump's position isn't dictated by the location of the pump, it is usually possible to shorten the pump's pickup tube to move the pickup and screen assembly as necessary to enable the sump to be altered. Sump changes are made easy for some engines by the availability of pans made for different models of the same engine, or for different chassis installations, that have sumps of a different shape or in different positions on the pan. Before making major alterations to a pan it might be wise to check with the local dealer that handles the make of engine being used to

In addition to the fuel tank, the battery, fuel pump and horn have been mounted in bed of this hot rod pickup to leave more space for the engine under hood up front.

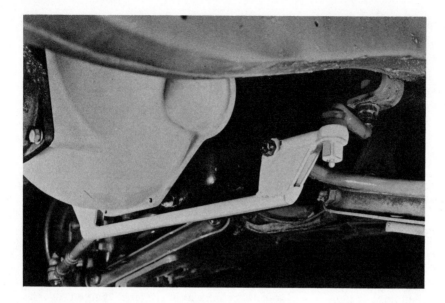

Dropped drag links are necessary in many installations to avoid interference with the pan oil sump.

determine whether a more suitable pan for the installation is available. When a pan's width causes interference with steering linkage parts it is often possible to heat the pan in the interference areas and pound recesses in it to provide the necessary clearance.

After alterations of any type have been made to a pan, the capacity of its sump must be restored to what it was originally by welding a compartment of suitable size to the side of the sump at some point where it won't cause interference with the steering linkage. The bottom of the compartment should be level with the bottom of the sump and oil flow between the compartment and the sump must be unrestricted.

A bad feature of some engines used for swaps is the location of their starting motor at the lower left side of their flywheel housing. This usually places the starter in a bad position in relation to the steering linkage of the chassis in which an engine of this type is being installed. Special housings are available for Oldsmobile engines, some Chryslers, and another make or two that enable the starting motor to be moved to the right side of the engine where it is out of the way of the steering linkage. Installation of a housing of this type is by far the easiest method of eliminating the starting motor problem.

Three general types of steering linkage are in use in cars that might be involved in an engine

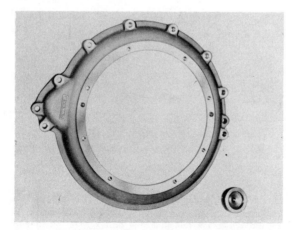

This is an engine housing adaptor to hook up a 1953-56 Buick powerplant to an early 1932-48 Ford transmission.

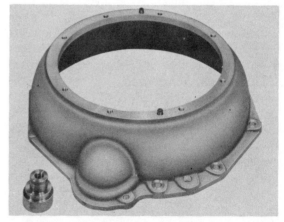

An extra deep housing adaptor is required to couple late-model Cad engines to early Ford or Merc transmissions.

swap. These include the linkage for solid axles that has a drag link parallel to the frame rails and a tie rod that connects the steering arms on the front wheels. This type of linkage is still used in many pickup trucks. Another is the so-called "cross steering" used in 1935 through 1948 Fords and many Mercurys. With this steering system the tie rod connects the steering gear on the left frame rail with the steering arm on the right wheel. A conventional tie rod then connects the right and left wheels. The third type is the late style that consists of a nearly horizontal pitman arm on the left side of the chassis and an idler arm on the right side of the chassis that is parallel to the pitman arm. The pitman arm and the idler arm are connected with a tie rod to which are connected short rods that run out to the steering arms. Linkage of this type usually causes the most headaches because as a rule it is quite far back in the chassis, in the area occupied by the oil pan sump on many of the favorite engines for swapping.

With conventional drag link steering in cars with solid front axles the point of interference between an engine and the steering mechanism is usually between some part of the left side of the engine and the steering gear itself or the gear's column. Usually the best solution to this condition is to move the steering gear away from the engine by altering the frame rail. This is done by fabricating a sturdy steel box of suitable dimensions and welding it to the outside of the frame so the steering gear can be bolted to the box in-

stead of to the frame. The frame rail must be cut so the steering gear can be moved to the left and it must be adequately reinforced so it will be as stiff as it was originally.

Interference experienced with cross steering systems is usually similar to that of solid axle steering plus the possibility that the tie rod might hit the engine's pan. Steering gears for cross steering linkage can usually be moved in the same manner described for gears for conventional drag link steering. Clearance for the tie rod should be provided by altering the oil pan but if this can't be done it may be necessary to bend the tie rod. When a tie rod must be bent it is generally advantageous to find one made of heavier material, such as a rod for a truck, or to make one from stronger material. The reason for using a stronger rod is that after a stock rod has been bent it will become springy in its bent areas. By using a stronger rod the springiness will be reduced, or eliminated altogether.

The accepted method of altering late model steering linkage is to "drop" the center section of the tie rod between the pitman arm and the idler arm so it will go around the pan's oil sump. This is done by making a new U-shaped center section for the rod from strong material and welding its ends to a standard tie rod. Reinforcing gussets are then welded in the corners between the new section and the ends of the tie rod. The center section of the tie rod is then removed by cutting it near the welds with a hacksaw. Tie rods altered in this manner are entirely satisfactory if the material used for the dropped section is strong enough and the welding is done by a competent welder. They provide the necessary pan clearance without the need for bending steering arms and otherwise rehashing the linkage. Changes of any type to the steering arms should be avoided because their strength is a critical factor and they determine the geometry of the linkage.

It is of utmost importance that alterations made to any part of a car's steering linkage to provide clearance for an engine be done correctly to ensure that the strength of the linkage won't be affected and that the correct steering geometry will be maintained. Weakened linkage can be extremely dangerous, as it might possibly break while the car was being driven, and incorrect

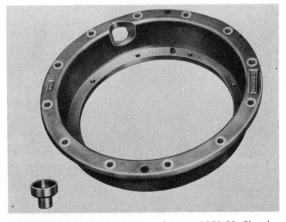

With this powerplant housing adaptor, 1951-53 Chrysler V8 engines can be aligned with early Ford transmissions.

AVAILABLE ENGINE TO

ENGINE	YEAR	TRANSMISSION	FLYWHEEL USED	CLUTCH PRESSURE PLATE
Buick	53-57 OHV V8's	Ford 32-48, Merc 39-50 Lincoln Zephyr and Continental 37-48	Stock Buick	Ford truck 11 inch
Cadillac	49-54 OHV V8's	Ford 32-48, Merc 39-50 Lincoln Zephyr and Continental 37-48	Stock Cad or Olds	Ford truck 11 inch
Cadillac	55-57 OHV V8's	Ford 32-48, Merc 39-50 Lincoln Zephyr and Continental 37-48	Stock 49-54 Cad or 55-57 Olds	Ford truck 11 inch
Chevrolet	All 6's	Ford 32-48, Merc 39-50 Lincoln Zephyr and Continental 37-48	Stock Chev	Ford 10 inch
Chevrolet	55-57 OHV V8's	Ford 32-48, Merc 39-50 Lincoln Zephyr and Continental 37-48	Stock Chev	49-50 Merc Borg & Beck
Chrysler	51-53 OHV V8's	Ford 32-48, Merc 39-50 Lincoln Zephyr and Continental 37-48	Dodge V8 pickup	Dodge truck 11 inch or Ford
Chrysler	54-57 OHV V8's	Ford 32-48, Merc 39-50 Lincoln Zephyr and Continental 37-48	Dodge V8 pickup	Dodge truck 11 inch or Ford truck
DeSoto	52-57 OHV V8's	Ford 32-48, Merc 39-50 Lincoln Zephyr and Continental 37-48	Dodge V8 pickup	Dodge truck 11 inch or Ford truck
Dodge	53-57 OHV V8's	Ford 32-48, Merc 39-50 Lincoln Zephyr and Continental 37-48	Dodge V8 pickup	Dodge truck 11 inch or Ford truck
Ford and Mercury	54-57 OHV V8's	Ford 32-48, Merc 39-50 Lincoln Zephyr and Continental 37-48	Stock Ford	Stock late Ford
GMC	All 6's	Ford 32-48, Merc 39-50 Lincoln Zephyr and Continental 37-48	Stock GMC	Ford 10 inch
Hudson	All OHV V8's	Ford 32-48, Merc 39-50 Lincoln Zephyr and Continental 37-48	Stock Hudson	Ford 10 inch
Lincoln—Ford truck F-8	All flathead V8's	Ford 32-48, Merc 39-50 Lincoln Zephyr and Continental 37-48	Stock Ford	Stock Ford truck
Lincoln	52-57 OHV V8's	Ford 32-48, Merc 39-50 Lincoln Zephyr and Continental 37-48	Stock Lincoln	Stock Ford or Lincoln
Mercury (and Fords)	49-53 flat-head V8's	Ford 32-48, Merc 39-50 Lincoln Zephyr and Continental 37-48	Stock Merc or Ford	Stock
Nash	All OHV V8's	Ford 32-48, Merc 39-50 Lincoln Zephyr and Continental 37-48	Stock Nash	Ford 10 inch
Oldsmobile	All OHV V8's	Ford 32-48, Merc 39-50 Lincoln Zephyr and Continental 37-48	Stock Olds	Ford truck 11 inch
Packard	All OHV V8's	Ford 32-48, Merc 39-50 Lincoln Zephyr and Continental 37-48	Stock Packard	Ford 10 inch
Plymouth	55-57 OHV V8's	Ford 32-48, Merc 39-50 Lincoln Zephyr and Continental 37-48	Dodge V8 truck	Dodge truck 11 inch or Ford truck
Pontiac	55-57 OHV V8's	Ford 32-48, Merc 39-50 Lincoln Zephyr and Continental 37-48	Stock Pontiac	49-50 Merc Bord & Beck
Studebaker	All OHV V8's except '56 Golden Hawk which is same as Packard	Ford 32-48, Merc 39-50 Lincoln Zephyr and Continental 37-48	Stock Stude	Ford 9 inch or special
Buick	All OHV V8's	Ford 49-57 Mercury 51-57	Stock Buick	Ford truck 11 inch
Cadillac	49-54 OHV V8's	Ford 49-57 Mercury 51-57	Stock Cad or pre-54 Olds	Ford truck 11 inch
Cadillac	55-57 OHV V8's	Ford 49-57 Mercury 51-57	Stock 55-57 Olds	Ford truck 11 inch or T-bird
Chevrolet	55-57 OHV V8's	Ford 49-57 Mercury 49-57	Stock	49-50 Merc Borg & Beck
Chrysler	51-53 OHV V8's	Ford 49-57 Mercury 51-57	Stock or Dodge V8 truck	Ford truck 11 inch or Dodge truck 11 inch
Chrysler	54-57 OHV V8's	Ford 49-57 Mercury 51-57	Stock or Dodge V8 truck	Ford truck 11 inch or Chrysler products 11 inch
DeSoto	52-57 OHV V8's	Ford 49-57 Mercury 51-57	Stock or Dodge V8 truck	Ford truck 11 inch or Chrysler products 11 inch
Dodge	53-57 OHV V8's	Ford 49-57 Mercury 51-57	Stock or Dodge V8 truck	Ford truck 11 inch or Chrysler products 11 inch
Lincoln	All OHV V8's	Ford 49-57 Mercury 51-57	Stock Lincoln	Stock
Oldsmobile	All OHV V8's	Ford 49-57 Mercury 51-57	Stock Olds of year to match engine	Olds 11 inch or Ford pickup 11 inch
Plymouth	55-57 OHV V8's	Ford 49-57 Mercury 51-57	Stock or Dodge V8 truck	Ford truck 11 inch or Chrysler products 11 inch
Cad & Olds	OVH V8's 49-54 Cad 49-57 Olds	Chev 37-54 standard shift transmission	Stock Cad or Olds	Stock
Cadillac	55-57 OHV V8's	Cad 51-53 standard shift transmission	Stock Cad	Stock Cad or Olds
Chrysler	51-53 OHV V8's	37-50 Cad or LaSalle std. shift transmission	Dodge V8 truck	Chrysler products 11 inch or Olds
Chrysler	54-57 OHV V8's	37-50 Cad or LaSalle std. shift transmission	Dodge V8 truck	Optional
Chrysler	51-53 OHV V8's	Cad or Olds Hydra-Matic transmission	Cad or Olds Hydro	None
Cad & Olds	OHV V8's 49-54 Cad; 49-57 Olds	Stude 53-54 automatic transmission	Cad or Olds Hydro flywheel	None
Cad & Olds	OHV V8's 49-54 Cad; 49-57 Olds	Stude 53-57 Commander std. shift transmission	Stock Cad or Olds	Cad or Olds
Cad & Olds	OHV V8's 49-54 Cad; 49-57 Olds	Early Cad or LaSalle	Stock Cad or Olds	Stock
Chrysler products	OHV V8's 54-57 Chry; 52-57 DeSoto; 53-57 Dodge; 55-57 Plym.	Cad or Olds Hydra-Matic	Cad or Olds Hydro flywheel	None
Chev V8	55-57 OHV V8's	Cad or LaSalle trans	Chev	Special

CHART COMPILED BY DEAN MOON

TRANSMISSION ADAPTORS

CLUTCH DISC	SPECIAL COMMENT	APPROXIMATE CURRENT PRICES	MANUFACTURER
Ford truck 11 inch	Re-drill Buick V8 flywheel to accept Ford clutch assembly	$55 to $65	1-2-4-6-7
Ford truck 11 inch	Steering must be moved outboard or additional adaptor used to switch starter to right side	$32 to $35	1-2-3-4-5-6-7
Ford truck 11 inch	Use 55-57 starter with Olds flywheel. Must use 49-54 Cad starter to match early flywheel. Some clutch hub discs require machining	$64.50	1-2-3-5-6-7
Ford 10 inch	In most cases, engine must be set back to clear radiator	$38 to $48	4-6
Ford 10 inch	Some steel plate adaptors are used in conjunction with Ford 8RT6392 bell housing	$42.50 to $59	1-2-4-5-6-7
Ford 11 inch truck	Slight grinding modification to Chrysler engine bell housing to clear Ford throw-out arm	$53 to $56	2-3-4-6-7
Ford 11 inch truck	Some adaptors move starter to right of engine for steering gear clearance	$57 to $74.50	2-4-5-6-7
Ford 11 inch truck	Some adaptors move starter to right of engine for steering gear clearance	$57 to $74.50	2-4-5-6-7
Optional Ford 11 inch truck	Some adaptors move starter to right of engine for steering gear clearance	$57 to $74.50	2-4-5-6-7
Ford, with right diameter and spline size	Pickup truck or T-bird pan, oil pump are needed in most installations for tie rod clearance	$59.50	1-2-4-5-6-7
Ford 10 inch	Same as Chev 6	$38	4-6
Ford 10 inch	Re-drill flywheel to accept Ford clutch assembly	$35	1
Stock Ford truck	Due to physical dimensions, extensive alterations are needed in early chassis	$52 to $55.25	3-4-6
Stock Ford or Lincoln	F8 truck pan, oil pump must be used for tie rod clearance	$52 to $55.25	3-4-6
Stock	No special adaptor needed. Use stock Ford housing 8RT6392. Installation requires pickup water pumps	$16.25	Ford part 8RT6392
Ford 10 inch	Re-drill flywheel to accept Ford pressure plate and disc	$35	1
Ford truck 11 inch	Use special adaptor available for moving starter to right side for steering clearance	$32 to $35	1-2-3-4-5-6-7
Ford 10 inch	Re-drill flywheel to accept Ford pressure plate	$35	1
Ford 11 inch	Some adaptors move starter to right of engine for steering clearance	$74.50	2-4-5-6-7
49-50 Merc Borg & Beck	Some adaptors use a steel plate in conjunction with stock Pontiac housing	$42.50	1-4-5
Ford 9 inch or special	Stu-V makes 10 inch clutch assembly. Use standard shift starter drive housing. '56 Golden Hawk uses Packard adaptor	$48 to $55	1-4-6
36-38 Chrysler products taxi disc. Borg-Warner #710	Use 52-54 Ford clutch linkage. Re-drill stock flywheel to use Ford pressure plate. Machine 3/32 inch off disc hub on flywheel side	$65	2-4-6-7
36-38 Chrysler products taxi disc. Borg-Warner #710	Machine 3/32 inch off disc hub on flywheel side. Use 49-53 Cad starter. Use 52-54 Ford clutch linkage	$53.50	1-2-3-4-5-6-7
T-bird	Use 52-54 Ford clutch linkage. Use 55-57 Cad starter	$77.75	1-2-3-6-7
Ford or Merc	Some adaptors are used in conjunction with stock Ford or Merc housing	$42.50	1-6
36-38 Chrysler products taxi disc. Borg-Warner #710	Starter motor remains on left side of engine with stock bell housing lower half. Housing must be notched for throw-out arm	$53.50 to $68.50	3-4
36-38 Chrysler products taxi disc. Borg-Warner #710	Use 52-54 Ford clutch linkage. Two-piece adaptors move starter to right for steering clearance	$75 to $81.75	2-4-6-7
36-38 Chrysler products taxi disc. Borg-Warner #710	Use 52-54 Ford clutch linkage. Two-piece adaptors move starter to right for steering clearance	$75 to $81.75	2-4-6-7
36-38 Chrysler products taxi disc. Borg-Warner #710	Use 52-54 Ford clutch linkage. Two-piece adaptors move starter to right for steering clearance	$75 to $81.75	2-4-6-7
Ford	Requires pan alterations for changes in most chassis or use F8 truck pan and oil pump	$69	3-4-6
Late Ford or Merc 11 inch, proper spline	Adaptor available for changing starter motor to right for steering clearance	$53.50	1-2-3-4-5-6
36-38 Chrysler products taxi disc. Borg-Warner #710	Use 52-54 Ford clutch linkage. Some adaptors move starter to right side for steering clearance	$75 to $81.85	2-4-6-7
Stock	Starter switch over adaptor available for Olds engines to give steering clearance. Places starter on right side of engine	$68 to $75	1-4
Stock Cad or Olds	Instructions with adaptor	$55	4
Olds 11 inch	Instructions with adaptor	$60 to $75	4-8
Optional	Two adaptors used. Chrysler to early Ford—Ford to LaSalle	$95 to $100	1-4
None	Adaptation requires some machine work to make Chrysler starter fit H-M flywheel	$69.50	2
None	Instructions with adaptor	$70	3
Stude truck 1½ ton	Instructions with adaptor	$70	3
Stock	Use stock bell housing. Uses stock Olds clutch release linkage kit, $12	$20	Olds part 558701 Cad part 1454141
None	Use '55 Cad bell housing number 1461477 with adaptor. H-M pilot shaft must be shortened as per instructions	$69.50	2
Borg & Beck	Adaptor spacer fits between Chev bell housing and Cad transmission	$25	4-8

ADAPTOR MANUFACTURERS: 1—Hildebrandt, 2—Cragar, 3—McBar, 4—Cook, 5—Wil-Cap, 6—Weber, 7—Harman & Collins, 8—Howard geometry can lead to all sorts of handling and tire wear problems.

Bolting the engine to the transmission is the simplest part of the job if the swap is one of those for which a special flywheel housing is available. After the housing has been bolted to the engine, the transmission is bolted to the housing, just as though stock parts were being used. For some installations it is necessary to bolt the housing to the transmission first and then the housing to the engine. If the installation is not one for which a special flywheel housing is available, a special housing or adaptor plate will have to be made. This can take a lot of time and effort but, fortunately, it is seldom necessary now.

Included with most special flywheel housings is an adaptor for fitting a pilot bearing or bushing of the correct type for the transmission to be used to the engine's crankshaft. These adaptors are made to fit in the original pilot bearing bore in the end of the shaft. If the shaft is fitted with a bushing or bearing, it will have to be removed so the adaptor can be installed. A slight problem might be experienced fitting the adaptor to crankshafts in some engines that are supposed to be fitted with an automatic transmission. This problem arises from the fact that the pilot bearing bore in these shafts wasn't enlarged to its finished diameter because it wasn't to be fitted with a pilot bearing. When undersize bores of this type are encountered, the easiest method of installing an adaptor is by turning the outer diameter of the portion of the adaptor that must be inserted in the crankshaft to a smaller diameter so it will fit in the bore. Care must be taken to not reduce the diameter too much because it must be a press fit in the crankshaft. If the adaptor should become loose in the shaft after the car had been driven for a while, it would allow the front end of the clutch shaft to move out of its normal plane and more than likely the gears in the transmission would be damaged.

Most engines used for swaps are equipped with a flywheel made for an automatic transmission. When such an engine is to be used with a stick-shift transmission its flywheel must be replaced with one designed for a clutch. Stock flywheels are available for all the more popular engines used for swap jobs. Also available for most of these engines are special aluminum alloy flywheels for the fellow who thinks he needs a light wheel. Aluminum wheels are considerably more expensive than stock types and generally not as durable.

Most special flywheels are designed for stock or Ford 11-inch clutch pressure plate assemblies. It is advisable to use a clutch with a large friction area so it will be able to transmit the high torque output of the new engine. When a pressure plate assembly different from that normally used on the flywheel is installed, it is necessary to drill new pressure plate mounting holes in the flywheel. This must be done accurately so the pressure plate will be concentric with the flywheel. Balance of the pressure plate and flywheel should be checked as an assembly and corrected as needed after the drilling has been done. The total pressure of the springs in a pressure plate assembly to be used for normal driving need not be as high as the pressure required for competition use. Too much pressure can raise the effort required on the clutch pedal to disengage the clutch to the point where driving becomes uncomfortable in heavy traffic.

Clutch discs must match their pressure plate in diameter and they must have a hub that has an opening of the correct diameter and with the proper number of splines to match the clutch shaft of the transmission to be used. Diameters of clutch shafts and the number of splines on them are standardized by the SAE. This often makes it possible to use a disc made originally for one make of car on the transmission of one or more other makes. In some instances it might be necessary to take a light cut from the ends of the hub so the hub won't interfere with the flywheel or the unsplined portion of the transmission's clutch shaft. When any special work is required for clutch throwout linkage installation, instructions are usually supplied with the flywheel housing for this part of the job.

Many types of special clutches for engines to be used for competition are available. These include pressure plate assemblies that have been reworked with stiffer springs, or that have additional springs to increase the pressure of the pressure plate on the disc; special discs with faces that are either bonded or bonded and riveted to the disc; and special double-disc clutches.

There isn't anything complicated about pressure plate assemblies that have beefed-up spring tension but it is advisable when an assembly of this type is used that it be bolted to a flywheel that hasn't been chopped excessively. The high pressure of the pressure plate housing pushing and pulling on a flywheel's rim when shifts are made can cause the flywheel to break. When this happens at high engine speeds the flywheel practically explodes. This occurs quite frequently in drag racing cars.

Bonded or bonded and riveted clutch discs are much stronger assemblies than stock discs, making them desirable for cars used strictly for drag racing or othed types of competition. The term "bonded" means that the friction facings have been cemented, or glued, to the steel surface of the clutch disc. This is a common method of attaching lining to brake shoes, eliminating the need for rivets. Bonding requires the use of a special cement and the application of heat to the friction facings and disc while they are clamped tightly together. The heat is applied by placing the members in a special oven for the required length of time.

On a clutch disc bonding offers the benefit of full-surface attachment of the friction plates to the disc instead of just at the rivets, as on a stock plate. This is a definite advantage as far as the strength of the assembly is concerned because it isn't uncommon for plates used with competition engines to tear loose from the disc in the areas between the rivets. Some disc assemblies are made doubly strong by both bonding and riveting the friction plates to the disc.

Bonded discs aren't good in a car used for normal driving because of the rough clutch action that results from their use. The reason for the rough action is that before the friction facings can be bonded to the discs, the flat steel springs used on stock discs to hold the facings away from the disc a slight amount must be removed. These springs are between the friction plates and the disc and their purpose is to provide a small amount of flexibility between the members of the assembly to enable the disc to take up as smoothly as possible the load it must transmit from the flywheel to the transmission. Without the springs there is a tendency for the clutch to chatter. In a competition car clutch chatter is a matter of small concern but in a car driven on the street most of the time it can become annoying. Chatter can also cause excessive wear in the transmission, universal joints, and the rear axle assembly.

Double-disc clutches are comparatively new to the hot rod field and they provide a definite improvement in dragsters and other cars in which the clutch is often overloaded. They consist of two driven discs that have high-quality friction facings (sometimes metallic facings), a special drive disc that is installed between the driven discs, and a pressure plate assembly that has a high total spring pressure. Special spacers that screw into the pressure plate mounting holes in the flywheel and which support the extra drive discs are supplied in the kits. The capscrews that normally secure the pressure plate assembly to the

These front motor mounts adapt an Olds V8 to a 1933-48 Ford chassis. Note strong construction to maintain rigidity.

These motor mounts will hold a late-model Cad V8 in 1949-53 Fords. Note mount holes line with frame holes.

flywheel screw into the outer ends of the spacers. A clutch of this type has double the friction area of a single-plate clutch, enabling it to transmit higher torque loads from the engine to the transmission.

After bolting the engine to the transmission, the front of the engine must be positioned vertically in relation to the frame so a determination can be made of what will be needed for front motormount supports. For many swaps this part of the job can be eliminated by buying a set of ready-made supports. Supports of this type are ready to be welded or bolted to the frame or one of its crossmembers and they are of the correct height.

If ready-made supports aren't available for a particular installation, the correct position for the engine in relation to the rails can be determined by loading the front of the car with enough weight to drop it to its original height. The front end of the engine is then raised or lowered as needed until the carburetor mounting flange on the intake manifold is level. This can be determined by removing the carburetor from the manifold and placing a small level on the flange so it is parallel to the engine's crankshaft. It is important that the chassis be at its correct height when the engine level is determined so that the carburetor flange on the manifold will be level when the weight of the engine, radiator, battery, hood, and other parts that were removed for the engine swap are in place on the car. It is more than likely that the front end of the car will be lower with the new engine than it was with its original engine but for best results it must be raised to its stock position by one or more of the methods that will be described later.

After the height of the engine in relation to the frame has been determined, measurements can be taken and suitable supports can be fabricated from pieces $3/16$ or $1/4$-inch flat steel plate. The supports can be made so they can be either welded or bolted to the frame. Welding is the quicker of the two methods but if it is planned to reinstall the stock engine in the car at a later date for resale purposes it is better to bolt the supports in place.

An engine to be used in a car fitted with a torque tube drive should be lined up so its crankshaft is centered in the frame in line with the driveshaft. If the engine is to be used with a Hotchkiss drive (open driveshaft) the engine can be moved sideways as much as an inch or an inch and a half to provide clearance for the steering gear or some other chassis part. It is also acceptable to set the engine at a slight angle in the frame in relation to the frame's centerline. When either of these things is done it is necessary to reposition the rear motormount, which is usually under the transmission, so it will not be in a bind.

Motormount insulators used between the engine and the supports on the frame should be of the type made for the engine. Sizes and qualities of motormount insulators vary for different engines and as their primary purpose is to suppress vibration, it is wise to use the correct ones.

Although stick-shift transmissions of the type that are standard in the chassis are generally used when an engine swap is made, it is becoming more popular now that automatic transmissions are so much more efficient than earlier types to use an automatic transmission instead. If an automatic transmission designed for the engine is being used, there won't be any difficulty connecting it to the engine. If the engine and transmission aren't made for each other, an adaptor housing will have to be provided to fit the transmission to the engine and the transmission's torque convertor or hydraulic coupling will have to be adapted to the engine's crankshaft. Parts for such conversions that adapt Oldsmobile or Cadillac Hydramatic transmissions and hydraulic couplings to many Chrysler engines are available.

After the engine and transmission have been joined together and lowered into the chassis it will probably be found that the stock rear motormount will have to be reworked to match the motormount pad on the transmission. If the transmission doesn't have a mounting pad, one that can be bolted to the transmission housing will have to be made.

Fitting the chassis' driveshaft to the automatic transmission may require a little ingenuity. Quite often standard parts that can be used for this purpose can be found by making inquiries at shops that specialize in automatic transmission repair work. This possibility is due to the variations in transmissions of the same make used in different makes of cars. Universal joint parts are often interchangeable between cars. One ex-

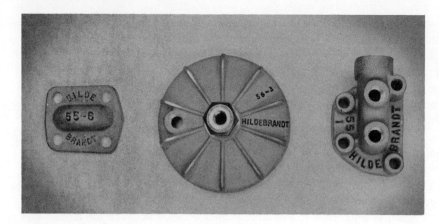

When late-model engines are adapted to early chassis, the full-flow oil filter may be in the way. These blockoffs (left to right) for Chrysler, Ford and Oldsmobile permit removal or relocation.

ample of this is that the front yoke of a universal joint that fits the output shaft of an Oldsmobile Hydramatic transmission matches the front universal joint of many '49 and later Ford driveshafts. There are many similar combinations. More than likely the length of the driveshaft will have to be changed for the new transmission. Many machine shops will do this.

Other transmissions that have become popular lately for engine swaps and for installation in cars fitted with their standard engines to be used for drag racing are early Cad and LaSalle stickshift boxes.

The last of the operations in the mechanical section is hooking up the exhaust system. The car must have a dual system if the new engine is to run as freely as it should and it would be wise to install a set of straight-through glass-packed mufflers. The mufflers should be long enough to quiet the engine so it can be driven around town without attracting the attention of police officers. New head pipes to connect the exhaust manifolds on headers to the mufflers must be made to suit the installation. The inside diameter of these pipes must be as large as that of pipes used in the exhaust system that would be connected to the engine if it were installed in the chassis for which it was built. Center pipes in the mufflers must be of adaquate diameter for the head pipes and in some instances it will be necessary to install larger tail pipes on the mufflers. At this point it would be foolish to restrict the engine's performance by hooking an inadequate exhaust system to it. As installing and modifying exhaust systems is a specialized sort of work; the average

fellow would be time and money ahead to have the exhaust system work done by the local muffler shop.

Section two in an engine swap job is concerned with the engine's lubrication system. Most modern V8's are fitted with a full-flow oil filter but quite often an engine can't be fitted into another chassis with its filter in the standard position. This means that the filter must be moved. Special adaptor plates for this purpose that bolt to the cylinder block in place of the filter are available for many engines. By using a plate of this type the filter can be moved to another part of the engine compartment. Neoprene hoses that have an inside diameter of not less than $\frac{1}{2}$-inch are then used to connect the filter to the engine.

When a filter must be moved in this manner it is a good idea to use the stock filter if possible, but if the stock filter can't be used, it can be replaced with one of a different type. This can be a filter made for a different engine or one of the universal full-flow filters made by Fram or one of the other filter manufacturers.

A full-flow oil filter is the best guarantee one can get for long engine life and when an engine is made to accommodate one of them it should be used. By-pass filters so popular before full-flow types become stock equipment filter such a small quantity of oil that they are practically valueless to an engine. A fellow might be tempted to leave a full-flow filter off his engine or to replace it with a by-pass type but neither of these makeshift methods should be considered.

Installation of an oil pressure indicator will be simplified if the gauge on the car's instrument panel has an adequate pressure range for the engine and the sending unit that was in the car's original engine can be adapted to the new engine. An engine sending unit of practically any type can be adapted to any engine by one means or another. If the threaded opening in the block is larger than the threaded portion of the sending unit, a threaded bushing can be used between the two members. If the opening in the block is smaller than the threaded portion of the sending unit or there isn't room near the opening for the unit, pipe fittings of the correct length and type can be used between the block and the unit. In extreme cases a satisfactory installation can be made by making a bracket that can be attached to the firewall to support the sending unit and then running a flexible neoprene hose with the correct fittings from the unit to the engine.

A special gauge can be installed if it isn't desirable to use the stock unit. This is easily done by mounting the gauge on the car's instrument panel and installing its sending unit in the engine with parts supplied with it. Gauges of this type can be either mechanical or electrical. If a mechanical gauge is used it is important that a flexible hose be installed between the engine and the body, or the hose can be run all the way to the gauge, so that movement of the engine in relation to the body will not eventually crack or break the line.

Section three is concerned with the cooling system. This deals with the radiator, heat indicator, and heater connections.

Most radiators in chassis involved in engine swap jobs have more than ample capacity to cool the new engine. The reason for this is that most of these chassis originally had flathead engines and flathead engines generally require greater radiator capacity than an overhead valve engine of considerably greater displacement.

It is seldom that the radiator has an inlet and outlet of the correct diameter and in the positions required by the new engine. Fittings of the wrong size can often be used by making reducers from steel tubing that can be installed between them and the radiator hoses. When this is done and the radiator has two inlets and two outlets and only one of each is needed for the new engine, the extra fittings can be plugged by installing short lengths of radiator hose of the correct size fitted with plugs fabricated from steel tubing.

The neatest appearing radiator installation is made when the radiator has the correct fittings for the engine. Fittings for this purpose can be installed in the radiator's tanks by any radiator repair man. At the same time the fittings are being installed, the radiator can be cleaned and checked for leaks, guaranteeing it will be in good condition and ready to give good service. The charge for alterations of this type and cleaning aren't so high that they shouldn't be considered.

Suitable flexible hoses of the many makes now available should be used between the engine and the radiator. These hoses adapt themselves to different fitting angularities and they reduce much of the strain normal engine movement exerts on a radiator's fittings. Radiator hoses that are too stiff for an installation can eventually crack the joints between radiator fittings and the radiator's tanks.

In most swaps it is possible to adapt the heat indicator sending unit from the original engine to the new engine. This simplifies the heat indicator problem. For swaps where this isn't possible, a special heat indicator can be used. Indicators of this type are made in both electrical and mechanical types. Either of them is easy to install.

Connecting the car's heater to the engine's cooling system is a simple matter of installing fittings of the correct size in the engine and then connecting these fittings with those on the heater with lengths of hose. Care must be taken to connect the fittings in the proper combinations so water flow through the heater will be in the correct direction.

Section four has to do with connecting the fuel line from the car's tank to the fuel pump on the new engine. Before this is done, the entire length of the fuel line on the car should be checked for damage. A line that is kinked, cracked, or otherwise damaged may not allow sufficient fuel to flow to the new engine. Damaged lines should be replaced or repaired.

The line from the tank can be extended as needed to within a few inches of the fuel pump by connecting a length of copper or steel tubing to it. Tubing used for this purpose should be of the same size as that in the car's fuel line. A regular flexible fuel hose or an eight or ten-inch length of neoprene hose is then installed between the end of the extended line and the fuel pump. If neoprene hose is used for this purpose its inside diameter should be the same as the outside diameter of the tubing. Its ends can be slipped over the end of the fuel line and the end of a short length of tubing that is connected to the fuel pump with suitable fittings. The hose is secured to the tubing with clamps. Clamps to hold the extended part of the fuel line to the frame should be installed every twelve inches or so along its length. This will prevent the tubing from vibrating and eventually breaking.

Copper and steel tubing are sometimes hard to work with for an installation of this type. A solution that can make the job much easier is to install neoprene hose between the fuel pump and the end of the fuel line, regardless of the gap that must be filled. Neoprene line is entirely satisfactory for such installations; however, it is wise to cover it with electrician's loom of the correct size to protect it from exterior damage. The hose must be clamped to the frame at several points along its length so it will be kept from vibrating and be held out of the way of any moving parts that might damage it.

Section five deals with what can be one of the more difficult parts of an engine swap job. This is the electrical system.

When an engine that has a six-volt electrical system is installed in a six-volt chassis, or a twelve-volt engine is installed in a twelve-volt chassis, the electrical system doesn't present any problems. But when a twelve-volt engine is installed in a six-volt chassis, many problems present themselves. The main problem is simply one of having a twelve-volt starter, generator, and ignition system and six-volt lights, radio, heater, gauges, etc. It isn't any trouble to install a twelve-volt battery in place of the six-volt unit but to change all the other components of the car's electrical system to twelve-volts is usually out of the question financially. The fact that this would be the ideal thing to do doesn't make it any less expensive.

The second best answer to the problem would be to convert the engine to six-volt operation. This would require changing the engine's starter, generator, and ignition coil. It's possible to adapt earlier model six-volt starters to many twelve-volt engines but if this move is contemplated it is wise to explore the possibilities before the

engine is installed in the chassis. The reason for this is that sometimes a six-volt starter will require a different flywheel than the one that is on the engine. If this is found to be the case after the engine is in the chassis it will take a lot of extra work to make the conversion. A few twelve-volt starters can be converted to six-volt operation by changing some of their internal parts but it will take a trip to the local parts store to find out if a specific starter can be given this treatment.

After the starter problem has been solved it would be a simple matter to mount the generator that was on the engine taken out of the chassis on the new engine. By making a special mounting bracket it shouldn't be any trouble to adapt practically any type of generator to any engine. The first thing to do would be to compare the pulleys on the six-volt and twelve-volt units to see whether they were for the same width belt. If the pulleys weren't the same width it might be possible to use the pulley from the twelve-volt generator on the six-volt unit or to buy one of the correct diameter and width that will fit the six-volt armature. The shafts in most makes of generators are fairly well standardized, making the pulleys sufficiently interchangeable for easy installation of one that will do the job. The diameter of the pulley can be important so an attempt should be made to keep the generator-to-crankshaft ratio with the new setup the same as it was on the engine for which the generator was made. When mounting the generator on the engine, be sure its pulley is in alignment with the crankshaft pulley. If the pulleys are out of alignment the belt will wear faster than it should and it may even climb off the pulleys when the engine is running.

Using the generator that came in the car on the new engine will make it possible to use the original generator regulator without any alterations. In fact, the car's entire electrical system, with possibly the exception of the starter switch and the wiring between the generator and its regulator, can be used without alterations.

Twelve-volt ignition coils installed as standard equipment on passenger cars cannot be used on six-volt current merely by leaving the twelve-volt resistor out of the circuit. Windings in these coils are designed for approximately eight volts and they will not put out the spark on six volts that a good six-volt coil will. No changes are necessary in a twelve-volt ignition distributor to enable it to be used with six volts but if a hotter spark than it will put out is needed it would be easy to install a special two-coil distributor and have the best.

Before we become too involved in this voltage problem, perhaps a short explanation of what goes on in a car's electrical system may make it easier to understand the principles involved and the reasons for the solutions recommended.

The rate of flow of electricity through a conductor, such as a length of wire or an accessory of any type, is measured in "amperes." The pressure of the flow, or the force that pushes amperes through the conductor, is "voltage." Before current can flow through an electrical circuit the circuit must be complete, or, in other words, a path for the current must be provided from one terminal post of the battery to the other. A circuit includes the battery, its cables, switches, the accessory for which the circuit is necessary, and the wires that connect these components. As long as the circuit is complete from one battery post to the other, current will flow and there will be both amperage and voltage in the circuit. When the circuit is broken, such as by opening a switch or disconnecting one of the wires or cables, current will cease to flow in the circuit. There will be voltage in the circuit but no amperage — there will be pressure but no flow.

The amount of electricity required to operate an electrical accessory is determined by the number of "watts" the accessory consumes in a second of time. This is the accessory's "power rating." To compute the number of watts required by any electrical device, multiply the number of volts in the circuit by the number of amperes flowing through it. For instance, if a six-volt radio requires 10 amperes for its operation, the power rating of the radio is sixty watts. An equivalent radio designed to operate on twelve volts would require only five amperes, which would give it, too, a power rating of sixty watts, although the amperage flow through the twelve-volt radio would be only half that through the six-volt type. Because of this lower amperage requirement of twelve-volt devices, the twelve-volt batteries made for automobiles have only half, or possibly a little more than half, the ampere-hour capacity of six-volt batteries. However, a twelve-volt battery is capable of as much work

as a six-volt type because although it can deliver only half as many amperes in a given time, it can push them with twice the force.

Voltage in a circuit for accessories that require a lower voltage than the battery delivers can be lowered by inserting a "resistor" in the circuit between the battery and the accessory. Resistors are made in different types, the most popular for automotive use being the wire-wound variety, such as those used with many ignition coils. A wire-wound resistor consists of a coil of special wire that has a high resistance to electrical flow wound on an insulator of some type. There is a terminal post at each end of the coil that enables the resistor to be inserted in a circuit.

Resistors are made in many capacities for different applications and it is important that the correct one be used. As the amperage flow through a resistor varies, the voltage delivered by it will vary also, the voltage going up as the amperage goes down; therefore, for the voltage to remain constant, the ampere flow must remain constant. This means that if amperage demand of the accessory served by the resistor should change, voltage in circuit would change.

It would seem as though it would be a simple matter to reduce the voltage of a twelve-volt battery to six volts with a resistor for the six-volt portion of mixed twelve-six-volt electrical system but the problem isn't so simple if the components served by the resistor are to function correctly. The reason for this is that the amperage flow through a car's electrical system varies with the number of lights and accessories that are in use at one time. If the system were served by a single resistor the voltage in the circuit would rise and fall according to the amperage load on the system and the lights and accessories wouldn't operate properly. It would be possible to use a resistor with each light bulb and each accessory in the car but this would involve many resistors of different capacities and quite an installation job. It's not practical to use resistors with fuel, oil pressure, or heat gauges because the amperage flow through the gauges and their sending units varies. The sending unit controls the flow of amperes through the indicating unit in the instrument panel and the indicating unit registers accordingly. The gauges would function if they were in series with the resistor but they would not give accurate readings.

An important disadvantage of using resistors to cut twelve-volt current to six-volts is that although the voltage of the current is cut by the resistor, amperage demand of the accessory served by the resistor is not. In other words, if a radio required 10 amperes at six-volts, its circuit would still require 10 amperes if it received current from a twelve-volt battery and a resistor. Power consumed by the radio and resistor would be ten times twelve, or 120 watts, instead of the normal 60 watts that would be consumed by an equivalent twelve-volt radio that would require only five amperes. Sixty of the 120 watts would be used by the radio and the other 60 would be dissipated by the resistor in the form of heat. This action would apply to any accessory or light bulb that was in series with a resistor, with the result that the load on a twelve-volt battery serving six-volt accessories through resistors would be twice what it would be if it were used with twelve-volt accessories. This extra load would be hard on the battery and generator and would shorten their life. Enough for theory.

If it isn't feasible or possible to convert the engine to six-volt operation, either the chassis components must be converted to twelve volts or a source of six-volt current must be provided for them. As stated before it is usually too expensive to convert all the chassis components to twelve volts so the only alternative is to provide six volts for them; however, some chassis components can be converted to twelve volts without too much trouble.

The source of six-volt current for a mixed twelve-six-volt electrical system would have to be either three of the six cells in a twelve-volt battery or a standard six-volt battery. An ideal solution to this problem would be two six-volt batteries connected in series. This arrangement would provide twelve volts for the twelve-volt portion of the system and one of the batteries could be used for the six-volt portion. Using two six-volt batteries in this manner would double the amperage-hour capacity of the twelve-volt part of the system, and one battery would provide full six-volt capacity. The twelve-volt generator would handle both batteries without any trouble.

Polarity of the electrical system, as determined by the side of the battery that is grounded, is important. Before the mass changeover by the industry to twelve volts, automobile manufactur-

ers used both positive and negative grounded systems but now they have all adopted the negative ground. Apparently the only reasons for the change were to eliminate confusion that existed in the service field when both polarities were used and to simplify the manufacture of generator regulators. Therefore, when converting a car to twelve volts, the negative post of the battery must be connected to ground, regardless of the polarity of the original system, because the generator regulator and ignition coil for the new engine are designed for a negative-grounded system.

Polarity doesn't make any difference to the generator as it will charge in any direction once it has been polarized by allowing current from the battery to flow through its field coils. This should be done whenever a generator has been installed on an engine after being removed for any purpose, or after its wires have been disconnected for any reason and then reconnected. Methods of polarizing generators vary with different types and care must be taken so as not to damage the generator's regulator. If the full current from the battery is allowed to flow through some regulator circuits it is possible that one or more of the point contact sets in the regulator will be burned or even welded together, so the wise thing to do is check with the local dealer that handles your make of engine for specific polarizing instructions.

Ignition coils are wound with a definite polarity in mind, and although they will create a spark on either polarity, the spark will be of greater intensity if the coil is wired correctly. This means that all the original equipment coils now in use on twelve-volt automobile engines are made to be used with a negative-grounded electrical system. Radios, heater motors, lights, and other accessories are not affected by polarity, so any of them can be used with either type of system. Some types of electric fuel pumps have a definite polarity that must correspond with the polarity of the car's electrical system.

If a standard twelve-volt battery is to be used in the car it will be necessary to fit it with a six-volt "tap" for the source of six-volt current. A tap is merely a means of connecting a cable to one of the battery's cell straps so current of the desired voltage can be taken from the battery. It isn't difficult to install a six-volt tap in a twelve-volt battery, the main thing to watch being that the tap is in the correct cell strap. The correct strap for six volts is easily determined because twelve-volt batteries have five straps and the tap must be in the third strap from either of the cells that have a terminal post. This is the strap that separates the third and fourth cells, counting from either of the cells that have posts.

To install a tap, carefully drill through the correct cell strap with a ¼-inch drill, taking care to not drill through the top of the cell, and then thread the hole with a 5⁄16-inch USS tap. Make a stud about an inch and a quarter long from a 5⁄16-inch copper bolt and screw one of its ends into the strap. Lock the stud in the strap with a flat washer and a nut run down snugly against the strap. All six-volt circuits in the car's electrical system will originate at this tap; however, the six-volt capacity will not be too great because of the low ampere-hour capacity of the battery.

If two six-volt batteries are to be used as the source of current, the positive post of the battery that is connected to ground must be connected to the negative post of the second battery with a suitable cable. This cable must be of the insulated type, such as is used between a battery and the starting motor solenoid, and it must have the correct terminals on its ends to fit the posts on the batteries. The conductor in the cable must be as large as the conductor in the main cable between the battery and the starter solenoid. The cable from the positive post of the second battery is connected to the battery post of the starter solenoid. Current for the six-volt part of the system can be taken from either end of the cable connecting the two batteries. The terminal on the end of the six-volt lead could be placed between either of the cable's terminals and the nut on the terminal's bolt. Battery cables for twelve-volt systems do not have to be as large as those for six-volt systems because they do not carry as much amperage but the cables and wires in the car that were used with the original six-volt system can be used with twelve volts with equal efficiency.

Several of the electrical circuits in an automobile receive their current from the "Accessory" post of the ignition switch. This is done so that current will flow to these circuits only when the ignition switch is in its "On" position. In a mixed twelve-six-volt system the ignition switch will be part of the twelve-volt portion so some arrangement will have to be made to accommodate the accessory circuits that must be controlled by the switch. This can be done by using a relay controlled by the ignition switch to complete the circuit between the source of six-volt current and the necessary accessories. The relay would be actuated by twelve-volt current but it would conduct six-volt current.

There are many types of relays available that could be used for such a purpose, including headlight and universal types. The relay should preferably be made for twelve-volt current but a six-volt type could be used without any trouble. A relay of this type has two circuits through it, one to complete the other.

The relay should be mounted in a position where the wires on the "Accessory" post of the ignition switch will reach its "Load" post. This particular post will be marked in various manners, depending on the relay, but the instructions with the relay will explain how it is to be wired. A wire will then have to be run from "Accessory" post of the ignition switch to the "Switch" post on the relay, and then unless the actuating winding in the relay is grounded through the relay's case, a "Ground" post on the relay will have to be grounded to the dash or some other metal part of the car with another short length of wire. Six-volt current for the relay must come from the six-volt tap on a twelve-volt battery or from one end of the cable that connects two six-volt batteries. The wire that serves the relay must be of at least 10 gauge because of the load it will carry and it must be connected to the relay's "Battery" terminal.

Now that we have the necessary sources of current for the various circuits in the car's electrical system, the only thing left to do is connect the circuits to the correct source according to the following recommendations.

Lighting Circuits

It would be wise to convert all the light bulbs in the car to twelve volts. This sounds as though it might be an expensive deal but actually the changeover could be made in the average car for seven or eight dollars. Twelve-volt bulbs will fit the six-volt sockets and no other changes would have to be made in the lighting circuits. Chances are the bulbs in the car will be old anyway and a change wouldn't hurt, especially as far as the headlights are concerned. It isn't widely known but light bulbs lose some of their brightness as they get older and sometimes they should be changed before they burn out just to restore the original brilliance of the lighting system. The original fuses and circuit breakers in the lighting circuits can be used with twelve-volt bulbs although the amperage draw of twelve-volt types is much less than that of six-volt types. A secondary advantage of twelve-volt bulbs is that they have a life expectancy of up to twice that of equivalent six-volt types.

Radio

A radio should be operated off twelve-volt current from a standard twelve-volt battery by installing a resistor of the correct capacity between the radio and the "Accessory" post of the ignition switch, which is a radio's normal source of current. Resistors for this purpose can be bought from almost any store that sells radio parts. A resistor should be installed according to the directions that are supplied with it. If two six-volt batteries were used it would be best to connect the radio to the "Load" post of the relay. This would eliminate the resistor and cut the power consumption of the radio in half.

Ignition Circuit

The ignition circuit would be stock. The only difference from the original six-volt circuit would be that the lead from the ignition switch to the ignition coil would be connected to the resistor for the twelve-volt coil. If a two-coil distributor were used, each coil would require its own resistor.

Starting Motor Control Circuit

Starting motor solenoids sometimes pose a problem when an engine change is made. Solenoids of some types are wound so that they are actuated by being grounded, and others must receive current to be actuated. The type of starter switch on the instrument panel is determined by the solenoid and it can be one of two general types: it can ground the circuit through the solenoid, or it can allow current to flow to the solenoid.

If the switch on the instrument panel were of the type that matched the solenoid on the starter of the new engine, it could be connected to the solenoid and be used without alterations, but if the switch and solenoid didn't match, another arrangement would have to be made. The most likely mismatched combination that would be encountered is a switch for a solenoid that must be grounded and a new solenoid that must receive current from the instrument panel switch. The solution to this problem is simple but it requires the use of both the old and new solenoids. The original solenoid and its switch are left as-is but the main cable from the battery to the solenoid is connected to the battery post on the new solenoid. A wire is then run from the six-volt tap on the battery, or from one end of the cable between two six-volt batteries, to the battery post on the original solenoid, and another wire is run from the starter post on the original solenoid to the switch post on the new solenoid. Then, when the original solenoid is actuated with the switch on the instrument panel, current flows from the battery post on the new solenoid, through the original solenoid, to the switch post on the new solenoid, causing the new solenoid to be actuated and close the circuit between its battery post and the starter.

Heater Motor, Overdrive Control, Heat Indicator, Oil Pressure Indicator, Fuel Level Indicator, Electric Fuel Pump

Circuits for these components must originate at the relay so current will not flow through them when the ignition switch is on. In the original installation they originated at the "Accessory" post of the ignition switch. They must be disconnected from this post and be connected to the "Load" post of the relay.

Window Motors, Seat Motors, Convertible Top Motors, Horn, Cigarette Lighter, Clock

If a standard twelve-volt battery is used, the circuits for these components must be connected to the six-volt tap on the battery. Their amperage draw is too high for them to be served by the relay and some of them must receive current when the ignition switch is "Off." If two six-volt batteries are used, the leads from these circuits must be connected to one end of the cable that connects the batteries together.

If the wires in any of the circuits have to be lengthened to reach the new source of current, wire with a conductor of the same size as that in the original wire must be used and the conductors must be joined with a regular connector that clamps to them or by soldering them together. It is important that the joint be tight so it will conduct the same amount of current as the rest of the circuit.

Chassis Modifications

Steps to take to compensate for the additional weight of the new engine will depend on the type of front suspension springs in the car. If the springs are of the leaf type it should be possible to raise the frame to its original height by either installing extra leaves in the springs or by using springs with thicker leaves. If the springs are of the coil type, springs wound from larger diameter wire can be installed. Quite often springs with different tensions are available for different models of an automobile. The dealer that handles the make of automobile in which the swap was made should have this information.

Sometimes, even with stiffer springs, a car fitted with coil springs won't come up to its original height. When this happens, additional height can be obtained by installing special shims available from parts stores and wheel alignment shops between one end of each spring and the member in which it seats. Also available are devices to increase the strength of the springs. These include rubber spacers that fit between the coils and helper springs that bolt to the frame and exert tension on one of the coils.

In rare instances it might be found that there is less weight on the car's front wheels with the new engine than there was with the original engine. There are several corrections for this condition. If the car is fitted with a leaf-type front spring, the frame can be lowered to its original height by removing a leaf or two from the spring or by having the spring re-arched. If the car has coil springs, the frame can be lowered by cutting part of a coil from one end of each of the springs or by installing springs wound from wire of a smaller diameter.

It is important that the front of the car be returned to its original height so that wheel alignment will not be affected. It would be a good idea after the car had been driven a few miles to have the alignment checked just to be sure that it was correct. This job can more than pay for itself in savings on tire wear.

Another worthwhile improvement to the front end if the new engine is heavier than the old one would be the installation of heavy-duty, double-acting shock absorbers. Stock shocks may not be capable of handling the forces created by the additional engine weight and the stiffer front springs.

After the car has been driven it will probably be found that its rear axle ratio is too low for normal driving. If this is the case, more enjoyment will be gained from the engine swap if gears of a higher ratio are installed. Cars to be used for drag racing or some other type of competition may require a lower ratio than that in the car. If this is so, it is a simple matter to install gears of the correct ratio.

CHAPTER THIRTEEN

Choosing the Right Transmission

Do stick shifts really have advantages over automatics? Problems of installation discussed including engine-transmission alignment.

ONE OF A HOT RODDER'S MAIN CONCERNS when he buys or builds a car is the car's transmission. It's a well-known fact that its transmission has much to do with a car's performance, and a hot rodder is definitely interested in performance. Transmissions available to hot rodders can be divided into two general types: automatic and synchromesh. In hot rod language a synchromesh transmission is a "stick-shift" transmission.

The types of cars for which a hot rodder could require a transmission are a passenger car used only for normal driving, a passenger car used for normal driving during the week and for drag racing on weekends, a passenger car used strictly for drag racing, a passenger car used strictly for straightaway competition, a competition car used strictly for drag racing, or a competition car used strictly for straightaway competition. Six classifications for the cars a hot rodder might own may seem to be too many but actually this isn't so. The cars in each classification have their own peculiar requirements as far as their transmission is concerned and a transmission that would be

entirely suitable for one might not be at all usable in another.

A hot rodder buying a new '58 or later automobile for normal driving would probably be satisfied with any automatic transmission except Buick's Dynaflow or Chevrolet's Powerglide or Turboglide. Buick and Chevrolet transmissions have too much slippage to enable a car to perform well but all the others provide acceptably good performance. Two-speed Fordomatics and Mercomatics and Chrysler product Torqueflite transmissions are extremely good.

A fellow buying a '58 or later automobile for normal driving and weekend drag use would have more of a problem. If he planned to run in the stock engine class he could more than likely get by quite well with one of the Torqueflites or a two-speed Fordomatic or Mercomatic. Hydra-Matics built after 1955 aren't as good for competition work as those built in 1955 or earlier years but in a stock car one of them might perform satisfactorily. If it is planned to rework the engine to any extent it would be wise to buy a stick-shift transmission, except for cars equipped

Group of transmissions around Transmission Expert Lou Sales is mostly of the converted Cadillac-La Salle variety. Transmission at the upper right is a Hydra-Matic. Most hot rodders prefer stick-shifts to the Hydra-Matics or torque converters.

with Hydra-Matics. The stock Hydra-Matic wouldn't be strong enough for competition work but it could be replaced with a '55 or earlier Hydra-Matic that had been reworked. Reworked Hydra-Matics are entirely satisfactory for this type of use.

All automatic transmissions, with the exception of Buick's Dynaflow, have positive gear ratios, just as stick-shift transmissions, but some of them have only two forward speeds compared to the three of most stick-shift boxes and the four of a rare few stick-shifts. All but Hydra-Matics have hydraulic torque converters that provide additional torque multiplication that is not positive in its ratio but instead varies with the loads on the engine and driveshaft. Dynaflow differs from the others in that it is all hydraulic torque converter.

Of the many factors that might make an automatic unsuitable for dragging, the hydraulic torque converter is the most important. The Hydra-Matic is the only automatic that has proven itself to be usable successfully on drag strips and the reason behind its success is that it is not penalized by a torque converter and that it has four forward speeds.

One of the drawbacks common to converters is their inability to withstand high engine speeds without coming apart. The pressure created by the oil in a converter's housing at high speed is so great that the housing may explode or the joint between it and the flywheel may start to leak. It's the end of the road when either of these things happens because when the oil in the converter drops to too low a level the converter can't transmit torque to the transmission. This can happen even with a stock engine if it is wound tighter than the safe speed for the converter. As a Hydra-Matic is coupled to the engine with a hydraulic coupling instead of with a converter, it isn't handicapped in this manner. The pressure in a coupling's housing doesn't increase appreciably with engine speed. The only additional pressure in a coupling's housing due to speed is the result of the centrifugal force of the oil and this isn't enough to blow the housing or its gasket.

Confusion exists in the minds of some hot rodders as to the difference between a hydraulic coupling and a hydraulic torque converter. While both these devices utilize oil to transmit torque from the engine's flywheel to the input shaft of the transmission, they differ greatly in their operation.

The only duty a hydraulic coupling has is to transmit torque from the engine to the transmission and while doing this it cushions the flow of torque so the torque will be transmitted to the transmission smoothly. It serves other purposes in that it enables the transmission to shift while under load and allows the car to be stopped without the necessity of disengaging the transmission from the engine by means of a clutch. At usable engine speeds the coupling transmits ap-

proximately 98 percent of the torque the engine feeds to it to the transmission.

Hydraulic torque converters transmit torque in much the same manner as hydraulic couplings but under certain conditions they also multiply the torque, just as it is multiplied by the gears in a transmission. The actual ratio of the multiplication varies with different converters but for most of them it ranges between 2 and 2½ to 1, which means that the maximum torque a converter can deliver varies between 2 and 2½ times the value of the torque at the engine's flywheel. The maximum multiplication occurs at a certain time when the flywheel is turning but the transmission shaft is stationary. This is when slippage between the crankshaft and the transmission is the highest and the efficiency of the converter is, therefore, lowest. As the speed of the transmission shaft increases to meet that of the crankshaft, the multiplication of the converter drops until it reaches practically the zero point. At this time the crankshaft and the transmission shaft are rotating at approximately the same speed and the slippage in the converter is at its minimum value, becoming, under this condition, a hydraulic coupling.

Converters are engineered, as far as the amount of torque multiplication they have is

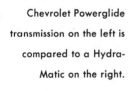

Chevrolet Powerglide transmission on the left is compared to a Hydra-Matic on the right.

Traction Masters extending from the rear axle to the forward end of the rear-spring anchor are a means of eliminating spring windup and wheel hop in stick-shift machines, thus enabling the hot rodder to get out of chute at fast pace.

concerned, to combine with the positive ratio in the transmissions to which they are coupled to give the correct overall ratio for the driving conditions that apply at the time. They are also engineered to transmit only the amount of torque the engines to which they are fitted can create, at the crankshaft speeds at which the torque is developed. When an engine is reworked to increase its torque, the balance between its torque output and its converter is upset. The converter isn't capable of handling the extra torque and a high percentage of the additional potential benefit to car performance is lost.

Having a torque converter between the engine and the transmission is the same as having a set of gears with an infinitely variable ratio ranging from the converter's maximum multiplication ratio to approximately 1 to 1, but over which the driver has no control, between the engine and the transmission.

Some torque converters have been improved immensely since they were first introduced and many of them have been tightened-up to the point where they slip only a fraction as much as they did. This tightening-up was made possible by the new engines that have so much more torque at low speeds than the older models. However, converters are still far from having a grip as positive as that of a good clutch.

A fellow installing an all-out modified engine in a passenger car that will be used strictly for drag racing has three logical transmission choices.

One of these is a reworked 1955 or earlier Hydra-Matic and the others are a stock or a special stick-shift box.

Performance provided by a reworked Hydra-Matic in a passenger car that can be expected to have a top speed at the end of the quarter between 110 and 115 mph can be as good as that provided by a stick-shift. And, if the car's driver isn't experienced in drag racing, a Hydra-Matic can provide a definite advantage. Getting out of the chute and to the finish line in the shortest time with a hot engine and a stick-shift in a fairly heavy car requires lots of practice but with a reworked Hydra-Matic anyone can stab the throttle and steer the car.

With a stick-shift the driver must know how to manipulate the clutch to get the car going smoothly, know when to shift gears so full advantage will be taken of the engine's torque, and know how to shift the gears so the period of time torque will not be conducted from the engine to the driveshaft will be reduced to the absolute minimum. The tires on the rear wheels have a tendency to break loose from the strip under the sudden application of torque when a clutch is engaged and the wheels sometimes hop up and down until the car gets moving fast enough for the tires to get a bite on the strip. If wheelspin isn't controlled correctly with the clutch and throttle, the guy in the next lane can be well on his way by the time the tires get a bite on the strip.

Wheel hop experience with a car that has a stick-shift transmission can be eliminated by the installation of Traction-masters on its rear axle. Traction-masters are a definite asset to any passenger car used for drag racing because of the way they control rear spring windup and wheel hop. Wheelspin can be reduced by using the correct tires, preferably slicks, on the rear wheels.

With a reworked Hydra-Matic, a car will usually get under way quickly and smoothly, with a minimum of wheelspin, because the transmission's hydraulic coupling cushions the flow of torque to the transmission and driveline and allows the tires to retain a better grip on the strip. This not only makes the car easier to drive but it also reduces the strain on its driveline.

Hydra-Matic transmissions have been made in more than one series but only the "R" series, which includes 1949 through '55 production is good for reworking. Only the four-speed models of the R series are suitable, and the '50 through '55's are the best of these. The "Jetaway" Hydra-Matics used in '56 and later cars have a change in them that makes them unsuitable for reworking. This change was made to eliminate the front clutch assembly and thereby make second to third speed shifts smoother. The clutch was replaced with a small hydraulic coupling. It is possible to replace a Jetaway in an Olds or Caddy with an earlier transmission if a better bite is needed.

A Hydra-Matic that has been reworked for drag use is nothing more than a self-shifting four-speed gearbox, with a hydraulic coupling that eliminates clutch trouble. However, to think that a Hydra-Matic that has been beefed-up for drag racing is going to be smooth around town is stretching the imagination a little too far, but one of them could be used for normal driving if one could stand the rough shifts. Another characteristic of Hydra-Matics is that they become more positive in their actions as car weight become less because there is less weight to oppose them.

Correctly set up, a Hydra-Matic will stand up better on a drag strip than a stick-shift because it doesn't take the beating a stick-shift does when its clutch is engaged to get the car under way and there is no gear clashing when shifts are made. A Hydra-Matic is much easier on the driveline than a stick-shift. The loss of U-joints, rear axle gears, and axle shafts is greatly reduced. This is the result of replacing the clutch with the hydraulic coupling, which takes the jerk out of the power application to the transmission and the rest of the driveline.

Cars with Hydra-Matic transmissions don't seem to be too sensitive about their rear axle ratio. With a low ratio the transmission will shift into high gear quicker than it would with a higher ratio. In this way it automatically compensates for the ratio by keeping the speed of the engine in the range where the engine can create sufficient power to move the car under steady acceleration. The most important thing about the ratio is to use one that reduces wheelspin when getting out of the chute to a minimum. Then the transmission can be adjusted to shift at the correct speeds for maximum torque at the rear wheels.

A hot rodder who would prefer a stick-shift transmission behind his reworked V8 can use a stock transmission or he can adapt one of the early Cadillac or La Salle boxes that have recently become so popular to it. Stick-shift transmissions used as standard equipment in 1958 automobiles are big, strong boxes that can take a lot of punishment. Many of them were made extra strong so they could be used in the racing kits supplied by the factories when the factories were sponsoring stock car racing teams.

The Cadillac and La Salle transmissions that are being installed in so many drag racing cars now are identical although they were used in both makes of cars. They were made in two types. Those built in 1937, which was the first model suitable for drag use, had a floor shift, and those built in 1938 and later were designed for a steering column shift. Most fellows installing a transmission in a drag car prefer a floor shift but in some areas floor shift Cad-La Salle boxes have become extremely hard to find. However, this isn't too much of a problem because there are conversion kits available for the column shift transmissions that enable them to be fitted with floor shift levers. These kits are entirely satisfactory and they eliminate all the springiness usually present in column shift linkage.

Cad-La Salle boxes have husky gears that never seem to break and their only weak point is their synchromesh shifting unit. Occasionally synchromesh will go out but this is a compara-

This column shift Cadillac-La Salle transmission has been reworked and has an adaptor plate for mounting behind a 1949-56 Ford powerplant.

tively small matter. Ratios of the gears are 2.39 in low and 1.53 in second. These are almost ideal for drag racing.

Other makes of stick-shift transmissions have been used for special installations but none of them are as sturdy as Cad-La Salle boxes. One of the more popular of these is the early Packard. It has ratios of 2.43 in low and 1.53 in second, which are very close to Cad-La Salle ratios. The main trouble with Packard transmissions is their weak case. The case can't seem to stand the strain of drag racing behind a hot, large displacement engine for very long. However, a Packard transmission should be entirely satisfactory behind a Chevy six or some other lower powered engine.

Another transmission in this group is the one used in '36 through '38 Buick Roadmaster or Century cars. Buick boxes have the same gear ratios as Cad-La Salle boxes but they require extensive reworking before they can be used. Parts required for this reworking include some from '41 through '48 Buick Roadmaster transmissions and a mainshaft, rear bearing retainer, and other miscellaneous parts from a '51 through '56 Olds transmission. Finding the necessary parts to rework a Buick box could be something

of a problem and it could be expensive. As with Packard boxes, Buick transmissions are recommended for engines with comparatively low torque outputs.

Before the Cad-La Salle boxes came along, Ford and Mercury stick-shift transmissions fitted with Lincoln gears were considered the ultimate for drag racing. The selection of gear ratios for them was more than ample but as the torque of the big ohv engines went up they started to give trouble by coming apart too frequently. They are still good behind a flathead V8 or Mercury but it isn't advisable to use one of them behind a reworked ohv V8.

A passenger car reworked for strictly straightaway running in dry lake or Bonneville competition isn't as critical as a drag car in its transmission requirements. A car used for straightaway running has ample room to pick up speed and severe use of its transmission isn't necessary to get it under way. For this reason it is possible to use a weaker transmission in a car of this type than could be used in a drag car. A stick-shift transmission should definitely be used in preference to an automatic because stick-shifts have less drag in high gear and their clutch provides a positive connection between the engine and the driveline. Torque loss in a hydraulic coupling of the type used with a Hydra-Matic transmission is practically nil at high speeds but the mass of mechanism that must be driven in the transmission can't help but cause some loss of torque between the converter and the driveshaft. A transmission with a torque converter wouldn't be at all suitable for an installation of this type because in addition to the extra torque required to drive the converter and transmission, the likelihood of exploding the converter housing or blowing the housing's gasket would always be present.

Many · competition cars built strictly for straightaway running don't have a transmission because they can be pushed to be started, and by replacing the transmission with an in-and-out box the clutch can also be eliminated. Elimination of the clutch in a car of this type is a good move because it is just one more thing to cause trouble. Straightaway cars that do have transmissions present much the same problems as passenger cars used for the same type of competition. As long as the car's clutch and the mainshaft in the transmission are strong enough to transmit the engine's torque to the driveshaft without slipping or failing, the transmission and clutch should be entirely satisfactory.

Of the competition cars built strictly for drag racing, there are a few dragsters that are capable of accelerating the full quarter-mile in high gear, but all the others must have a sturdy transmission

and clutch. Transmissions of any type or make that will hold up under the beating the transmission in a dragster or other competition drag car must take are limited in number. There aren't any automatics up to the task, although there were some experiments at one time with Chrysler torque converters. The converters were used without their transmissions so that only the multiplication in the converter itself was used to get the car out of the chute. None of these experiments were too successful.

At the present time the only stick-shift transmission suitable for use in dragsters and other fast competition drag machines are Cad-La Salle boxes. With one of these transmissions and a good double-plate clutch, transmission and clutch troubles can be practically eliminated.

A common transmission conversion nowadays is the replacing of an automatic transmission in a passenger car with a stick-shift box. A fellow usually decides to make such a conversion after he has tried his automatic at the drags a few times and found that it left much to be desired. As a rule, these conversions involve a stick-shift transmission made originally for the car but in some instances it may be decided to install a Cad-La Salle or one of the other special boxes. Regardless of the type of transmission used, such conversions are an involved procedure because it is necessary to install a clutch pedal and the necessary clutch and gearshift linkage along with the transmission. When a stock transmission is to be used it is sometimes possible to find a

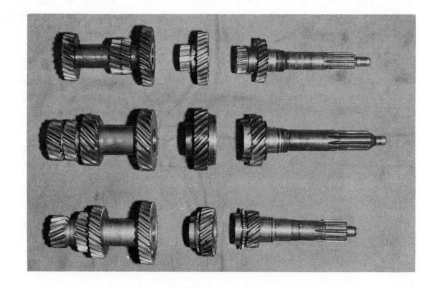

Cluster, second and main drive gears are (top to bottom) Chevrolet, La Salle, and Lincoln Zephyr. Note larger size of the La Salle gears.

fellow with the same make and model of car who has a stick-shift and is willing to trade it for an automatic. When such a trade can be made, the expense of making the conversion is greatly reduced and the difficulties of finding the many necessary parts for the clutch and gearshift linkage are eliminated.

Installation of a Cad-La Salle or other special stick-shift box is simplified for a few makes of engines by the availability of adaptors that enable the transmission to be bolted to the stock flywheel housing. For many of these installations it is necessary to have the transmission's mainshaft shortened and resplined for the car's universal joint. One or two adaptors for connecting the transmissions to driveshafts of different kinds are also available and usually the driveshaft length has to be altered to match the transmission. Shortening the mainshaft and altering the driveshaft's length are jobs that require special equipment but most machine shops should be able to handle them. It is usually necessary to rework the stock rear motormount bracket or build a new one to accommodate the transmission. An installation of this sort is a lot of work but transmission trouble is usually a thing of the past once it has been made.

When installing a stick-shift transmission of any kind on an engine there are certain precautions that should be taken to ensure that it will be correctly aligned with the engine's block and crankshaft. Methods of doing this differ for different makes of engines but the general idea with all of them is to make sure the center of the bore in the rear flange of the flywheel housing that aligns the transmission with the engine is in line with the centerline of the crankshaft, and that the rear surface of the housing to which the transmission bolts is exactly perpendicular to the centerline of the crankshaft. These things are checked by bolting the housing to the cylinder block and then clamping a dial indicator to the flywheel flange on the crankshaft so the indicator will rotate with the shaft.

Concentricity of the housing's bore with the crankshaft is checked by adjusting the indicator so its plunger button contacts the middle of the bore's face. Then, as the crankshaft is rotated, the indicator travels around the bore and indicates in thousandths of any inch any misalignment between the members. Alignment of the housing's rear face is checked by adjusting the indicator so its button contacts the area of the face around the bore. Then, as the crankshaft is rotated, the indicator shows the amount of misalignment, if any, between the face and the crankshaft. Permissible amounts of misalignment between these members vary for different makes and models of engines, as do the methods of correcting the alignment. The only way a fellow can learn these things is by looking them up in a shop manual for his engine.

Flywheel alignment must also be checked after the flywheel has been bolted to the crankshaft. This is done by bolting the wheel to the shaft with the specified torque on its bolts or nuts and then mounting a dial indicator on the cylinder block or flywheel housing in such a position that its plunger button rests on the surface of the wheel. For most engines the button should rest on the area of the wheel contacted by the clutch disc, near the larger diameter of the area, but for others it may be specified that the indicator should contact the wheel in another area. Then, as the crankshaft is rotated, any amount the flywheel's face deviates from a plane perpendicular to the centerline of the crankshaft will be shown by the indicator.

If flywheel runout is more than that specified in the shop manual for the engine, the wheel must be removed and its mounting flange and the flange on the crankshaft checked for burrs or foreign material that might prevent the wheel from seating on the shaft as it should. Some flywheels can be rotated 180 degrees in relation to the crankshaft. If this is possible with the engine being worked on, it could be tried to determine whether it would reduce the runout to within specifications. Care must be taken when rotating the crankshaft to hold it either toward or away from the cylinder block so it can't float back and forth in its main bearings. If the shaft is allowed to move back and forth, the crankshaft end play will be measured as flywheel runout.

CHAPTER FOURTEEN

Building Your Own Hot Rod

Choosing the basic car. Chassis, body,
suspension modifications. Building for street
or competition, or both. Examples of some of the best.

Don Francisco, well-known hot rod expert, examines suspension and steering setup on one of the many hot rods.

TELLING A FELLOW how to build a hot rod is just about as ridiculous as telling him what he should eat for breakfast. No two hot rodders have the same likes and dislikes and this is the reason there are as different hot rods as there are hot rodders. The only thing that all hot rods have in common is an engine that has been reworked to make the car perform better, or a larger displacement engine of a different make that was installed with normal engine swap methods.

A fellow can want a hot rod for several different uses and for each use there are many different ways in which he can accomplish his goal. If hot rods were divided into groups according to the reason for which they were built, the largest group would include those for normal driving, the second would include cars for drag racing, in the third group would probably be cars for track racing, and cars for straightaway competition such as on a dry lake or at Bonneville would comprise the smallest group. It's practically impossible to reduce hot rods to any smaller denomination than this because a hot rod of

This competition roadster
considered to be a classic
in the hot rod field, features
a 1927 Model T body and
other early Ford components.

nearly any body type can fit into any of the groups. Exceptions to this would be dragsters, Bonneville streamliners, and track roadsters.

Since the time of the Model T there have been several cars that hot rodders have accepted over other types and makes as basis for modifications. It wouldn't be unreasonable to consider some of these cars, which are all of Ford origin, as hot rod "classics." That all the classics are Fords is more than just a coincidence because the name Ford has been synonymous with hot rods for longer than the present generation can remember. The reasons for this are the result of the way Fords are built and merchandised. Fords have always been small cars, and it is one of the first considerations for a hot rod that it be small. By being small, Fords have also been of com-

paratively light weight. This also fits into hot rod requirements. Fords have always been among the industry's lowest priced full-size automobiles and, for this reason, Ford has built and sold more passenger cars than any other manufacturer. This has made used and wrecked Fords plentiful and cheap, and price has always been something a hot rodder has had to consider. Through some quirk of fate, Fords have always had engines that are easy to work on and that are highly adaptable to hot rodding techniques. The engines respond readily to improvements and they stay together remarkably well when subjcted to normal hot rod abuse. Added together, these things make a combination that until recently no other car could come near equalling. But now, Chevrolet, with its compara-

Driver of competition T
is protected by a sturdy
roll bar. Bars at
rear are provided to
start engine by
pushing car.

tively new and exceptionally adaptable V8 engine, may possibly take over Ford's position at the top of the hot rod ladder.

Chevrolet has paralleled Ford in car size, weight, production, price, and appearance for many years but until 1955 they were handicapped by engines and transmissions that only a Ford-hater could like. When a Ford owner told a Chevy lover that he had better paint his stovebolt green so he could hide it in the grass alongside the road and watch the Fords go by, he meant what he said. Six-hole Chevys couldn't stay close to a Ford, and even when they were reworked, a reworked Ford would go around them. But when Chevy engineers got the go-ahead from the big-wheels that determine policy to modernize their powerplants for 1955, the result was a terrific blow to Ford superiority. To this date Ford hasn't been able to completely recover their former performance edge.

Starting with the Model T, the first of the Ford classic hot rods was the '27 T roadster. The only part of this car that actually qualifies as

Cockpit of competition T roadster is gutted to save weight. Tank on right is for fuel. Note heavy shield over flywheel and clutch to protect driver from fragmentation of parts.

Engine in classic hot rod is much modified 1953 De Soto equipped with four Stromberg 97 carburetors, Scintilla Vertex magneto, racing pistons, and special camshaft. Small opening in radiator shield admits air for drag racing.

Husky front suspension on this hot rod includes large tubular shock absorbers and Dodge tubular front axle.

Engine in combination street and competition roadster is modified 1956 Lincoln equipped with a McCulloch supercharger and two, four-barrel carburetors concealed by the pressure housings on top of the engine.

being a classic is its body. At one time roadster bodies of this vintage were very much in demand for both street rods and competition cars. Next was the Model A roadster. It was used in its entirety, first with reworked Model A engines and then with reworked Model B and flathead V8's. It was a favorite for street and competition. After the Model A came the '32 roadster and three-window coupe. The roadster was much more popular than the coupe for both street and competition but enough of the coupes were used to qualify it as a classic. Next were '34 three-window coupes, then '36 three-window coupes, and then '40 coupes and sedans. At one time coupes of all these years were very popular and it was common practice to chop their tops. They made good cars for street or competition.

The last of the classics were '49 and '50 Ford coupes and sedans. These were the cars that were instrumental in starting the tremendous move to engine swapping. Later model Fords and other makes of cars were used for countless engine swaps after 1950 but there's something lacking about these later models that keeps them out of the classic category.

All the classics mentioned have been used in various forms for competition of all types. Model A and '32 roadsters were used when hot rod track racing was first started but it wasn't long before they were replaced by cars that had

Model T roadster bodies and special frames. And later builders of the faster cars gradually changed from stock bodies to special bodies they made themselves. The first of these special bodies were narrowed stock bodies. A slice was taken lengthwise out of a roadster body and then the two sides were welded together, leaving just enough room for the driver. Next were the airplane belly tanks. Special frames were made for the tanks, which were in halves, and one half was used for the bottom of the body and the other half was used for the top. Holes were cut in the tank for the axles, exhaust pipes, the driver's head, and anything else that wouldn't fit within its confines. These were the early "streamliners."

The last and most professional appearing of the special bodies are the enclosed wheel streamliners built for Bonneville. These streamliners consistently run over 200 miles per hour and the fastest one to date has turned 272 mph. Some of them have aluminum body panels and others are constructed of fiberglass.

Many hot rods for competition purposes are built from the ground up. All of them use standard passenger car running-gear components but the components may be extensively modified to conform to the car's specifications. Frames for cars of this type are often from '32 or Model A Fords, narrowed, shortened, and otherwise modified. Frames built after '32 consist of members

Lincoln-powered roadster has 1929 Ford Model A body. Plugs at end of exhaust stacks may be removed for competition. With plugs in place, exhaust is routed through dual set of mufflers.

Flathead 1940 Ford engine is set back in the frame on this Model A bodied roadster to equalize weight. Model A frame was modified to make frame low. Besides being a creditable competition machine, roadster has been a winner at shows.

Front-end of Ford hot rod features completely chromed axle with ends of I-beam section filled, heavy-duty shock absorbers, and hydraulic brakes. Note carbs above hood.

that are too heavy for competition hot rod use. A shortage of early frames and a desire for something better has led many fellows to build frames from lengths of steel tubing. Members for frames of this type are cut from the steel tubing and welded together to form a unit of adequate strength and stiffness for the application.

Most competition hot rods have roadster or coupe bodies, in standard or modified form, with special noses and hoods to give them some degree of streamlining. Many of them are fitted with full belly pans. Others have special bodies ranging from a cockpit between or even behind the rear wheels, as is customary in modern dragster design, to covered wheel streamliner bodies.

Suspension can consist of leaf, torsion bar, or coil springs, but torsion bar and coil springs are definitely in the minority. The front spring is usually some model of Ford transverse, or "cross" spring, or a special spring of similar design. The number of leaves in the spring vary according to the weight of the car and the stiffness desired and the spring is mounted either ahead of, above, or behind the front axle. On track cars the shackle at the left end of the spring is anchored so it can't move to prevent the frame from moving sideways in relation to the axle when the cars are in turns. The mount on the frame for the spring is usually of the "suicide" type that consists of a bracket welded to the forward side of the frame's front crossmember. Some of these brackets, especially on track cars, are adjustable so the frame can be raised or lowered in relation to the spring and axle. This is done to enable the car's handling characteristics to be changed.

Dragsters usually don't have any rear suspension. The frame is bolted tight to brackets welded to the rear axle housings. This same construction is also used for some straightaway cars and streamliners. Drag and straightaway cars that have rear springs usually have a spring of the cross type similar to the one on the front. Rear cross springs are longer and stiffer than those used on the front of the car and they can be mounted ahead of, above, or behind the axle assembly. Rear spring brackets on the frames of track and some straightaway and drag cars are adjustable to permit the frame to be raised or lowered in relation to the axle so the car will

handle better for track racing and so the rear tires can get the best possible bite for drag racing and straightaway running.

When torsion bars are used as suspension members they are mounted either parallel to the frame rails or parallel to the axles. One of their ends is fitted with an arm that is shackled to the axle and the other end is locked to the frame with an adjustable device that permits the car to be raised or lowered by twisting the anchored ends. For track racing, the axle end of the arm on the bar that supports the left front of the frame is usually connected to the axle without a shackle. Connecting the arm to the axle in this manner serves the same purpose as the solid shackle at the left end of a transverse leaf spring.

Cars with torsion bar suspension are fitted with a transverse radius rod. One end of the rod is connected to the frame and the other end is connected to the axle. This rod is parallel to the axle and its end that is connected to the frame is on the opposite side of the chassis from the axle end. This makes the rod as long as practical means permit so that the arc its ends

Cockpit of roadster shows dual purpose of car. Hand pump on driveline tunnel pressurizes separate competition fuel system. Glove compartment was utilized as space for extra instrumentation.

Another example of the classic group of hot rods is this roadster based on a 1932 Ford chassis and body. Often referred to as the "deuce" because of its model year, this car is an excellent example of a functionally and cleanly designed hot rod.

Engine in "deuce" is a 1955 Chevrolet V8 utilizing a special camshaft and three carburetors. Exhaust system bypasses mufflers when caps are removed from the chromed exhaust stacks.

pass through as the frame moves up and down in relation to the axle causes the frame and axle to be moved a minimum distance sideways in relation to each other.

Transverse radius rods have been eliminated on the rear ends of most professional racing cars by the substitution of an arrangement commonly called a "Watt's" linkage but which is actually a "Robert's" linkage. Both Watt's and Robert's linkages are devices designed to produce straight line motion. The Robert's linkage that is used is comprised of members pivoted at points of attachment on the frame and axle and so-arranged geometrically that the frame and axle can move vertically in relation to each other with only minute transverse movement.

Coil springs are seen only rarely on competition hot rods when they are used, mountings are provided on the frame and axles to accommodate them. Perhaps one of the reasons for the

scarcity of coil spring suspensions on cars of this type is the general unavailability of springs of the correct size and tension for such installations.

Front and rear axles connected to their frames with transverse leaf springs, torsion bars, or coil springs must be fitted with longitudinal radius rods, or torque arms, that hold them in their correct longitudinal position in relation to the frame. These rods also control torsional movement of the front axle resulting from brake applications and torsional movement of some rear axles resulting from brake applications and the torque reaction of the ring and pinion gears in the axle assembly.

Radius rods for front axles sometimes consist of a standard '48 or earlier Ford "wishbone" that has been split at its rear end. The ends are spread apart and fitted with ball joints that are connected to the frame rails. Rods of this type

Rear-end of 1932 Ford shows typical body revision which places special taillights in the decklid. While being basically interested in performance, many hot rodders have been just as enthusiastic when it comes to dressing up their machines.

Three-window, 1932 Ford coupe is popular base material for hot rodders. Body of this extensively modified machine has been channeled to place it six inches lower on the frame.

Stock 1952 Oldsmobile engine powers the three-window hot rod coupe. Only engine modification is hand-formed exhaust headers which collect spent gases in single-tubed system running to aft section of car.

Exhaust system of 1932 Ford appears complicated. Note removable cap in tubing at front of door and tail pipe extensions from mufflers. Most states require fenders for street use.

Custom upholstery and carpeting dress up 1932 Ford interior. Note special seats set on floor to compensate for low headroom resulting from chopped top.

The Glass Slipper, world record holding Class C (183 to 305 cubic inches) dragster, is beautifully streamlined and constructed. Note tubular front axle, light but strong radius rods, and extra-heavy steering drag link.

are said to be "strapped." For some installations special rods that serve the same purpose as a split wishbone are made from lengths of steel tubing welded together to provide the required strength and stiffness.

Some front radius rods are of the parallelogram type, which means that two rods are used for each end of the axle. The axle ends of each pair of rods are connected to a bracket either bolted or welded to the axle so that one rod is above the axle and the other is below it. Frame ends of the rods are connected to the frame rails or brackets welded or bolted to the rails. Ball joints that permit unlimited vertical movement of the rod ends and some torsional movement of the members to which the rods are connected

Glass Slipper is shown on start of runs which broke world record for standing-start kilometer. Car averaged speed of 106.428 miles per hour over distance and was timed at 168.85 miles per hour at the finish line.

are used at both ends of all the rods. The rods in each pair are parallel to each other and separated approximately six inches.

With strapped front radius rods that are solidly connected to the axle, vertical movement of the frame and axle in relation to each other causes some longitudinal movement of the axle in relation to the frame and also changes the axle's caster angle. In addition to this, when movement of one end of the axle in relation to the frame is greater or in a different direction to movement of the opposite end of the axle, a twisting effort is exerted on the axle and the rods. This twist must be absorbed by either the radius rods or the axle beam. This is not a good condition because the twisting effort may eventually cause one or more of the members to break and it acts with the same effect as a stabilizer bar (sway bar) to resist movement of one end of the axle in relation to the other. This stabilizing effect isn't good because it upsets the balance of the suspension members as a unit. Each of the members should do its job without help from any of the others: the spring should support the load of the frame, the radius rods should do nothing more than locate the front axle in relation to

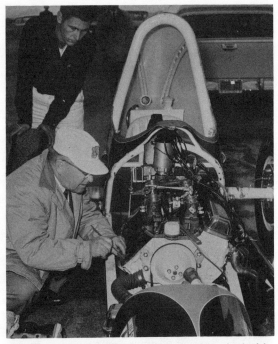

Modified Chevrolet engine in Glass Slipper is checked by official following record run to ascertain it to be in specified displacement class. Body of machine is fiberglass.

Body work on Money Oldsmobile dragster is not beautiful, but this did not prevent it from covering quarter mile from a standing start in 10.42 seconds and reaching a speed of 141.5 miles per hour to capture top honors in the 1957 National Championship Drag Meet held at Oklahoma City. This annual event, incidentally, attracts machines from all over country.

Money Oldsmobile uses light-weight motorcycle wheels at front. At right, Wally Parks, president of National Hot Rod Association and editor of Hod Rod magazine, congratulates driver and team at end of championship run.

Masters Dragliner starts run in Championship meet. Well-engineered-and-streamlined machine has topped 123 mph at end of quarter mile from standing start. Power is a modified 1955 Chevrolet V8. Radiators are not used on dragsters.

Front-end of Masters Dragliner is characterized by light-weight construction. Rear axle is solidly mounted to frame without springs. Driver sits in enclosed cockpit behind the rear axle.

Hot Rod Magazine Special is world record holder in Class B (305 to 448 cubic inches). Typical of dragsters, front-end weight has been reduced by drilling lightening holes in axle and eliminating front brakes. These fellows are members of the crew which helped to engineer, build, and maintain this outstanding dragster.

the frame and control any torque moment in it resulting from brake applications, and chassis roll should be held within the desired limits with a suitable stabilizer bar.

With front axle radius rods of the parallelogram type, vertical movement of the axle and

Engine in dragster is a supercharged Chrysler V8. Crew member is shown here siphoning methanol fuel from tank. Methanol was used for testing; it was replaced by nitromethane mixture for the highly successful record runs.

frame in relation to each other effects slight longitudinal movement of the axle in relation to the frame but the axle's caster angle remains constant; there is no twisting effort on axle or rods.

The wishbone type radius rods used on the front of '48 and earlier Fords combine the axle and radius rods into a solid unit. The ends of the axle can move up and down in any direction in relation to the frame without subjecting the axle beam to any twisting effort. The problem with such an arrangement is that in most hot rods there isn't any place to mount the rear end of the wishbone, which must be midway between the frame rails and at the correct height above the road surface. Height of the rear end of the wishbone is important because it controls the caster angle of the axle. If at all possible, a wishbone radius rod should be used instead of strapped rods to eliminate the possibility of cracking or breaking the front suspension members and to guarantee freedom of movement of the members.

Radius rods for a rear axle assembly are subject to the same problems and conditions that

This is the warm-up run of the Hot Rod Magazine Special. Car holds world record for standing start kilometer by covering distance at an average speed of 123.556 miles per hour. Speed at the end of run reached 182.22 mph.

apply to front radius rods. When a torque tube drive is used, the torque tube transmits fore and aft axle movement to the transmission and axle assembly and resists twisting effort exerted on the assembly by the ring and pinion gears. If the engine is rigidly mounted to the frame, or its fore and aft movement is controlled by radius rods between it and the frame and the torque tube doesn't have a slip joint, rear radius rods aren't actually necessary except to take some of the bending effort exerted on the rear axle assembly by the wheels as they push on the ends of the housing to move the car forward or pull on them to stop the car when the brakes are applied. Rods for this purpose can be connected to the axle assembly near its outer ends and be joined solidly to the torque tube.

If the engine in a car that has a torque tube drive isn't mounted solidly enough to transmit driving and braking forces from the torque tube to the frame, radius rods can be connected directly to the frame. The ideal way of doing this is to make the radius rods in the form of a wishbone. The wishbone's rear ends are fastened to

the axle housings, close to the wheels, in some manner that allows some twisting of the axle in relation to the arms, and its front end is pivotally mounted so the center of the pivot is on a vertical line through the center of the universal joint and as close to the joint as possible. With an arrangement of this type the torque tube and driveshaft must be fitted with slip joints that will enable their length to change to compensate for longitudinal movement of the rear axle assembly caused by the wishbone as the axle moves up and down in relation to the frame.

Rear axle radius rods that are connected to the frame and used with a torque tube drive must be pivotally mounted on the axle to eliminate the creation of a twisting effort on the rear axle assembly as one wheel moves more or less than the other wheel in relation to the frame. The centers of the joints on the front ends of the rods should be on a transverse line through the center of the universal joint. To be on the safe side, the torque tube and driveshaft used with an arrangement of this type should have slip joints so that their length can compensate

Dragsters of this type where driver sits back of the rear axle are sometimes called "slingshots." Note the two-piece steering drag link, designed to eliminate vibrational whip and erratic steering possible if a single unit of this length had been used. This dragster shows excellent workmanship.

Radius rods used on an axle fitted with an open driveshaft and springs of any type other than longitudinal leaf springs must control the full amount of torque exerted on the axle assembly by the ring and pinion gears. This means that the rods must be strong and sturdily mounted at both their axle and frame ends. However, when the front ends of the rods are connected to the frame rails, the same problem of torsion in the axle assembly when one end of the axle is higher or lower in relation to the frame than the other end exists with an open driveshaft as with an assembly that has a torque tube. Unless some flexibility is provided between the rods and the axle, such a condition will eventually cause the rods to be torn loose from the axle housing or for some other part of the assembly to be damaged. The best arrangement for an axle of this type is a wishbone that connects to a point midway between the frame rails. When a wishbone is used, the axle assembly will rotate slightly as it moves up and down in relation to the frame but compensation for this movement will be made in the universal joints at each end of the driveshaft.

Action of the frame and axles in relation to each other must be controlled by shock absorbers. Shock absorbers of several types that are suitable for competition hot rods are available. These include tubular direct-acting and lever types. Tubular shocks are available in several lengths and ranges of movement and many companies that specialize in shock absorber installations and repair work can change the valves in them for different applications. Some tube shocks are adjustable to three different degrees of resistance.

One popular lever shock is the Houdaille that was standard equipment 1948 Ford, Mercury, and Lincoln cars. Shocks of this type are converted by some shock absorber companies to 50-50 action. Resistance provided by these shocks is adjustable while they are in place on the car.

Shock absorbers are one of the most important parts in any suspension system and they become even more critical on a competition hot rod. They should be mounted as close to the wheels as possible so their arm or piston shaft will be moved the maximum distance for each amount of wheel movement and they must have a range of move-

automatically for any fore and aft movement of the rear axle assembly caused by the radius rods.

Radius rods that form a true parallelogram cannot be used on rear axles that are fitted with torque tubes. The reason for this is that an axle with a torque tube must pivot as it moves in relation to the frame so that the centerline of its pinion shaft can remain aimed at the center of the universal joint. With a parallelogram arrangement the axle would be held so that it couldn't rotate as it should. Parallelogram rods are good on an axle fitted with a Hotchkiss drive (open driveshaft) because an axle of this type should be held so its pinion shaft is somewhere near parallel to the transmission mainshaft.

Needle-nosed dragster is excellent example of hot rod technique and craftsmanship. Power-to-weight ratio in this machine is about 2 7/16 pounds per horsepower as compared to the 14-pound average of stock passenger cars. Engine is much-modified Chrysler.

ment that is adequate for the distance the axles can move. Shocks that are easily adjusted have a definite advantage over non-adjustable types because they simplify changes in chassis stiffness that might be necessary during some types of competition.

Front axles used for most competition hot rods are Model A or early Ford V8 fitted with spindles of the type to match the brakes and hubs that are to be used. Sometimes a special axle is made from chrome-moly tubing. Ends for the kingpins and brackets for spring shackles, radius rods,

Matched Ford roadster and coupe are competition hot rods powered by six-cylinder GMC engines. Modifications include magneto ignition and fuel injection systems. Twin machines show typical hot rod craftsmanship and pride in appearance.

Model T body on this roadster not only has been channeled to lower it on chassis but also lengthened and widened a full six inches. Grille shell is 1932 Ford. Note "free" exhaust setup enabling engine to operate with minimum back pressure.

Front-end details of T-bodied roadster show chromed shocks, axle, steering linkage. Lack of fenders might eliminate use of this machine on the streets in some states.

Rear-end of T-roadster has modified 1932 Ford suspension system, including oversize hydraulic shock absorbers. Note typical hot rodder technique of chroming many vital parts.

Modified flathead Ford engine powers T-bodied car. Equipment includes four-carburetor manifold, special camshaft, racing pistons. Excellent care and craftsmanship indicated.

and shock absorbers are welded to the tube. Axles of this type must be made by a man who knows what he is doing so that the brackets and end pieces will be fitted correctly to the tube and so the welding will be trustworthy.

Rear axle assemblies are usually some model of Ford fitted with a "quick-change" center section. A quick-change center section is a special aluminum ring gear housing to which standard Model A or '32 through '48 Ford axle housings can be bolted. Incorporated in the center section is a pair of spur gears between a stub driveshaft and the pinion gear shaft. Changing the spur gears in sets changes the final ratio between the driveshaft and the axle shafts. The gears can be changed by merely removing a small cover on the rear of the ring gear housing; hence the term

This drag coupe is called the "Holey One" because of hundreds of lightening holes in its chassis structure. Designers went all-out to decrease frontal area by chopping top to the barest minimum, narrowing the hood to a V-point.

quick-change. A quick-change rear end simplifies rear axle gear ratio changes that are often so necessary in most types of hot rod competition.

For some types of competition it is desirable to eliminate the differential effect in the rear axle gear assembly so that both axles will be driven at the same speed. This is done by welding the spider gears in the standard differential assembly to their shafts so they can't turn, or by installing a "spool" ring gear carrier in the axle assembly. A spool takes the place of the standard ring gear carrier and differential assembly to provide a solid connection between the ring gear and both axle shafts. Axle assemblies with welded spider gears or a spool are called "locked" rear ends.

A locked rear end is a necessity for track racing so that engine torque will be transmitted to the track's surface by both rear wheels. If one wheel should lose traction for any reason, the other wheel will drive the car. Some fellows like a locked rear end for drag racing but for other drag drivers they are strictly poison. Drivers of dry lakes and Bonneville straightaway cars are also divided in their opinions of locked rear ends.

Brakes are an important part of any hot rod but their importance depends on the type of use for which the hot rod is being built. Cars for straightaway running and the lighter cars for drag use are often fitted with only two-wheel brakes. Straightaway cars have ample room in which to stop and owners of the lighter drag cars don't

Modified Dodge V8 engine in drag coupe has fuel injection, other full-race equipment. Note quick-change rear axle center section, exhaust stacks, nearly slick racing tires.

like to use brakes on the front wheels because of their extra weight. Heavier drag cars usually require four-wheel brakes for safety's sake.

Ideal brakes for competition hot rods are the spot types now available. Brakes of this type are fairly light in weight but their main advantage over drum brakes is their resistance to fade due to heat. Fade resistance could be important in a really fast drag car and it is the main reason that drum brakes are no longer used on hot rod or professional track racing cars.

Drum brakes used on any type of hot rod should be hydraulically actuated. Mechanically actuated brakes are too difficult to adjust and maintain in adjustment and they don't have the stopping ability of the better hydraulic types.

An exceptionally good brake that can be

Driving position in some competition hot rods is sometimes located in center of body for best possible weight distribution. Note heavy tubular roll bar, pressure fuel system.

Competition hot rod cockpit is stripped of all but the essentials. Center steering requires special mounting for gear. Throttle pedal is aluminum casting. Note chrome.

This is another example of a body gutted for competition and equipped with a center driving position. Note fuel tank, safety fire equipment, and seat-belt for driver.

Fiat body on this dragster presents an odd appearance because of aft placement on frame. The car is in coupe class.

adapted to most 1948 and earlier Ford spindles and rear axle assemblies are the twelve-inch Bendix hydraulics that were used on 1939 and later Lincoln Zephyrs. These brakes have ample lining area to provide maximum stopping ability for any hot rod. When used on four wheels, it is sometimes necessary to reduce their effectiveness by shortening the lining on some of the shoes.

Wheels used on competition cars vary between stock steel wheels and special magnesium alloy wheels. Stock wheels are considerably cheaper than mag types and they fit stock hubs without

any difficulty. Mag wheels have the advantage of being lighter in weight and stronger, and they are available in types for knock-off hubs for quick wheel changing.

Engine placement in competition hot rods varies for the type of competition. In dragsters the engine is placed as far back in the chassis as it can be and still be connected to the rear axle assembly. In other drag cars with more conventional bodies the engine is usually placed quite far back in the chassis but not as far as in dragsters. Engine placement isn't as critical

Another oddity is dragster with American Austin body which puts machine in coupe class. Driver's head fits through top.

Unusual location of engine instrumentation on this rear-engined dragster allows mechanic crew-member to check engine conditions prior to runs on strip.

for straightaway running as for dragging but enough of the car's weight must be on its rear wheels to enable the wheels to get the traction they will require to drive the car at high speeds. There must also be enough weight on the front wheels to give the car directional stability. If there weren't enough weight on the front wheels the car would be hard to hold in a straight line. This may not sound right in view of the exceptionally light front ends of some dragsters and the speeds these cars are now running but it must be remembered that most of these cars have exceptionally long wheelbases that gives what weight they do have at the front end a leverage advantage that helps the wheels stay on the ground, and that they are driven under full throttle for only a quarter of a mile. Even under these conditions most dragsters are difficult to drive because of their light front ends. On a mile-run through a trap on a dry lake or on a two or three-mile run to the trap at Bonneville a dragster would more than likely become altogether too spooky for any driver in his right mind.

Cars for track racing have a very definite weight distribution problem that affects both their traction and handling ability. The usual practice with these cars is to install the firewall, which is also the rear motormount support, very near a point midway between the centers of the car's front and rear axles. Weight distribution is then fairly well divided between the car's front and rear wheels to give the rear wheels adequate traction to drive the car and to give all four wheels adequate side bite so the car can get through the turns as it should. Raising and lowering the frame in relation to the axles as described previously has an influence on the distribution of the car's weight on its axles; once the engine position has been established, minor variations in weight distribution are accomplished in this manner. Weight is also distributed on the car's individual wheels by "wedging" the frame. This is done by twisting the frame on its spring mounts or by adjusting the torsion bars so that the left wheels carry more weight than the right wheels when the car is going down the straightaway. This is done to help compensate for some of the weight shift in the chassis when the car is in turns.

Modifications to a hot rod to be used for normal driving are must less extensive than those for a competition car. These usually include the

Rear-engined dragster is powered by a completely modified but seldom used Chevrolet six-cylinder engine. Car shows low frontal area and overall excellent construction details.

installation of hydraulic brakes on cars equipped originally with mechanical brakes, installation of efficient shock absorbers of either tubular type, installation of a stiffer stabilizer bar, installation of a transverse radius rod on cars equipped with transverse springs, and, in some instances, installation of stiffer front and rear springs.

Few hot rodders resort to the practice of radically lowering a road car by hacking up its suspension members but for those who find such action appealing it should be pointed out that lowering should be done in moderation because it has many evils to condemn it and few virtues to recommend it. It can spoil a car's riding ability, throw its front wheels out of alignment, destroy its driveshaft alignment, upset the angularity of its carburetor, and reduce its road clearance. These things often add up to a car that is uncomfortable to ride in, dangerous to drive, rough on its tires, and that can't be driven on rough roads or in and out of some driveways. Lowering isn't for hot rods: leave it to the squirrels.

The overall height of some cars with stock bodies that are used for competition is lowered by "channeling" the body over the car's frame.

Front end of Chevrolet six dragster characterized by light, strong construction. Note lightening holes in shock arm.

Rear-end of Chevrolet dragster shows solid-mounted rear axle bolted to end of frame side rails. Rear axle has quick-change center section allowing different ratios to be used.

This streamliner is one of the fastest cars in the world, having topped two hundred seventy miles per hour at the Bonneville salt flats. The hot rod machine is powered by three 296-cubic-inch Mercury engines.

This allows the frame to remain in its original position in relation to its axles. The only difficult thing about channeling is that it requires considerable modifications to the body in that the body's floor has to be cut loose from the body shell and then raised in relation to the shell the amount the shell is to be channeled over the frame. With some frames it is necessary to reposition their body mounting brackets for the channeled body. Any way you look at this job, it's a lot of work.

Tops on coupes and sedans are often "chopped" to reduce the car's overall height and frontal area. Chopping a top involves taking a horizontal slice out of the top and then rewelding the severed piece back onto the body, it is a job that few amateurs can do well. Rules for most types of competition specify how much a top can be chopped and still be legal for different competition classes.

Stock bodied cars to be used strictly for competition are usually "gutted." A body is gutted by removing its headliner, door panels, seats that the driver won't need, floor mats, and anything else that has weight and can be removed. Usually the heavy standard front seat is removed and a lightweight bucket seat installed in a comfortable position for the driver. Gutted cars aren't too comfortable to ride in from the standpoint of noise and rattles but their lower weight usually pays off in competition events.

Safety devices required in a car by most competition associations include a sturdy roll bar that will protect the driver in case the car should roll, a seat belt that will hold him in his seat regardless of the position the car might be in, a flywheel housing cover in some drag cars, and, quite often, a fire extinguisher readly accessible to the driver. Safety regulations have usually been found the hard way to be necessary and a smart hot rodder will comply with them to the best of his ability. All a fellow with average intelligence has to do is imagine his car upside down at a hundred-plus miles per hour and its top folding down around his ears, or nothing between his head and the pavement but a mighty thin crash helmet, or pieces of the flywheel and clutch assembly from his car ripping through his feet and legs. With visions of this sort in mind it shouldn't take him long to decide that required safety equipment is cheap insurance for living his allotted span on this lump of dirt we call Earth.

CHAPTER FIFTEEN

The ABC's of Trouble Shooting

Every possible engine malfunction
problem is discussed in
easy-to-understand detail.

IN THE OLD DAYS a mechanic had to be part smart, part psychic, and part lucky to determine what was wrong when a car's engine stopped running. Today, all he has to do is connect a few electronic gadgets to the engine's vital parts, flip a switch or two, and watch a few dials and gauges. If he knows what the dials and gauges mean, he can pick out the faulty part without even getting his hands dirty. But despite the vast improvements made for the mechanic engaged in the art of trouble shooting, it's still the same old story for the fellow who's car quits on the road. If he doesn't have a nodding acquaintance with the things that go on in the engine and other components of the modern automobile, he's stuck until someone comes along to give him a hand; however, if he has at least an idea of what makes a car run, and a little help, he might not be afoot too long. He can more than likely determine what's wrong and make a temporary repair so the car will run at least to the next garage. The purpose of this chapter is to provide that little bit of help.

Among the things it's nice to have along when such an emergency occurs are a flashlight in good condition, a small and medium size screwdriver, a small hammer, a pair of pliers, a set of end or combination box-end wrenches including sizes from 5/16 to at least 11/16 of an inch, a 10 or 12-inch adjustable end wrench, and a pocket knife with a sharp blade. Along with these basic tools, one should have a few spare parts, including a distributor rotor, a distributor cap, a condenser, an ignition coil, a five or six-foot length of about 12-gauge primary wire with snap clips on its ends, a fuel pump filter bowl gasket, a complete fuel pump, a few feet of soft iron "bailing" wire, an ignition distributor "pigtail" lead, a fan belt, and a few miscellaneous nuts and washers. In addition to the tools and parts listed you can add others you might need for your particular car. Take a look under the hood someday and go over in your mind what could possibly happen on the road and what you would need to correct the condition. The spare parts wouldn't need to be new. As long as you knew they would

A preliminary test of the ignition system is made by checking for a spark between one of the spark plug wires and its plug.

operate as they are supposed to for at least a few hundred miles they would be good enough for spares.

For highway trouble shooting, a car can be considered as two basic parts: the engine, and the driveline. The driveline includes the clutch, transmission, universal joints, and the rear axle assembly. If the engine quits running, look for trouble in it and its accessories; if the engine runs but the car won't move look for trouble in the driveline.

The basic requirements upon which an automobile engine depends to run are a mixture of fuel and air in its cylinders, a high voltage spark across the gap in its spark plugs, and correct timing of the spark at the plugs in relation to the position of the pistons in its cylinders. The fuel-to-air ratio of the mixture in the cylinders must be within certain limits or the mixture will not ignite when the spark occurs at the spark plugs.

It has been said that ninety percent of the failures and tune up difficulties suffered by auto-

mobile engines originate in their ignition systems and there is little evidence to indicate otherwise. However, a trouble shooter has a definite advantage if he knows how an engine acted during its death throes. Did it die quietly and quickly, indicating a positive break in the primary or secondary circuit of its ignition system; or did it die noisily and slowly, backfiring through the exhaust system as it fired intermittently, indicating a loose connection in its ignition circuit, a defective condenser, or possibly a faulty ignition coil; or did it die slowly and quietly, only to restart and run a few more revolutions and die again, indicating a lack of fuel in its carburetor; or did it gradually and quietly lose speed and power the last few miles before it died, indicating either a stoppage in one of its fuel lines or a faulty fuel pump? Let's start trouble shooting!

Ignition System

Make a preliminary check of the ignition system to determine whether it is at fault by pulling one of the spark plug cables off its plug and holding its end approximately a quarter of an inch from some grounded part of the engine or frame while cranking the engine with the starter with the ignition switch on. Fat blue sparks jumping regularly from the cable to the ground would indicate that the ignition system was OK and the trouble lies elsewhere. Weak sparks from the cable, detected by moving the cable closer to the grounded surface, or no sparks at all, would indicate an abnormal condition in the ignition system that must be corrected. Failure of the starting motor to crank the engine at its normal speed would indicate that something was wrong with the starting motor or its controls, the battery, or the battery's cables.

Battery and Cables

Assuming the starter doesn't act as it should, check the battery and its cables. It's not likely that a low battery or bad cables would be the cause of a running engine's dying but such a thing isn't impossible. The battery is the heart of the car's electrical system and, therefore, the functions of the many components in the system are dependent on its condition.

A battery going dead because of an internal short may turn the engine sluggishly but it will die quickly under repeated starting. Confirmation of battery condition can be made by turning on the headlights. If the battery is nearly dead, the lights will stay on but become dim when the starter is engaged. Solution: A new battery. Possibility: Push the car to start the engine.

The battery may be in good condition but still not crank the engine. With the lights on, engage the starter. If the lights stay bright, there is something wrong with either the starter solenoid or the starting motor; but if the lights go out — not just dim but completely out — there is either a poor connection between one of the battery's posts and the plates in one of the cells, or there is a bad electrical connection between one of the posts and its cables, or the conductor in one of the cables is badly corroded or partially broken at some point. To find the trouble if the lights go out, check the connections at the ends of each battery cable for corrosion and tightness. If all

Testing the battery for life by shorting its terminal posts with a pair of pliers. Do this gently to prevent damaging the battery.

With the distributor cap off, crank engine over and watch distributor shaft to determine if it is rotating as it should.

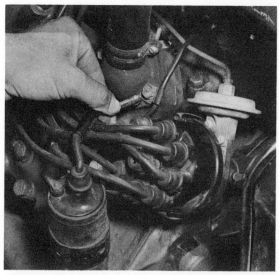

Checking for spark at the end of the coil lead while engine is being cranked by starter with ignition switch on.

the connections seem to be tight, try to move the posts in the battery to determine whether they have broken loose from the plates.

In the event that all these points seem to be in good order, remove the cables from the battery and scrape the outside of the posts and the inside of the cable terminals to remove any insulating scale or corrosion and replace the cables on the posts. It's possible for an electrical connection to be mechanically tight but not electrically tight. If possible, have someone hold the starter button down while you're checking the various cables and connections. Then, when you move the loose or faulty part, the starter will engage, indicating you have found the trouble.

Another possibility is that the lights won't come on at all. This would indicate a stone-dead battery, a cable that has come completely loose or has been severed, or a battery post that has broken loose from the battery plates.

To determine whether the battery is dead, use the handles of a pair of pliers, or some other conductor, to span from one of the posts to the other. Touch one of the posts lightly to prevent damaging the battery in case it isn't dead. A shower of sparks at the post will prove the battery to be very much alive — at least live enough to make the lights glow a little. A complete lack of sparks at the post is proof the battery is dead or one of its posts is broken inside the cell. If

one of the posts seems to be loose in the case, push it down solidly into the case and touch the conductor to the posts again. Sparks at the posts this time means the loose post is the cause of the trouble, but a lack of sparks is a good indication that the battery is dead. A dead battery won't be much help to you but a battery with a loose post can often be used long enough to reach civilization by wedging or tying the post in a position where it makes contact with its plates.

When sparks at the battery post show the battery isn't dead, check the connections at each end of its cables as described previously. Have the light switch in its "ON" position while checking the connections. Then, if you should make contact at the faulty connection while moving the cables about, the lights will light up and possibly sparks will be seen at the connection. If an inspection of the cable connections fails to disclose the trouble, trace each cable along its length to find any spot that may have been severed in some manner or been eaten through by corrosion. Bad connections can be corrected by tightening them or cleaning their contact surfaces and a severed or corroded cable can often be wired or clamped together as a temporary measure.

Ignition Wiring

If, during the preliminary test, the starting motor cranked the engine in a normal manner but the sparks that jumped from the end of the spark plug cable to ground were short and thin, or there weren't any sparks at all, make a visual inspection of the ignition system wiring. If all the secondary cables seem to be in place in the coil and distributor cap and on the spark plugs, and the primary wires are attached to the coil and distributor posts, try to move each wire and cable to determine whether all connections are tight.

Ignition Distributor Shaft

If everything seems to be in order as far as the wiring is concerned, remove the cap from the distributor and crank the engine, with the ignition switch off, while watching the rotor and breaker cam in the distributor. The rotor and cam should rotate when the starting motor spins the crankshaft, but if they don't you've found the trouble and you might as well close the hood and start looking for a tow to town.

Failure of a distributor shaft to rotate with the engine's crankshaft can be the result of stripped timing gears, or a broken timing chain, depending on the type of camshaft drive used in the engine, or a failure in the distributor drive mechanism between the camshaft and the distributor shaft. Failures in the distributor drive can be caused by the distributor shaft's "freezing" in its bushings, locking so tightly to the bushings and resisting movement so stubbornly that the driving gear or other mechanism on the lower end of the shaft breaks.

Distributor Cap and Rotor

However, let's be more inclined toward the comparatively cheerful side and assume that when the engine is cranked, the breaker cam and rotor perform properly. Replace the distributor cap, pull the coil secondary lead out of the cap and hold it near a grounded surface. Then, with the ignition switch on, sparks should fly hot and fast from the end of the lead when the engine is cranked. If sparks fly, the trouble is in the distributor cap or rotor.

Check the top of the cap for cracks or carbon paths around the coil socket, badly burned or corroded contact surfaces in the socket, or accumulations of moisture, grease, or dirt on and around the sockets. Remove the cap and check its interior surface for cracks and carbon paths originating at the coil terminal, and accumulations of moisture or grease. Solution: a temporary repair can often be effected when a cap is short-circuited by a crack or carbon path by drilling a hole completely through the cap. Center the hole (about $\frac{5}{16}$-inch in diameter) on the crack or path, midway between the terminals it connects.

Using small screwdriver to loosen dirt or corrosion that might have collected in coil lead socket in distributor cap.

Putting the "eagle eye" on distributor rotor to determine if it is cracked, has carbon paths, or is otherwise defective.

Checking the coil-to-distributor secondary lead for continuity by touching its two ends to battery's terminal posts.

The hole — possibly made with a pocket knife, in a pinch — acts as an air-gap resistance which the spark won't jump at normal driving speeds. If moisture, or an accumulation of grease, is acting as a conductor to allow the current to short to ground, dry or clean the cap with a cloth.

Perhaps the cap is clean and in good condition. In this case inspect the rotor closely for broken or missing cap contacts, cracks, or carbon paths; also, it's possible the rotor may be broken into two or more pieces. Secondary current from the coil terminal in the cap may not be able to reach the rotor if the rotor has a missing contact, and

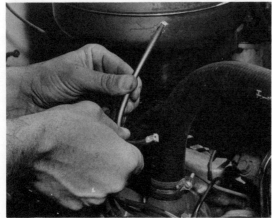

Flexing a coil-to-distributor secondary lead that won't conduct current to locate broken place or gap in conductor.

current reaching a rotor with good contacts may be short-circuiting through a crack or along a carbon path to the distributor shaft or breaker cam. Another possibility is that the locating tang in the rotor has broken, allowing the rotor to turn on the distributor shaft and deliver the secondary current from the coil to the wrong cylinder. This condition can be detected by trying to turn the rotor on the shaft. Solution: The spare rotor in the tool box. You forgot? Then you'd better be an ingenious devil. Carbon paths can sometimes be scraped for temporary relief, but a cracked or broken rotor presents an almost impossible problem. A rotor damaged so it can turn on the distributor shaft might be used long enough to get the car home by aligning it correctly on the shaft and wedging it in place.

Coil Tower

Now let's consider the possibility that there weren't any sparks between the coil wire and the grounded surface when the last check was made. In that case it's probably safe to assume that the distributor cap and rotor are in satisfactory operating condition and that the socket tower on the coil for the secondary lead may be at fault. Inspect the exterior surface of the socket for cracks, carbon paths, moisture, grease, or other defects. Inspect the interior of the socket for badly burned or corroded contact surfaces. Solution: Scrape carbon paths on the exterior of the socket, or remove moisture or grease from the socket with a cloth. Contact surfaces inside the socket may be scraped to expose bare metal. A cracked coil may pose a problem—you might try a little ingenuity, but if this fails, look for a tow.

Coil Lead

If the coil and its socket seem to be in good condition, check the cable between the coil and the distributor cap to determine whether it is conducting current. Do this by holding one of the cable's ends on the hot terminal of the starting motor solenoid and brushing its other end lightly against a grounded surface. Sparks will be seen at its grounded end if current is passing through the cable. If sparks are not seen during this check, the conductor in the cable is probably severed at some point. Solution: A defective coil-distributor cable can sometimes be made to work by feeling along its length to find the break in its conductor and then cutting the cable in two at that point. Quite often one end of the cable will be found to be long enough to reach from the coil to the distributor. Strip the insulation from a half-inch of the conductor at the cable's snipped end, separate the conductor's strands and fold them back alongside the insulation, and insert the end in the coil or distributor socket. If neither of the pieces of cable is long enough to be usable, splice the conductors of the two pieces together and support the cable so the splice is at least an inch from any grounded surface when its ends are in the coil and distributor cap.

Presuming that everything up to this point seems to be in serviceable condition, continue your search for the weak link by checking the ignition system primary circuit. Start at the distributor, as this is where most primary failures seem to originate, and work back to the battery.

Ignition Distributor Primary Circuit

Remove the distributor cap and look at the primary wires in the distributor to determine whether they are connected to their terminals as they should be. If all the wires seem to be properly connected, check the connections for tightness. Solution: Replace on its terminal any wire that has become disconnected, or tighten any connection that is loose.

Breaker Points

Inspect the breaker points in the distributor next. These overworked and neglected parts can stall an engine in a number of ways. Common breaker point defects are: not opening, not closing, becoming non-conductive, and becoming shorted.

To determine whether the points are opening, watch the point arm while the engine is being cranked with the starter, ignition switch off. The points must open a visible amount as each lobe of the breaker cam passes under the rubbing block on the movable point arm. A double check can be made by holding the distributor cap end of the coil secondary lead near a ground while the engine is being cranked with the starter, ignition switch on. If there aren't any sparks at the grounded end of the wire and the points don't

Watching distributor points to see if they open and close as they should while engine is cranked with the starter.

seem to be opening, try opening them with a screwdriver. Don't short the points to the distributor cam or breaker plate or this check will be ineffective, and don't touch the blade of the screwdriver or you may get a shock. If the reason the engine won't run is because the points aren't opening, there should be a spark between coil wire end and ground each time the points are opened with the screwdriver.

There are many reasons why points won't open but perhaps the most common of these is that the fiber rubbing block on the movable

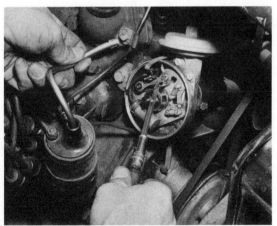

Using a screwdriver to open and close distributor points manually while watching the end of coil lead for sparks.

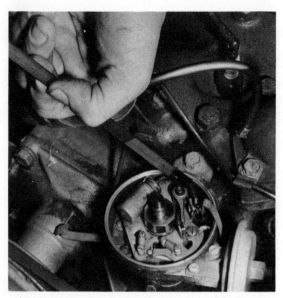

Lubricating the distributor point pivot with oil from engine crankcase so that the points will move freely on the pivot.

point arm has worn and become shortened to the point where it will no longer contact the lobes on the breaker cam and lift the arm as the cam rotates. A sure-fire cure for this condition is to adjust the movable point so the points do open when the cam rotates.

Failure of points to open can also be caused by a loose or broken rubbing block on the point arm. The cure for either of these conditions is not too positive without installing a new point arm but it may be possible to tighten a loose rubbing block or adjust the points so they will open even though the block is loose. A piece of wood or other nonconducting material taped or tied to the point arm in place of the broken block might enable the car to run under its own power far enough for a replacement part to be found. Another reason for points not opening could be that the adjustable point had become loose and vibrated toward the movable arm, closing the gap. This particular type of failure is possible but not too likely. Solution: Adjust the points so they open, and lock the adjustable point in place.

One more possibility exists in the category of points failing to open. This condition is quite common and usually traceable to a tired or mismatched ignition condenser that causes a peak to be built up on one of the points and a pit to be created in the other. When the points are

closed, the peak fits in the pit and current flows from one point to the other, and when the peak and pit aren't too large or of odd shape, current flow is interrupted as usual when the points open. However, it's possible for the peak and pit to grow to such size and shape that current flow between the points is not interrupted when the point arm moves to separate them. When the points become deformed in this manner a casual examination to determine whether they open may result in a wrong diagnosis. Solution: Restore the make-and-break operation of the points by filing or scraping the peak away, or possibly by adjusting the points so they separate farther when they are open.

Points covered with oil, grease, magnetic metallic particles, or other conductive materials may also fail to interrupt the primary circuit when they are open. Points in such condition can be cleaned with a clean cloth. When cleaning points with a cloth take care to prevent lint or threads from the cloth from becoming lodged between them. An unbelievably tiny piece of lint can cause a pair of points to remain separated so that current will not flow from one to the other.

Ignition failure caused by breaker points not closing can usually be determined visually. The cause for such a failure could be a broken or displaced spring on the movable point arm or a movable arm that had frozen on its pivot pin. The ends of a broken spring could possibly be clipped together with a small clip made from a piece of tin can or sheet metal, or a spring that had come loose from its anchor point at one end could be secured in its correct position. A point arm frozen on its pivot pin can usually be loosened by placing a drop of oil, from the crankcase if necessary, on the top of the pin and gently working the arm back and forth so the oil can work its way between the pin and the bushing in the point arm.

Another cause of points failing to close could be that the adjustable point had come loose, permitting it to be pounded so far out of adjustment by the movable arm that the rubbing block on the movable arm finally rested on the breaker cam all the time and held the points apart. Here, again, correct the condition by adjusting the points so they open and close as they should and lock the adjustable point in position.

A set of points may appear to be opening and closing perfectly when the engine is cranked by the starter but it's entirely possible that they are not making and breaking the flow of current through the primary circuit. To determine whether current is flowing through the points when they are closed, turn on the ignition switch, hold the distributor end of the coil secondary lead near a ground, and then bridge the gap between the movable point arm and the breaker plate with a screwdriver. If current isn't flowing through the points, sparks will be seen around the screwdriver each time contact is made between the point arm and the breaker plate and a spark will jump from the coil lead to ground each time contact between the arm and plate is broken. If current is flowing through the points, sparks won't be seen at the screwdriver and a spark won't be created at the coil lead when the connection between the point arm and the breaker plate is broken. To restore the points to usefulness, if current isn't flowing through them, either file or scrape their contact surfaces to remove any oxidation or foreign substance that may be on them.

Still another condition may exist when breaker points are opening and closing correctly but aren't making and breaking the primary circuit. With this condition, primary current is flowing all the time the ignition switch is on, regardless of whether the points are open or closed, indicating that the movable point arm, the condenser, or some other part of the primary circuit is shorted to a grounded surface. With the primary circuit shorted in this manner there won't be any sparks from the coil lead when the engine is cranked with the starting motor, with the ignition switch on. To determine whether it's the points that are at fault when this condition is found, it's necessary to remove the other possible sources of trouble from the circuit.

The first step in isolating the points is disconnecting the condenser lead from the terminal on the points, or distributor housing, as the case may be, to eliminate the condenser from the circuit. Now crank the engine with the starter, ignition switch on, and watch for sparks between the coil secondary lead and ground. Hold the coil lead within approximately an eighth of an inch of the grounded surface during this test because sec-

ondary current created by the ignition coil when the condenser is out of the circuit is weak and scrawny and incapable of jumping wide gaps, nor is it capable of jumping the comparatively narrow spark plug gap when there is compression pressure in the cylinders.

If sparks are seen at the secondary lead after the condenser has been disconnected, the trouble is in the condenser, but if sparks are not seen, look for a shorted point assembly. Continue by removing the lead that connects the point assembly to the primary terminal on the distributor housing from the points. Then, if the point arm is shorted, there should be current at the lead and weak sparks should be created at the coil wire when the free end of the lead is brushed back and forth against a grounded surface. If this check indicates that the point arm is shorted and there is no visible fault to cause the condition, remove the point assembly from the distributor and examine it more closely. Look for any condition that would allow current to flow from the point arm, its spring, or terminal for the primary lead, to the pin on which the arm pivots or to any other grounded surface in the distributor. If something wrong is found, correct it if possible and replace the points; if there is no fault apparent, or the fault cannot be corrected, it looks as though you'll need another point assembly to get going again.

Other than what you've just read, there isn't much more that can happen to a set of breaker points unless they just disintegrate for some reason and go up in smoke, or they literally fall apart. The balance of the primary circuit is comparatively simple and easy to check.

Ignition Condenser

The ignition condenser, usually housed out of the weather in the distributor but sometimes mounted on the outside of the distributor housing, is not an unusual source of engine failure. A condenser is basically a simple device but there are several ways in which it can become defective. However, as far as you're concerned when the engine in your car stops running, the condenser is either working or it isn't, and if it isn't, its actions are following one or the other of two patterns: it is shorting the primary circuit to ground because it is shorted internally, or it is no longer effective in the circuit because it has an open circuit internally or externally. The breaker points cannot open the primary circuit when the condenser is shorted internally because the circuit is grounded through the condenser.

An internally shorted condenser can be detected, as explained previously in the test for shorted breaker points, by disconnecting the condenser lead from the points or primary terminal on the distributor and checking for a spark at the coil lead by cranking the engine with the switch on. If there are weak sparks at the lead when the condenser is out of the circuit but none when it is in the circuit, the condenser is defective. The only thing to do with a bad condenser is replace it with another.

A condenser with an internal or external open circuit in an otherwise normal primary circuit can be detected by the weak spark delivered by the coil secondary lead when the engine is cranked, switch on. The spark will be of the same size and intensity as the spark created when the condenser is taken out of the circuit. Check the condenser for an external open circuit by inspecting the joint between the end of the conductor in its lead and the terminal attached to the lead, and the tightness of the terminal where it connects to the primary circuit. Check the lead for a broken conductor and looseness in the condenser case. Also, inspect the connection between the condenser and the breaker plate of the distributor housing for tightness. The condenser's case must be grounded or the condenser cannot operate. Be sure the condenser is not loose in its clamp and that there isn't any corrosion between the clamp and case that might insulate the case from being grounded. If all these points seem to be in good order, the trouble must be inside the condenser.

External condenser difficulties can usually be temporarily corrected to enable the engine to run at least long enough to propel the car back to civilization. A loose terminal on a lead can be clamped onto the lead with a pair of pliers and loose connections can be tightened. A lead that is loose in the condenser could possibly be pushed into the condenser and wedged in place. A clamp that is loose on a condenser's case can be bent so it holds the condenser more tightly, and a corroded case can be scraped to restore electrical conductivity between it and the clamp.

An open circuit inside a condenser presents a more difficult problem, however, that can be corrected only by replacing the condenser.

Primary Circuit Wiring

The main function of the primary circuit between the ignition switch and the breaker points in the distributor is to conduct current to the ignition coil and then from the coil to the points. There should be current in the circuit at all times when the ignition switch is on. Apparently the trouble that stopped your journey wasn't in the distributor points or condenser or you'd be on your way now, one way or another, so let's check the rest of the primary circuit to find the difficulty.

Distributor "Pigtail" Lead

An occasional troublemaker in the primary circuit is the "pigtail" lead in the distributor. The pigtail is a short wire that connects the terminal on the breaker points to the primary terminal on the distributor housing. In nearly all modern distributors the pigtail must be formed from a flexible type of wire so it will not hamper movement of the breaker plate and point assembly when the plate is rotated back and forth by the vacuum spark advance mechanism when the engine is running. It's this frequent, almost continual movement of the breaker plate that has given the pigtail its bad reputation. After a few million cycles of back and forth movement of the plate, the metal conductor in the pigtail begins to suffer from metal fatigue and, quite often, it breaks. If one isn't familiar with this particular type of failure the difficulty can sometimes be hard to locate because the broken ends of the pigtail will often make and break contact while the engine is running, causing the engine to hesitate, run awhile, hesitate again, and so on. In some instances the engine dies for keeps when the pigtail lets go.

A broken pigtail can often be found by flexing the wire with the fingers at closely spaced points along its length. If a break cannot be found in the pigtail by this mechanical method, perhaps it can be found electrically. Crank the engine to a point where the breaker points are closed, turn the ignition switch on, and then hold the distributor end of the coil secondary lead near a grounded surface with one hand while flexing the pigtail with the other. A break in the pigtail is indicated if an occasional weak spark occurs at the coil lead. A broken pigtail can often be snipped in two at the break and the two ends stripped and twisted together for a temporary repair. Don't shorten the pigtail too much, though, or it may be pulled apart when the breaker plates move. Also, it is essential to tape the spliced portion or support it in some manner so it can't contact a grounded surface and short the primary circuit.

In the event that wiggling the pigtail didn't cause any sparks at the coil lead, it's possible the pigtail either isn't broken, or that if it is broken, contact was not made between its ends when it was moved. To find which of these possibilities exists, continue the check, with the breaker points closed, by making and breaking contact between the distributor housing end of the pigtail, at the terminal on the housing, and the breaker plate with a screwdriver. If the pigtail is broken and not conducting current, sparks will fly around the screwdriver and the coil cable when contact between the plate and the terminal is broken; but if the pigtail is conducting current, there won't be any activity at the screwdriver or coil lead. Try opening and closing the points with a screwdriver, taking care to not touch any grounded surface with the screwdriver's blade. If the pigtail is conducting current, big fat sparks will fly at the coil lead when the points are opened; if the pigtail is not conducting current, there won't be any sparks.

Distributor Primary Terminal

Presuming the pigtail passes its tests with top grades down the line, the next part of the circuit to receive consideration is the insulated primary terminal that passes through the side of the distributor housing. The primary lead from the ignition coil connects to the outside of the terminal and the pigtail connects to its end in the distributor. It's possible, but not too common, for insulating members of the terminal to break and allow primary current from the coil to flow into the distributor housing instead of to the pigtail and points.

A quick check of a shorted distributor terminal can be made by cranking the engine to a

point where the breaker points are open, turning on the ignition switch, and then making contact between the end of the terminal and the breaker plate or distributor housing with a screwdriver. If sparks fly around the end of the screwdriver as contact with the terminal is made and broken, current is flowing through the terminal and it is probably alright. However, if there aren't any sparks around the screwdriver, either the terminal is shorted or there isn't any current in the primary circuit. To find which of these possibilities exists, disconnect the primary wire from the outer end of the terminal and touch the end of its conductor to the distributor housing. Sparks will be seen if there is current in the wire, but there won't be any sparks if the wire is not carrying current. A sure indication that the terminal is shorted will be seen if sparks fly when the wire is touched to its outer end when the distributor points are open.

A distributor housing terminal that was shorted because one of its members was broken or missing would be difficult to repair without the proper parts. Perhaps the best thing to do in such an instance would be to remove the terminal entirely from the distributor and run the primary lead from the coil through the hole in the housing and connect it directly to the pigtail. The splice between the lead and the pigtail would

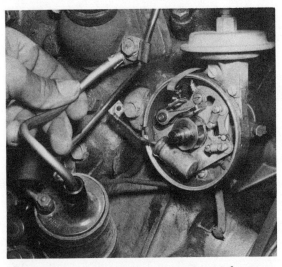

Cranking the engine with the starter, with condenser lead disconnected, and checking for a spark at the coil wire. If weak sparks are seen, the system, less condenser, is okay.

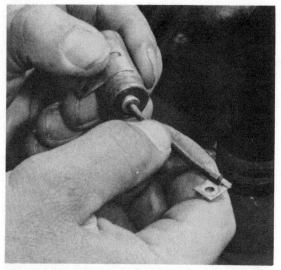

Inspecting the lead wire of a suspicious condenser for indications of loose or otherwise faulty connections at its ends. Some of these faults are repaired easily but others are not.

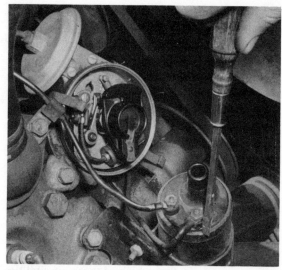

Checking the distributor post of the coil for current, with ignition switch on and the points in the distributor open, by shorting the terminal post to the steel case of the coil.

have to be insulated with tape or some other material so it wouldn't become shorted by contacting the breaker plate or distributor housing.

Distributor Primary Lead

The primary lead between the coil and the distributor seldom gives trouble but if the difficulty hasn't been found up to this point, check the lead next. With the breaker points open, or the lead disconnected from the distributor, and the ignition switch on, it should be possible to detect current at either of the lead's ends. Touch the distributor end of the wire to the distributor housing or some other grounded surface, or if the wire is still attached to the distributor, bridge the gap between its terminal and the distributor housing with a screwdriver. Sparks should fly when either of these things is done; if they don't, either the primary current in the circuit isn't reaching the wire or there is something wrong with the wire. With one end of a screwdriver resting on a grounded surface, touch its shank to the distributor terminal on the coil. Sparks will be seen if current is reaching the terminal.

When sparks are seen at both ends of the coil-to-distributor wire, it is carrying current; however, when sparks are seen at the coil end only, check the wire and the terminals on its ends for defects. It's possible for the conductor in a wire to be loose in the terminal crimped to its end, and it's also possible for the conductor to become severed at some point along the wire's length. With the wire connected to the coil and distributor, crank the engine to close the breaker points and turn the ignition switch on. Then check each end of the wire by trying to move the conductor in its terminal. If sparks are seen between the conductor and either of the terminals, crimp the terminal tightly onto the conductor with a pair of pliers. If the terminals are tight on the conductor, hold or prop the distributor end of the coil secondary lead near a grounded surface and check the wire by flexing and bending it at closely spaced points along its length. When contact is made and then broken at any severed spot in the wire's conductor, sparks will jump from the coil's secondary cable. Repair the wire by cutting it in two at the break and twisting the two ends of the conductor together.

Also examine the wire for any chafed or worn spots in its insulation where the conductor might be unprotected and contacting some grounded part of the automobile. These spots often occur where wires pass through clips or other devices installed to hold them in place, or where they accidently contact moving parts such as those in the throttle linkage.

Ignition Coil — Primary Winding

Flow of primary current through the ignition coil can be easily checked by holding the point of a screwdriver against a grounded surface and touching its shank against one and then the other of the coil's two primary terminals. Use care, though, when shorting the coil's "Bat." terminal to prevent damaging the car's ignition switch, ammeter, or wiring. Shorting an ignition system at any point between the coil and battery with a screwdriver or other device that doesn't have a built-in resistance is a touchy operation because the full fury of the battery is involved. Wires can become red hot almost instantaneously when full battery current flows through them, and ammeters and ignition switches can be burned-out just as quickly. When tests are made by shorting any part of the circuit on the distributor side of the coil, the resistance of the coil's primary winding reduces the amperage flow through the circuit to such a low value that the entire circuit can handle the current safely, but when the circuit is shorted on the battery side of the coil the resistance of the coil winding has no effect on the current's flow and damage can result.

The ideal device for checking ignition primary circuits and other low amperage circuits consists of an ordinary single-filament light bulb in series with a pair of flexible wire leads. Touching the free end of one of the leads to a grounded surface and the other lead to a terminal or the conductor in one of the wires of the primary circuit will cause the bulb to burn if there is current in the circuit; however, when tests are made on the distributor side of the coil it's necessary for the distributor points to be separated before the bulb will burn. When the points are closed, current from the coil's primary winding flows directly to ground and there isn't enough left over to light the bulb. Such a device can be used with complete safety at any point in the ignition primary circuit because the resistance of the filament in the bulb limits the flow of current through the circuit to a maximum well within the circuit's capacity.

It's nice to know what tools and equipment you should have for a certain task but, unfortunately, such knowledge is of little value when you're stalled on a lonely road, miles from the nearest help, and the necessary equipment isn't at hand. Under such circumstances you've got to do as well as you can with what you have. If it becomes necessary to determine whether a part of the ignition circuit on the battery side of the coil is hot or not the quickest method of doing

Checking the switch side of the coil for current, with the ignition switch on, by cautiously shorting the coil post to steel case of the coil. Sparks should fly when this is done.

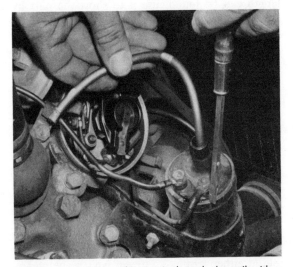

Making and breaking the circuit through the coil with a screwdriver while watching the end of coil wire for sparks. If sparks are seen at the coil wire, the coil circuit is okay.

Checking the switch-to-coil lead for current by flicking its end against a grounded surface. If sparks are seen when the wire touches ground, circuit from the battery is okay.

so is by shorting it to ground, but knowing that parts of the circuit can be damaged in this manner may help you prevent such damage. If a large conductor, such as a screwdriver, must be used as the shorting medium, protect the circuit by touching the part to be checked as lightly and for as short a time as possible by merely flicking the shorting device past the part so contact is made and broken as quickly as possible.

If a piece of stranded wire of practically any length can be found, use it to short the part by holding one end of the wire's conductor on a grounded surface and touching the part with just one strand of the conductor's other end. It's possible the strand may go up in smoke when it touches the part being tested but this is of little consequence and merely shows there is current at the part; also, destruction of the strand will serve as a visual demonstration of the terrific potentiality of the battery when its force is not limited by a resistance of some sort.

Getting back to the ignition coil, current should be detected at both its primary terminals when they are shorted to ground. For this check, the ignition switch must be on and the points in the distributor separated. If sparks aren't visible at either terminal, current isn't reaching the coil, but if sparks are visible at the terminal marked "Bat." and not at the "Dist." terminal, something is wrong with the coil's primary wind-

ing or one of its terminals. Examine the top surface of the coil for cracks or other defects around the primary terminals and check the terminal studs to determine whether they have broken loose from the coil. The terminal studs on most coils have a hole drilled through their center, with the end of the primary winding passing through the hole and soldered to the stud. Drilling the studs in this manner weakens them and it isn't too hard for a strong-arm mechanic to twist one of them off or fracture one or both more than slightly when tightening the terminal nuts. A stud partially broken through when its lead was installed could possibly break in service and sever the wire soldered to it. However, a terminal broken in this manner would be noticed immediately unless the stud managed to remain lodged in the coil cover and retain a respectable appearance.

A coil with a cracked cover that has caused the coil to drop dead, or with internally shorted or open-circuited primary windings that have accomplished the same result, is of no use to anyone and holds little promise of ever being any good again. If your coil is in either of these conditions, start looking for another coil or grab a tow to the nearest settlement.

Another possibility that exists and which must be considered when checking the primary circuit of a coil is that of the primary winding's being shorted in such a manner that current can flow from one of the coil's primary terminals to the other without passing through enough of the winding to allow the coil to create a secondary charge. Such a condition is almost impossible to detect without the proper testing equipment but a roadside test that will serve the purpose can be made. This test won't put the finger specifically on the primary winding but it will test the coil as a whole and who cares what part of a coil has gone sour as long at it won't work?

To test the coil alone, isolate it as much as possible from the rest of the ignition circuit by removing the coil-to-distributor wire from the coil terminal. With the ignition switch on, gently ground the coil's "Bat." terminal to make sure the coil is receiving current, as indicated by sparks at the terminal, and then, while holding the distributor end of the coil secondary lead near a grounded surface, touch a grounded screwdriver to the coil's "Dist." terminal. Sparks between the "Dist." terminal and the screwdriver will indicate that current is flowing through the coil's primary winding, and a weak spark between the coil's secondary lead and ground each time the screwdriver is moved away from the terminal will indicate the coil is creating a secondary voltage.

A lack of sparks at a coil's "Dist." terminal when the terminal is grounded, and when it is known there is current at the "Bat." terminal, is definite proof the coil's primary winding is either open-circuited or grounded in the coil. When the "Dist." terminal is receiving current, failure to produce a spark at the secondary lead after the "Dist." terminal has been grounded and then open-circuited again proves that either the coil's primary winding is shorted or that its secondary winding is shorted or open-circuited. In either case you're the loser because the coil is no longer serviceable and it will have to be replaced before the engine will run again.

Coil-to-Switch Circuit

Returning to the original coil test procedure, a lack of sparks when the coil's "Bat." terminal was grounded, with the ignition switch on, would indicate there wasn't any current at the terminal. To determine the reason for there not being any current at the coil, it's necessary to check the circuit between the coil and the ignition switch; however, the circuit may be either one of two types. If the circuit in your car is of the simpler type that consists merely of a wire that connects the coil to the switch, check for current at the wire's switch end by lightly shorting the "Ign." terminal of the switch. If there is current at the switch end of the coil wire but not at the coil end, look for a break in the wire or for a loose terminal on one or both ends of the wire. Splice the conductor at a break or tighten loose terminals to correct such conditions. Finding a break in a switch-to-coil wire might not be as simple as it seems, however, because in most stock cars this wire is bound tightly with many others in a "loom" or "harness." It wouldn't make sense, though, except in a case of dire necessity, to rip the loom apart in an attempt to find a bad spot in the wire when it would be so much easier to disconnect the wire at both its ends and install a new one. The new wire can be taped to the

loom at several spots to prevent it becoming entangled in moving parts under the hood or from contacting hot surfaces.

The procedure for checking the second type of coil-to-switch circuit, which varies from the single-wire type in that a resistor of some sort has been inserted in the circuit, requires that the resistor be checked for current at each of its two terminal posts. Some ignition system resistors are mounted in the engine compartment, either on the engine or firewall, whereas others are mounted on the passenger side of the firewall.

Most ignition system resistors consist of a coil of wire of a special alloy wound on a suitable support but another type that once was quite popular consists of a light bulb in a bakelite container. Current from the ignition switch flows through the filament in the bulb before it reaches the ignition coil. There was also an ignition coil, not used as original equipment but sold for replacement purposes, that contained a light bulb in its case. The bulb acted as a built-in resistor in the primary circuit, just as an externally mounted bulb would, and it could be replaced by removing a cap from the coil case.

One of the first things to check when an engine with a light bulb in its ignition circuit drops dead is the bulb. Current flow to the primary winding in the ignition coil would be interrupted, just as though the ignition switch had been turned off, if the bulb should burn out. With the ignition switch on and the breaker points closed, or the terminal post on the coil side of the bulb's case grounded, the bulb should glow. If current can be detected on the switch side of the bulb and bulb doesn't glow, chances are it is burned out and needs replacing. A quick, permanent repair can be made by installing a new bulb of the same type, and a temporary repair can be made if a new bulb isn't handy by placing the wires on the two posts of the bulb's case on one of the posts. This will allow the current flowing from the switch to by-pass the bulb and flow directly to the coil.

A bulb mounted in a coil case could be by-passed by stuffing a piece of tinfoil or other material capable of conducting electricity in the bulb's socket so a connection would be made between the socket's center terminals and its sides. An alternative method would be to break the glass portion of the bulb and bend the two heavy leads that conduct current to the filaments so they would stay in contact with each other. Remember, though, that these are just temporary repairs and that a new bulb should be installed as soon as possible to prevent damage to the coil.

With the ignition switch on, it should be possible to detect current at the "Bat." terminal of the coil, at both terminals of either a bulb type or wire coil resistor, and at the "Ign." post of the ignition switch. Lack of current at the coil when current can be detected at the coil side of the resistor would indicate a loose or corroded connection between the post on the coil and the wire between it and the resistor, or loose terminals on the ends of the wire, or a severed conductor in the wire. Clean and tighten bad connections, tighten loose terminals with a pair of pliers, or repair a wire that has a severed conductor by splicing the conductor's two ends together or by replacing the wire. Current at the switch side of a resistor but not at its coil side is proof that the resistor is not passing current, possibly as a result of a loose connection or a broken conductor in the resistor. If the difficulty isn't readily apparent, perhaps the best thing to do is attach the wires on the resistor's two terminal posts to one of the posts as a temporary means of getting going again and then replace the resistor with a new one as soon as possible.

Lack of current at the switch side of the resistor when the switch post is definitely hot would indicate the same type of difficulties and repairs described for the resistor-to-coil wire.

There is another possibility that must be considered when checking the switch-to-coil part of the circuit and that is that the insulation of the wire has worn through at some spot, allowing the conductor in the wire to short against some grounded surface. However, you can rest assured there won't be any mystery when this happens because a short bad enough to stop an engine cold will cause the wire to become so hot that its insulation will char or possibly burst into flame. In the event of charring or flames, turn off the ignition quickly and extinguish the fire. After the wire has cooled and its bare sections have been taped or moved away from grounded surfaces, it may be possible to use it long enough to get the car home; however, a charred or burnt wire should be replaced as soon as possible to prevent a recurrence of the trouble.

Ignition Switch

Ignition switches seldom give any trouble but it's not impossible for one to go haywire. If, when the ignition switch is in its "ON" position, current can be detected at its "Bat." terminal but not at its "Ing." terminal, something is wrong with it. If the circuit through the switch can't be completed by flipping it on and off a few times, a temporary measure can be accomplished by removing the switch-to-coil wire from the switch's "Ign." terminal and placing it on the "Bat." terminal. Changing the wires in this manner bypasses the switch and eliminates it from the circuit. When the time comes to stop the engine it will be necessary to disconnect the coil wire from either the switch or the coil.

Ignition Switch to Solenoid Circuit

Lack of current at the "Bat." terminal of the ignition switch would prove something to be at fault in the circuit between the switch and its source of current. You know the battery and its cables are alright because they were the first things you checked. That narrows the possibilities down to the ammeter and the wires between the switch and the hot post of the starting motor solenoid. Not all cars are wired so their ignition circuit originates at the starting motor solenoid and passes through the ammeter but any circuit that varies from this pattern can usually be easily traced and its wires and connections checked in the same manner as those in more conventional circuits.

Most automotive-type ammeters have two terminals to which are connected the wires that serve all but one of the electrical circuits on the automobile—the lone circuit that does not include the ammeter is the starting motor circuit because of its high amperage requirements. A wire from the hot side of the starting motor solenoid is usually connected to one of the ammeter's terminals, and wires to the ignition system, lights, generator, and electrical accessories are connected to the other terminal. By wiring the ammeter in this manner all current flow necessary to operate the automobile, with the exception of that required by the starting motor, passes through the ammeter.

When an ammeter is correctly wired, both its terminals are hot at all times; therefore, there should always be current in the wires connected to the terminals. To continue the check of the ignition primary circuit, test for current at the "cold" terminal of the ammeter—this is the terminal to which the wires leading to the various switches and accessories are connected. Rather than shorting this terminal because of its usual inaccessibility and the possibility of damaging the ammeter, turn the headlights off and on or work the brake pedal to operate the stoplights while watching the ammeter hand. If the lights come on as they should and the ammeter hand moves toward the discharge side of the meter's scale, the ammeter is in usable condition; however, be sure to watch for movement of the ammeter hand when the lights go on and off because it's possible for lights to be wired in such a manner that their circuits do not include the ammeter. If this should be the case, the actions of the lights would not give any indication of the ammeter's condition and it would be necessary to check the ammeter at its terminals by shorting or some other means to determine its condition.

An indication of current at the ammeter's cold terminal and a lack of current at the ignition switch will prove that something is wrong with the wire that connects the switch to the ammeter. The wire's conductor may be broken or the terminals on its ends may not be making contact with the conductor. With the ignition switch on and the breaker points in the distributor closed, check for loose terminals by trying to move the wire's conductor in its terminals. Any looseness at these points should be indicated by sparks between the conductor and terminal and movement of the ammeter hand. Loose terminals can be tightened by squeezing them with a pair of pliers. A broken conductor in the wire might be found by flexing the wire at closely spaced points along its length.

A broken wire can be cut and spliced for a temporary repair; however, the wire may be part of a wiring loom and impossible to check without separating that part of the loom. If this is the case, merely disconnect the wire at each of its ends and install a new wire, or disconnect the coil wire from the ignition switch and run it directly to the ammeter. To stop an engine when its coil wire is connected to the ammeter, it's necessary to disconnect the wire from either the meter or the coil.

In rare cases where the ammeter is burned-out or otherwise damaged so that current isn't being conducted from one of its terminal posts to the other, it can be easily removed from the circuit by connecting all the wires originally attached to its two posts to either one of the posts. Changing the wires in this manner will not affect the operation of any of the car's many electrical circuits in any way whatsoever with the exception that amperage flow in the circuits will not be shown by the meter.

The wire between the ammeter and the starting motor solenoid, or other source of current, is the last link in the primary circuit. If current cannot be detected at the ammeter end of the wire, check the wire for loose terminals, broken conductor, or a completely severed spot at some point along its length. This wire, too, may be in a loom, making it difficult to check for a broken conductor; if so, install another wire if possible. If a suitable length of wire isn't available for replacement purposes, tear the loom apart to find the defect and repair the wire. When a car is disabled by such a defect don't try to run the engine by running a hot wire directly from the starting motor solenoid to the coil because the circuit between the generator and the battery is not complete without the ammeter-to-solenoid lead and some types of generators cannot be operated on an open circuit in this manner without being damaged.

Carburetor flooding can often be stopped by tapping carburetor near needle seat with wrench or whatever else is handy. This is a quick, easy cure that should be permanent.

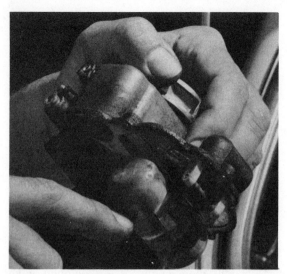

The float of a flooding carburetor can be checked for freedom of movement by lifting it with finger then letting it drop. If it binds, loosen it so that it is free to move.

Ignition Timing

It's possible for an ignition system to be in perfect condition and throw big fat sparks from the spark plug cables but be so far out of time with the engine that the engine won't run. Such a condition is comparatively rare but not at all impossible. It could be caused by a distributor coming loose in its mounting and rotating out of position, or, more rarely still, by an extremely loose timing chain that has jumped a few teeth on one of its sprockets. An ignition system out of time because the distributor has slipped can be retimed again without too much effort but a system out of time because the timing chain has jumped teeth is a more serious problem that will require a new chain and considerable work for its installation.

A distributor that has come loose and moved can be easily detected by grasping the distributor and trying to rotate it in its mounting. To get the engine running again rotate the distributor back to its original position and tighten its securing mechanism. The direction to rotate the distributor may pose a problem, however, unless there is something to indicate the position its housing occupied before it slipped. If you're not the lucky type and must guess which way to turn the distributor, it would seem logical to turn it against any force that might tend to move it, such as the force exerted by a steel vacuum line, rather than

with such a force. With the distributor in its new position, try to start the engine. If the engine runs at all, you know you're on the right track, but if it doesn't, turn the distributor in the opposite direction, back past the position it was in when the engine stalled, and try again. Once the engine starts it may be necessary to rotate the distributor one way or the other a slight amount to correct any advanced or retarded condition so the engine will pull well enough to propel the car to the garage where the timing can be adjusted more accurately.

That's about all there is to checking the engine's electrical system. If there had been anything wrong with the system, you would have found it. The next section is concerned with checking the engine's fuel system, cooling system, and other mechanical things that can stall a car.

The purpose of the fuel system is to deliver fuel and air mixture to the engine's cylinders in the correct proportions to form a combustible mixture. If something in the system failed, it's possible the cylinders were receiving too much fuel, or not enough fuel, or were not receiving enough air.

Fuel Gauge

The first thing to check in the fuel system is the fuel gauge on the instrument panel. If the gauge registers empty the chances are you have found the trouble. The solution to this predicament is obvious. But if the gauge indicates there is fuel in the tank the trouble probably lies in some other part of the system. It's not impossible for a fuel gauge to register incorrectly, though, so make sure there is fuel in the tank by pulling the tank's cap and checking.

Preliminary Inspection

Once you have determined the fuel condition and have satisfied yourself that there is sufficient fuel to run the engine, take a look at the carburetor and fuel pump. Look for raw fuel on the carburetor or pump and also inspect the flexible fuel hose between the carburetor and the line from the tank. If any of these members is wet with fuel you have more than likely found the source of trouble. A wet carburetor is "flooded," a wet fuel pump is either leaking around its diaphragm or through a hole in the diaphragm, and a wet flexible hose probably has a leak at some point. The odor of gasoline is usually quite strong in the engine compartment of a car that has a leaky fuel system.

If the carburetor is flooded, the engine is receiving too much fuel in proportion to the quantity of air inducted into the cylinders and the air-fuel ratio of the mixture is too "rich" for the mixture to burn. If the fuel pump is leaking it may not be capable of delivering fuel to the carburetor, and if the flexible hose is leaking it may be allowing air to enter the fuel line and reduce the pumping capacity of the pump. Let's consider the possibility of a flooded carburetor first.

Flooded Carburetor

The usual cause of a flooded carburetor is a piece of dirt or other foreign material between the carburetor's float needle and its seat. In some carburetors it's possible for the float to drag on the side of the float bowl and fail to close the needle. In the event the needle doesn't seal properly on its seat, the fuel pump continues to pump fuel into the carburetor and the fuel level in the float bowl rises to the point where fuel flows into the intake manifold by way of the carburetor's main discharge nozzles. When a carburetor floods in this manner fuel may also flow out of the vent holes in its bowl cover and seep through its throttle valve shaft bores.

An engine stalled by a flooded carburetor can generally be started again by lightly tapping the fuel line fitting and the carburetor bowl in the area around the float needle seat with a wrench or a small hammer. Tapping the bowl in this manner will usually dislodge whatever is under the needle and allow it to seat and stop the flow of fuel. Tapping the carburetor will, in most instances, also jar a stuck float loose so it will function properly. After tapping the carburetor, try to start the engine while holding the throttle all the way open. Holding the throttle open while cranking the engine with the starter allows the maximum quantity of air to be drawn into the cylinders to overcome the excess fuel condition.

In some cases it is possible that the flooding cannot be stopped by tapping on the carburetor.

Checking needle and seat for foreign material that might keep the needle from seating to shut off the flow of gasoline into the carburetor. It takes only a minute piece of dirt or other matter to hold the needle off the seat, with consequent flooding of the carburetor. Also, check the seat to be sure it is tight in the cover or body of the carburetor; if it isn't, it is possible for fuel to flow around it and into the bowl of the unit.

When this revolting condition exists it becomes necessary to take the bowl cover off the carburetor and see what cooks inside. When it is necessary to disconnect choke linkage to remove the bowl cover take a good look at the linkage before removing it so you will be able to reinstall it correctly.

Some carburetors are so constructed that the float and needle assembly are attached to the bowl cover but in others the float and needle are in the bowl. With either type remove the float and inspect it for any damage that might prevent it from closing the needle, such as a broken arm or pivot, and shake it to determine whether it has developed a leak and become partially filled with fuel. A float filled with gasoline loses it buoyancy and becomes a sinker instead of a float and therefore cannot force the needle against its seat when the fuel in the carburetor bowl is at its correct level. If the float is filled with gas, drain it and attempt to seal the hole.

Presuming the float is in usable condition, inspect the needle and its seat for anything that might hold the needle off the seat. Check both the inlet and outlet sides of the seat because there might be a piece of solid matter half in and half out of its fuel opening that is causing all the trouble. Remove anything in the seat or on the needle and reassemble the carburetor.

Another type of engine flooding can be the result of a lack of air in the carburetor. This could be caused by a restriction in the carburetor throat, above the discharge nozzles, or in the air cleaner. About the only thing that could cause a restriction in the carburetor throat would be the choke valve. If the valve should close when the engine was running, manifold vacuum would cause fuel to flow freely from the carburetor's main discharge nozzles and raw fuel would be inducted into the engine's cylinders. A closed choke valve should be easy to find after the air cleaner has been removed from the carburetor but if the valve is found to be open and it is of the manually operated type, try to move it to see whether its lever is held securely by the control cable. If the lever has slipped on the cable or the cable housing has slipped in its clamp or something has broken and allowed the valve to move freely, correct the condition if possible or secure the valve in its open position with a piece of wire. A choke valve of the auto-

matic type could fail, and close or not open, from any number of causes and perhaps the best thing to do in such an instance would be to temporarily secure it in its open position, just as a manually operated choke would be.

Leaking Fuel Pump

A fuel pump can leak either externally or internally; however, many pumps are so designed that when they leak internally the fuel can flow through drain holes in the pump housing and onto the outside of the engine rather than into the crankcase where it can dilute the lubricating oil. An external leak could be the result of loose fittings in the inlet or outlet side of the pump, loose valve caps, loose screws around the circumference of the diaphragm housing, a crack in the housing, a loose filter bowl, a cracked filter bowl, or a defective filter bowl gasket. Leaks in the carburetor side of the pump would have to be very bad to cause the engine to stall but on the vacuum, or tank, side a leak doesn't have to be too pronounced to allow the pump to pull air instead of fuel. A defective filter bowl gasket or cracked bowl will pose more of a problem because they are on the vacuum side of the pump and must be sealed more securely if the pump is to operate well enough to get the car to a source of new parts. Ordinary tape and sealers used in automotive work and possibly on hand when such a thing might happen are of little use for such sealing jobs because they are soluble in gasoline and lose their adhesive and sealing properties when exposed to it.

Internal leaks in a pump are the result of a hole or other flaw in the diaphragm that exerts the pressure on the fuel to force it to the carburetor. When a diaphragm is in this condition the pump is dead and unless a spare is handy the car is dead too.

Leaking Flexible Fuel Hose

A leaking flexible hose places you in almost the same position as a cracked filter bowl or a defective bowl gasket. The leak must be sealed air-tight but the problem is finding a way to do the sealing. If the leak happened to be in the middle of the hose it might be possible to cut the hose in two at the leak, insert a short length of copper or steel tubing in the two ends of the

If the choke valve should close when the engine is running, the engine will be flooded. Check the choke mechanism by moving it back and forth to see if the choke valve opens and stays open.

hose, and then clamp the hose to the tubing with wire wrapped around it and twisted together. In some cars it might be possible to eliminate the flexible fuel line entirely by bending the line from the tank to make it connect directly to the fuel pump. This is a temporary measure, however, because movement of the engine in relation to the frame would soon cause the fuel line to crack or break.

Check for Fuel in Carburetor

The first thing to do when checking the carburetor to see if there is fuel in its float bowl is remove its air cleaner and work the throttle linkage back and forth a few times while looking into its air horn. As the throttle is opened a small stream of gasoline should squirt from the accelerating pump nozzles. If the carburetor is of the single-throat type it will have only one nozzle but if it is a dual or four-throat unit it will have two nozzles. Fuel squirting from the nozzles in solid streams indicates that there is fuel in the carburetor bowl, whereas a lack of fuel proves the carburetor bowl to be empty, indicating trouble between the carburetor and the fuel tank.

Dirt or Water in Carburetor

If liquid does squirt from the nozzles when the throttle is opened and the engine won't run there is a possibility that the main metering jets in the carburetor bowl are plugged or that there is water in the bowl. It's not improbable for the metering jet of a single-throat carburetor to become plugged with dirt or other foreign material but it is rare that both jets of a dual-throat unit would plug at the same time. This could happen if an unusually large quantity of dirt or sediment should collect in the bowl for some reason but such an occurrence isn't too likely. It is much more possible for sufficient water to collect in the bowl to stop the engine. Water is heavier than gasoline and therefore it will remain on the bottom of a carburetor bowl.

No Fuel in Carburetor

When movement of the throttle does not produce any fuel at the accelerating pump nozzles the first thing to do is disconnect the fuel line at the carburetor and crank the engine with the starter while watching the end of the fuel line. A solid stream of fuel should spurt from the end of the line at regular intervals as the crankshaft rotates. If fuel does flow from the line the trouble may lie in the carburetor float needle and seat assembly, or if the carburetor has a filtering screen, the screen may be plugged with dirt or lint. The filter screens in some carburetors can be removed for cleaning only by unscrewing the fuel line fitting or the needle seat from the bowl but in others it can be reached by merely unscrewing a large cap usually located near the fuel inlet fitting. If your carburetor does not have a filter screen and it is possible to do so, remove the fuel line fitting from the carburetor and check it to determine whether it is plugged. If the line is open, remove the bowl cover from the carburetor and inspect the float for free movement. It's possible but not too probable for a float to stick and hold its needle on its seat. If this is the case locate the bind and loosen the float so it can operate as it should. If the float is free remove it and the needle and seat and check the seat and fuel passage in the carburetor for any obstruction that would prevent the fuel from reaching the float bowl.

Plugged Tank Vent

Assuming that fuel did not squirt from the fuel line when the engine was cranked, remove the filter cap from the fuel tank and repeat the check by cranking the engine again. Allow the starter to operate at least thirty seconds to give the fuel pump a chance to fill itself and the line to the carburetor. The theory behind repeating the test with the fuel tank uncapped is to completely eliminate the possibility of the tank's not being adequately vented. If by chance the vent in the tank should become plugged in some manner, air would not be able to enter the tank to replace the fuel drawn from it by the fuel pump. A vacuum would be created in the tank and fuel would cease to flow to the pump.

Actually the pump does not draw fuel from the tank. It forces the air in the fuel line out of the line and creates a partial vacuum, or low pressure, in the line. Then, atmospheric pressure, acting on the surface of the fuel in the tank, pushes fuel into the fuel line and into the pump. The diaphragm in the pump then forces the fuel into the carburetor. It is absolutely necessary, therefore, that the tank be vented to allow atmos-

pheric pressure to enter it if the fuel is to flow to the pump. In any case, make sure the tank is vented.

Fuel Lines and Fittings

If removing the tank cap didn't change the situation, disconnect the pump end of the line from the pump and blow through it from the carburetor end. If the line is plugged so that air cannot be blown through it, try opening it with a piece of wire or other material; however, it's not too common for this line to become plugged. If you can blow through the line without any trouble it's possible that the fuel pump is inoperative, has a plugged fuel passage or fitting, or is not receiving fuel from the tank. To determine whether the pump or a lack of fuel is causing the trouble, disconnect the pump from the tank line and try to force fuel through the line by blowing, with the mouth, into tank filler opening.

On many older cars, blowing into the fuel tank is easy because the filler opening is readily accessible but on most later models it presents a problem because the filler openings are hidden in recesses. Sometimes a tire pump can be used to build up pressure in a tank. When a pump is used it is necessary to wrap a cloth around its hose and hold the cloth tightly against the filler opening to seal the opening so the air pressure won't escape. The vent openings of externally vented tanks will have to be plugged before pressure can be created in the tank. This can be done by holding a finger over the opening. If it so happens that it is impossible to blow into the filler opening, an alternative method is, if possible, to blow into the pump end of the line. This method isn't the best because if there is an obstruction in the line it will be blown back into the tank where it may cause trouble again, instead of out of the line. However, at a time like this the main idea is to clear the line in any way possible to get the car rolling again. When blowing into the pump end of the line a gurgling should be heard in the tank as the air escapes through the fuel. If pressure can be held in the line, it is plugged.

Obstructed Flexible Fuel Hose

If the pump-to-tank line seems to be clear so fuel can pass freely through it, remove the flexible fuel hose from the pump and check it for obstructions by blowing through it.

Fuel Pump

Check the fuel pump and its fittings if the fuel hose seems to be in good condition. If you can manage to do so, wet the end of a finger and seal the inlet fitting on the pump with it and then crank the engine with the starter. This may be hard or impossible to do if you are alone. With some cars it is possible to operate the starter from the engine compartment by grounding the switch terminal on its solenoid or connecting one terminal to the other with a short length of wire or a pair of pliers or a wrench. Be sure the engine is out of gear and your hands and arms are clear of the fan and generator pulley and their belts before engaging the starter. As the engine is cranked a vacuum should be created in the side of the pump sealed with the finger and you should be able to feel the vacuum on the finger. If there is any doubt as to whether the pump has created a vacuum, move the finger slightly so air can enter the fitting. If there was a vacuum in the pump the air will be heard entering the pump. A lack of vacuum indicates either an inoperative pump or an obstruction in the pump.

If the pump doesn't seem to be working, check the nut or clamp that holds the filter bowl on the pump for tightness. Tighten the nut or clamp if it seems to be loose and repeat the check for vacuum by cranking the engine again while holding a finger over the pump's inlet fitting. If the pump builds up a vacuum now the trouble may have been an air leak between the bowl and the pump. Reconnect the line from the tank to the pump and crank the engine again to see if the pump will pick up fuel. If fuel is pumped out of the outlet side of the pump you'll soon be on the road again, but if it isn't, remove the fitting on the tank side of the pump and inspect it for foreign material that may have plugged it. If the fitting is clean, examine the passage in the pump. It is seldom that this part of a pump will become plugged because it empties directly into the filter portion. If all is well so far, remove the filter bowl and filtering element and check the bowl for water and other sediment and check the filtering element for collections of matter that might prevent fuel from flowing through it. A filtering element so thoroughly plugged that it cannot be

cleaned with the tools at hand can be left out of the pump temporarily to get the car running again.

A fuel filter of the accessory type that may have been installed in the fuel line at some time or other should be checked in the same manner as the filter on the fuel pump.

About the only things left to disable a fuel pump would be the mechanical parts in its operating linkage or valve assemblies. Failures in these parts could include frozen linkage, broken linkage, a broken diaphragm spring, a stuck valve, a broken valve, or a broken valve spring. Frozen linkage is easily recognized because the lever that actuates the pump diaphragm will not move when this condition exists. Don't be confused, however, by the normal resistance of the lever because in some pumps, especially those with vacuum units, the lever is quite hard to move. Regardless of the type of pump on the engine the linkage will have some free movement if it is not frozen. Frozen linkage can usually be worked loose so it will operate satisfactorily by exerting pressure on it in one direction and then the other until it will move through its full range. A vacuum can be created in the pump by holding a finger over the fuel inlet and working the arm by hand if the linkage and the rest of the pump is in operating condition.

A broken diaphragm spring in a pump that does not have an integral vacuum pump can be detected by the lack of resistance to movement of the pump actuating arm. It will be necessary to dismantle the fuel section of a double-unit pump to find a broken diaphragm spring because the resistance of the spring in the vacuum section is much greater than that of the fuel spring.

If the pump's linkage and diaphragm spring seem to be in good condition but a vacuum cannot be created in it by operating the linkage by hand, it's possible one of its valves or valve springs is broken or jammed. To check the valves it is necessary to remove the top portion of the pump from the lower part. Remove the valve cages and the valve assemblies one at a time and inspect them for damage. If either of the valves seems to be stuck, it is a simple matter to free it and restore the pump to operating condition. If one of the valves is broken, you may have trouble on your hands and may need another pump or a

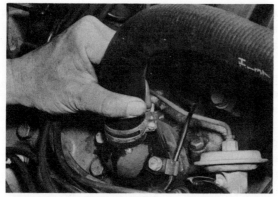

Radiator hoses and other fittings in an engine's cooling system are natural spots for leaks that can drain system and cause overheating. Replace hose, fittings to correct.

Pump Actuating Linkage

A pump in perfect condition won't pump fuel if the stroke of its actuating lever is too short. Such a condition is the result of a worn lobe on the camshaft or worn intermediate linkage between the camshaft and the pump arm. The cure for a worn cam lobe is a new camshaft but worn intermediate linkage, such as the pushrod used in 1932 to '48 Ford V8's and '39 through '48 Mercurys, can cause the same trouble as a worn cam lobe. More than one car of these categories has been driven home, and often farther, after a simple temporary repair had been made. The simple repair that corrects for the combined wear in these parts is to insert a thin nut, or a piece of metal, tin foil, or any other solid material, in the socket to lift the arm a slight amount in relation to the upper end of the rod. The material used for this purpose should be approximately $\frac{1}{16}$ of an inch thick to guarantee adequate stroke and it must be wedged tightly in the pump socket so it will not fall out of the socket when the pump is being installed on the engine.

tow to town unless some sort of material from which a new valve can be fashioned is available. A broken valve spring could possibly be made to work by stretching the longer of the two halves to make it long enough to hold the valve against its seat.

Making a quick check of the fuel pump to see if it will create a vacuum by sealing its inlet and then cranking the engine. If the pump will not create a vacuum, it is defective in some way.

Overheating

There are four general types of engine overheating. The most common of these is caused by hot weather and the other three are the results of loss of water from the cooling system, impaired water circulation, or impaired air circulation.

Lack of Water

Overheating due to lack of water in the cooling system can be caused by either an internal or external leak. An internal leak is usually through a blown head gasket but sometimes it can be through a crack in the cylinder block or head. These defects either allow the water to leak into one or more of the cylinders and then be blown out of the exhaust system, or allow compression and combustion pressures to create a pressure in the cooling system and blow water out of the radiator. Either of these conditions is serious enough to end any journey. The repairs required are a new head gasket or suitable measures to close the crack. Some cracks are not repairable and a new block or head will have to be installed.

External leaks that allow water to escape from a cooling system can be through either a loose, cracked, or broken radiator or heater hose, a worn water pump, broken radiator, loose drain plug, rusted Welch plug, or a loose fitting that allows the water to leak past the fitting's gasket.

Stop-leak solutions poured into a radiator seldom have any effect on leaks of any size but if the leak can be slowed down it may be possible to stop it altogether with one of these solutions.

If the radiator has a pressure cap it may be possible, after all temporary repairs have been made, to slow the leak considerably by wedging the small valve in the cap's inner part in an open position with a small piece of wood or other material. The purpose of this valve is to allow air to enter the radiator after the engine has been shut down and the coolant in the engine and radiator is cooling. Under some conditions it would be possible for a vacuum to be created in the cooling system when the coolant was cooling if air were not allowed to enter the radiator in this manner. By wedging the valve open it will not be possible for the normal high pressure to be created in the radiator as the engine temperature rises and the coolant expands and, therefore,

there will not be any pressure in the cooling system to force water out of any leaks that might be in the radiator.

Rusted Welch plugs are common causes of water leaks but as a rule they cause slow leaks that can be plugged with a piece of wood whittled to size and forced into the hole in the plug. Before making a wooden plug for a hole in a Welch plug stick a screwdriver or some other sharp instrument into the hole and wiggle it around to enlarge the hole as much as possible and eliminate any material around the hole that may be almost rusted away. By doing this the wooden plug will have a better chance of sealing the leak by having comparatively sound material to seat against.

If a gasket in some part of the cooling system is bad it may not be possible to stop the leak without replacing the gasket. For most fittings that use gaskets a simple gasket can be made from a piece of magazine cover or similar material. Remove the fitting and cut or tear the paper to match its outer shape and the shape of the opening it covers. Clean the mating surfaces of the fitting and the surface it bolts to and then bolt the fitting and its gasket in place.

Restricted Water Flow

The third cause of overheating is restricted water flow through the cooling system. This can be caused by a radiator that is plugged with deposits of rust or foreign material, by a radiator hose that has become swollen internally and stopped or reduced the flow of water, by a fan or water pump belt that is broken or slipping and not turning the water pump, by a thermostat that has stuck in the closed position, by a water distributor tube in the cylinder block that has rusted through and broken, or by a water pump that has corroded or otherwise damaged impeller blades.

There isn't much that can be done with a radiator that is plugged internally without a professional "boil-out" treatment. Sometimes a radiator will become partially plugged and be unable to cool an engine at high speeds but still have sufficient capacity to cool satisfactorily at lower speeds.

A radiator hose that has swollen internally and blocked the flow of water could possibly be removed from the engine and part of its inner surface removed to make a passage for the water. Such a hose would probably be stiff on the outside and therefore would have to be removed from the engine with care to prevent its being damaged to the extent that it couldn't be reused. If the inside of the hose had become swollen because of oil in the cooling system it's possible the outside of the hose would be soft and squishy.

A loose fan belt doesn't pose much of a problem because it can be tightened to correct the condition. In most cars the fan belt also runs the generator; therefore, if the fan belt is slipping it is more than likely that the battery will be low too because the generator hasn't been charging as it should. It's not uncommon on older engines for the fan belt to become oily and slippery from oil that has been thrown or has leaked out of the engine. If the belt on your engine is in this condition and won't turn the water pump and generator, try to wipe it off with a cloth or rub dirt into its friction surfaces to dry it and make it a little more sticky. It may also be necessary to tighten

the belt to make it grab the pulleys better. Another possibility with a fan belt is that the belt is of the wrong type or that it has worn on its sides to the point where it is bottoming in the pulleys and not getting a bite on the sides of the pulleys as it should.

Thermostats don't stick in the closed position too often but when one does it can cause an engine to overheat in a hurry. The best thing to do if there is any doubt about the condition of a thermostat is remove it temporarily from the engine so it cannot restrict the flow of water to the radiator.

Many engines of the six-cyinder variety have a water distributor tube in the water jacket that directs coolant from the water pump to exhaust valve seats and other hot spots in the engine. The tube serves another purpose of carrying cool water from the pump at the front of the engine to the rear of the cylinder block so the rear cylinders will receive their share of cooling. It's not uncommon for these tubes to become rusted and finally break in two at some point along

Loose or broken oil filter fittings and lines are fine spots for oil leaks. Loose fittings can usually be tightened but a broken line will have to be replaced to correct condition.

their length. When this happens the rear portion of the engine will overheat and rapidly bring the water in the cooling system to a boil. The only cure for this condition is a new tube that can be installed only after the water pump and radiator have been removed.

A defective water pump that has a broken impeller or damaged impeller blades that can't move the water through the engine is another of those things that cannot be easily repaired on the road.

Restricted Air Flow

The fourth condition that can cause an engine to overheat is partial or complete clogging of the air passages through the radiator core. This can be caused by mud, dirt, leaves, bugs, paper, or anything else that has an opportunity to collect on the radiator in sufficient quantity to block the flow of air through the core. Such a condition is easy to detect and the obvious solution is to clean the core with any available means so that air may again flow through it.

Loss of Oil Pressure

Loss of oil pressure can make itself known by failure of the hand on the oil pressure gauge to move, by the lighting-up of a warning light on the instrument panel, or by strange sounds coming from the engine. Nothing else can be worse on an engine than running it without oil pressure, so at the first sign of such a condition turn off the ignition, park the car and start an investigation.

Loss of oil pressure can be the result of lack of oil in the crankcase, oil pump failure, or a faulty pressure relief valve in the engine's lubrication system. The first thing to check is the level of the oil in the crankcase. If there is oil in the engine, the trouble may be of too serious a nature for roadside repairs. But if the crankcase is dry, it may be because the oil was used by normal consumption, or that it leaked out through a defective joint between the engine block and one of its covers, or was pumped out through a flaw in the pressure portion of the lubrication system. It's also possible that the drain plug in the crankcase might have fallen out.

The method of repairing a broken oil line will depend on the type of line it is and where it goes.

A split or broken tube for an oil pressure gauge could be disconnected completely and a plug screwed into the cylinder block, or the tube could be squeezed together, on the block side of the break, with a pair of pliers to seal its end. It wouldn't be possible to squeeze the end of a hose together, so a plug would probably be needed if the break were in a hose. A broken line to or from an oil filter can be treated in the same manner as a gauge line; however, if the filter is of the full-flow type used on most late model engines, the engine cannot be run with either of the filter lines sealed or disconnected because all the oil that lubricates the engine flows through the lines and the filter.

Lack of oil pressure when there is oil in the crankcase would indicate a failure in the pump or relief valve assembly or a plugged oil pump screen. Another possibility is a faulty gauge that is failing to show pressure when it should but such a failure is rare. To check the gauge it is only necessary to loosen one of the connections in the line between the engine and the gauge and start the engine for an instant. If there is pressure in the system, oil will flow from the connection, indicating a bad gauge, but if there is no oil at the connection, the gauge is probably all right. You can't harm the engine by running it with a bad gauge but be sure there is pressure in the engine's oiling system before you do.

Worn-out or Broken Internal Parts

An engine stalled by a broken or worn-out internal part is a dead duck and an attempt to make a roadside repair is justified only in a case of extreme necessity. We've all heard stories of how a burned out connecting rod bearing was repaired with a piece of the driver's leather belt or a piece of bacon rind, and how a broken piston was removed and the spark plug in that cylinder disconnected, and other just as odd repairs made so a car could be driven out of the wilderness and back to civilization, but a fellow would have to be way out on a limb to take the time to resort to such temporary measures.

If your car stalls and you have reason to believe the cause is a burned out rod bearing or a broken rod, crankshaft, piston, or other equally vital part, don't waste time trying to figure out a temporary repair. Get the car home the best way you can and repair the damage correctly.

CHAPTER SIXTEEN

Racing Tire Problems

*How to get the best possible traction
for race track and drag strip competition.
The five musts of big-time competition.*

No MATTER HOW HOT the machinery in a racing roadster or dragster may be, there still remains the problem of transmitting its power to the ground in the most efficient manner. This brings up the extremely important matter of tires. How do you figure the proper width and diameter of a racing slick in relation to horsepower? How can you get the best traction; the most service; the most safety?

Most hot rodders seem to feel that the width of a dragster slick is the most important problem. Offhand they guess that the way to get maximum traction is to use the widest possible tire. If they do this it is quite possible that they will end up with too much width and more traction than they have horsepower to use, which will reduce their car's ability to accelerate and cause undue strain on the clutch and rear end.

Actually, a slick's tread should never be more than one inch wider than the rim of the wheel on which the tire will be used. A rim's width is the distance between the inside surfaces of its flanges. One inch wider than the rim is the absolute maximum. The ideal is a tread the same

width as the rim. When the wheel is too narrow for the tread width it may overcome the friction between the rim and the beads of the tire. This would allow the wheel to rotate within the tire, swallow a inner tube's valve stem, and possibly throw the tire—an event that can be highly dangerous at speed of 150 miles per hour. Tires adhere better to magnesium wheels than to steel; however, to be on the safe side, the inch-to-inch tread to rim formula should also be followed with mag wheels.

Thread width is only one consideration. To obtain maximum traction there are other rules to be followed:

Correct Tread Design. Treads must be designed for the specific track and type of use. Drag slicks are smooth with sharp block shoulders on both edges. Track slicks for roadster racing on asphalt are smooth with one round shoulder and one block shoulder. Dirt track tires have deep waffle pattern treads. Front tires for roadsters and dragsters usually have standard or straight ribbed treads. Deflated slicks should have a slightly concave tread. A tread that was flat when

Checking for out-of-round wheel. A crayon held on rigid support will mark out-of-round points on a rotating wheel. Mag wheels hold shape better than steel.

Checking wheel's balance. Spirit level bubble on hub of a static balancer shows wheel's heaviest, lightest points. Points are marked "H" and "L" and will be opposed to points "H" and "L" on the tire.

Tire balance is checked. Tire and deflated tube are rotated on spindle. It naturally comes to a rest with a heavy spot at bottom. Marked casing is mounted on similarly marked wheel. Heaviest part of tire is mounted at light point of the wheel to obtain a practical balance job.

the tire was deflated would hump in the middle when the tire was inflated, but a concave tread becomes flat when inflated and bears flat on a track's surface.

Correct Outside Diameter. The outside diameter of the rear tires must be established in relationship to the gear ratio and engine rpm. Too great an outside diameter prevents the car's engine from attaining its speed of maximum horsepower output. The tire, mounted and inflated, should be measured horizontally across its diameter; its relationship to the gear ratio and rpm for certain car speeds can then be established with a special slide rule obtainable from most speed parts supply houses.

Correct Air Pressure. Inflation pressures must be correct in relation to the weight of the car, size of the tire, and the type of racing. Tubeless nylon casings, with the inner liner left in and fitted with inner tubes, are recommended. Tubes must be used because tubeless tires tend to lose air at high speeds. The casing is punctured in

three places with an ice pick to allow the extra air pressure that would build up around the tube as a result of the heat generated by racing speeds to escape. An additional advantage of the strong construction of tubeless tires and the inflexibility of nylon cord is that convex humping at midtread is alleviated.

Air pressure should be checked regularly because a valve cone will tend to lose air at high speeds due to centrifugal force. If the pressure falls too low there is a possibility the valve stem may be swallowed and the tire disintegrated. Incidentally, valve caps are always recommended. If pressures listed give too much traction, the pressure may be increased five pounds to slightly hump the tread. Roll and heat build-up are more pronounced when initial pressures are too low. Pressures on the high side are safer but may cause some loss of roadability.

Any change in temperature varies the pressure in the tires; allowances should be made for this effect.

Recommended Pressures

Track Slick:
Asphalt ....38 lbs.
Dirt ....25 lbs.
Dirt Track ....25 lbs.
Drag Slicks:
6 x 7.10 ....30 lbs.
6½ x 7.10 ....25 lbs.
7 x 8.00 ....30 lbs.
7½ x 8.00 ....25 lbs.
8 x 8.00 ....22 lbs.

Correct Balance and Weight. Slicks should be as perfectly paired in size and weight as possible. Before mounting, the static balance of the wheel and tire should be checked separately and marked with chalk so the heavy point of the tire can be mounted opposite the heavy point of the wheel. Tires should always be balanced with the tube installed. The tube also has a heavy point and this can be opposed to the heavy point on the tire. Adding a cold patch to the tube can help shift the balance to where it is needed most.

Attempts to true out-of-round tires should not be made. At different depths, the tread has different cure hardnesses. A 50 shore hardness at the surface may be reduced to a 40 shore hardness ¼-inch below. Shaving into the softer rubber will cause irregular wear and eventually intensify balance problems. If a new tire or recap is out of round, it should be returned for an adjustment. Wheels should also be checked for an out-of-round condition. This is easily done by rotating the wheel near a piece of crayon held against a solid support. When the crayon is held the proper distance from an out-of-round wheel, only the high spots will be marked. If the crayon marks the entire circumference, the wheel is true. Steel wheels are the worst out-of-round offenders; magnesium wheels are up to three times stronger than steel wheels and they hold their shape better.

A big factor in determining the most efficient tire sizes is the car's weight distribution. Important differences depend on the frame extension and location of the engine. Other important factors are the car's suspension, wheel size, gear ratios, horsepower, height, width, and weight. To sift these facts and come up with the proper tire formula is a job for an expert. Bruce Alexander, 4017 McArthur Blvd., Oakland 19, California, is just such an expert. He has been help-

Measuring wheel width to decide what size slicks to employ. Proper wheel width is measured from the inside of rim flanges — not outside. Wheel in photo is 7½-inch mag.

Measuring the width of the tire's tread. Too much tread width for width of rim is usual error. An inch to inch relationship has been found to be best for competition.

Measuring the full outside diameter of a racing tire. Always measure horizontally while the tire is inflated, on a wheel. Too much outside diameter results in the loss of horsepower.

ing hot rodders with tire problems for 12 years and answers their questions by mail.

Correct Maintenance: No one must be reminded that a pair of new racing slicks may be worth several hundred dollars and that recaps are worth only a fraction as much. Towing over long distances on the highway can cause a needless tire expense if the car can be carried on a trailer, but if the car must be towed, remove its slicks. It is good sense to cover tires from the hot sun when not in use. Between seasons, the wheels should be jacked-up and the tires deflated. When tires are changed, an approved mounting ma-

chine should be used. Hammering or prying at the beads must be avoided to prevent bead breakage. A lubricant should never be used to ease a tire onto its rim because it will reduce the all-important friction between the tire and the rim. Soapstone should be lightly fogged onto a tube before it is inserted into its casing but too much should not be used as it might form lumps that will stick the tube to the tire at high speeds.

Tires present some knotty but not insurmountable problems to the serious-minded hot rodder. Careful planning can net a better performance in competition that make this effort worth while.

Hot Rod Glossary

~~~~~~

A

A-Bone—Model A Ford
Alky—methanol, alcohol

B

Bent-Eight—any V8 engine
Binders—brakes
Blower—supercharger
Blown engine—engine using a supercharger
Bobbed—cut or shortened, usually applied to fenders
Boost—manifold pressure supplied by supercharger
Boots—tires
Bottom-end—engine crankshaft, main bearings, and
   connecting rod bearings
Box—transmission

C

Cam—camshaft
Channeled—body floor repositioned to lower overall
   height
Chopped—cut down, such as removing portion of body
   top for lowering, or removing material from flywheel
Crank—abbreviation for crankshaft

D

Deuce—1932 Ford
Dog clutch—in-out type clutch using gear shift to couple
   engine to driveshaft
Dohc—Double overhead camshaft
Dragster—car built exclusively for drag racing

F

Filled—gaps in welded body panel joints concealed
Filled axle—dropped front axle with portions of "I"
   beam section filled with metal for added strength
Flathead—L-head or side-valve engine
Forked-eight—V8 engine
Four-banger—four-cylinder engine
Full house—much modified engine

G

Gear box—transmission
Grind—cam lobe contour (street grind, full-race grind,
   etc.)

H

Header—exhaust manifold designed for free-flow of exhaust gases

I

Igniter—ignition distributor

J

Jug—carburetor
Juice—nitromethane and other fuel additives

219

L

Lay rubber—spin wheels on pavement
Locked rear-end—rear axle with gears modified to eliminate differential action

M

Mag—magneto
Mill—any engine
Molded—body contours and panel joints worked into continuous smooth surface

N

Nitro—nitromethane

O

Off the line—start of drag race
Ohc—overhead camshaft
Ohv—overhead valves
Over-bore—engine with cylinder diameters enlarged over stock dimensions

P

Peaked—ornamental raised bead worked into metal
Pop the clutch—engage clutch suddenly
Ported—enlarged passages between manifold and valves
Pot—carburetor

Q

Quick-change rear-end—rear axle equipped with gears in center section that may be changed quickly to alter ratios

R

Rag-top—convertible
Rail-job—dragster without body
Relieved—passages cut in cylinder block to aid flow of fuel-air mixture to cylinder

S

Sectioned—section of metal removed from body to reduce overall height
Setup—carburetor(s) and manifold
Shaved—ornamentation and hardware removed from portions of body
Six-holer—six-cylinder engine
Skins—tires
Slicks—wide, smooth-tread racing tires
Slingshot—dragster with driving position behind rear axle
Slug—piston
Smoothed—similar to shaved
Speed shift—shift rapidly without releasing accelerator pedal
Stick shift—manual shift transmission
Stove-bolt—Chevrolet engine
Stroker—engine with overstock length stroke

T

T-bone—model T Ford
Tach—tachometer (revolutions-per-minute indicator)

Index